COLERIDGE'S WRITINGS

General Editor: John Beer

Volume 4: On Religion and Psychology

COLERIDGE'S WRITINGS

Myriad-minded in his intellectual interests, Coleridge often passed quickly from one subject to another, so that the range and mass of the materials he left can be bewildering to later readers. *Coleridge's Writings* is a series addressed to those who wish to have a guide to his important statements on particular subjects. Each volume presents his writings in a major field of human knowledge or thought, tracing the development of his ideas. Connections are also made with relevant writings in the period, suggesting the extent to which Coleridge was either summing up, contributing to or reacting against current developments. Each volume is produced by a specialist in the field; the general editor is John Beer, Professor of English Literature at Cambridge, who has published various studies of Coleridge's thought and poetry.

Volume 1   *On Politics and Society*
                edited by John Morrow

Volume 2   *On Humanity*
                edited by Anya Taylor

Volume 3   *On Language*
                edited by A. C. Goodson

Volume 4   *On Religion and Psychology*
                edited by John Beer

Coleridge's Writings

Volume 4

On Religion and Psychology

Edited by

John Beer
Emeritus Professor of English Literature
University of Cambridge
and Fellow of Peterhouse

First published 2002 by
PALGRAVE
Houndmills, Basingstoke, Hampshire RG21 6XS and
175 Fifth Avenue, New York, N. Y. 10010
Companies and representatives throughout the world

PALGRAVE is the new global academic imprint of
St. Martin's Press LLC Scholarly and Reference Division and
Palgrave Publishers Ltd (formerly Macmillan Press Ltd).

ISBN 0–333–73490–4

This book is printed on paper suitable for recycling and
made from fully managed and sustained forest sources.

A catalogue record for this book is available
from the British Library.

A catalogue record for this book is available
from the Library of Congress.

10   9   8   7   6   5   4   3   2   1
11   10   09   08   07   06   05   04   03   02

Printed and bound in Great Britain by
Antony Rowe Ltd, Chippenham, Wiltshire

Contents

Foreword

The appearance of hitherto unpublished material in the last hundred years has brought out more fully the range and complexity of Coleridge's intelligence and knowledge. The *Notebooks* and *Collected Works*, both now well on the way to completion, together with the *Collected Letters*, have made it increasingly evident that this was the most extraordinary English mind of the time. The specialist or more general student who wishes to know what Coleridge had to say on a particular subject may, however, find the sheer mass of materials bewildering, since in his less formal writings he passed quickly from one subject to another. *Coleridge's Writings* is a series addressed to such readers. In each volume a particular area of Coleridge's interest is explored, with an attempt to present his most significant statements and to show the development of his thought on the subject in question.

Of all the multifarious interests Coleridge showed in his career religion could be said to have been the deepest and most lasting. Intended originally for the Church, he remained preoccupied by his thinking on the subject for long stretches of his life, particularly during his later years. Even his poetry—for which he is of course best known—cannot fully be understood without taking this substratum into account. He was also, to a degree quite unusual in his time, preoccupied by the life of the mind. Accordingly, while the attempt here is to present a conspectus of his religious thinking the chief focus is on that area where it ran side by side with psychological inquiry.

The shifts in his intellectual and religious positions were marked by varying amounts of attention to religion in his writings. During the early years there were a few notebook entries and letters, coupled with his writing for the 1795 Lectures in Bristol. During the years of dialogue with Wordsworth, comments of a religious nature were spread across notebooks, letters and general writings; following the Malta years the Christian element intensified, particularly with the writing of *The Friend*. Whereas in other volumes of this series the materials have been reasonably limited, here they overflow abundantly. There are many entries in the notebooks and marginal comments in religious books, his new absorption being marked both by the *Lay Sermons* and then by his most important published work on the subject, the *Aids to Reflection*.

Concurrent with his work towards this came a great deal of criticism of and commentary on the Bible—so much so that it is hoped to produce another volume of *Coleridge's Writings* devoted exclusively to it.

In his last years he was increasingly exercised by the desire to produce a significant religious work: his 'Opus Maximum', sometimes referred to as his 'Assertion of Religion'. At the time of compilation of the present volume this was still unpublished in full, though a number of extracts had appeared in other places. The serious student of Coleridge's religious thought will want to consult the new volume—particularly on topics such as the Trinity—but it will in itself be so extensive as to preclude the extracting of more than one or two passages for a volume such as this. In the same way, topics raised in this volume can in many cases be pursued at greater length in the pages of works such as *The Friend*, the *Lectures on the History of Philosophy* or *On the Constitution of the Church and State*. Here, as always, the editorial work in the Princeton edition will be found invaluable by the reader who wishes to inquire further.

I wish to express my gratitude to Princeton University Press and Oxford University Press for permission to reproduce extracts from Coleridgean texts; to Samantha Harvey for assistance with selection of extracts from the Letters; and to Hazel Dunn for help with the preparation of the typescript.

J. B. B.
General Editor

List of Abbreviations

AR	Coleridge, *Aids to Reflection* [1825], ed. John Beer, *CC* 9 (1993)
BL	Coleridge, *Biographia Literaria* [1817], ed. James Engell and Walter Jackson Bate, *CC* 7 (2 vols. 1983)
CC	*The Collected Works of Samuel Taylor Coleridge*, general ed. Kathleen Coburn, associate ed. Bart Winer (Princeton N.J. and London 1969–)
CL	Coleridge, *Collected Letters*, ed. E.L. Griggs (6 vols., Oxford 1956–71)
CM	Coleridge, *Marginalia*, ed. George Whalley, *CC* 12 (5 vols. so far published out of a projected 6, 1980–)
CN	Coleridge, *Notebooks*, ed. Kathleen Coburn (4 vols. so far published out of a projected 5, Princeton, N.J. and London 1959–; volume 5 from draft)
C&S	Coleridge, *On the Constitution of the Church and State* [1829], ed. John Colmer, *CC* 10 (1976)
Friend	Coleridge, *The Friend* [1809–18], ed. Barbara Rooke, *CC* 4 (2 vols. 1969)
HW	*The Complete Works of William Hazlitt*, ed. P.P. Howe (21 vols. 1930–4)
Lects (1795)	Coleridge, *Lectures 1795: On Politics and Religion*, ed. Lewis Patton and Peter Mann, *CC* 1 (1971)
LS	Coleridge, *Lay Sermons* [1816–17], ed. R.J. White, *CC* 6 (1972)
PW (Beer)	Coleridge, *Poems*, ed. J.B. Beer, new edn, Everyman (2000)
SWF	Coleridge, *Shorter Works and Fragments*, ed. H.J. Jackson and J.R. de J. Jackson, *CC* 11 (1995)
TT	Coleridge, *Table Talk*, ed. Carl Woodring, *CC* 14 (2 vols. 1990)
〈 〉	Coleridge's additions to his text
[ ]	Matter added by editor

Coleridge's Life

The following outline records some crucial events in Coleridge's career, particularly in relation to his writings on religion. Full chronologies are printed in the various volumes of the Princeton *Collected Coleridge*.

1772   Coleridge born (21 October).

1781   (Oct)   Death of Coleridge's father.

1782   (until 1791)   School at Christ's Hospital, London.

1791   (until late 1794)   At Jesus College, Cambridge.

1794   (June)   Welsh tour; meeting with Southey at Oxford initiates pantisocratic scheme.

1795   (Jan)   Bristol Lectures begun;
(May–June)   'Six Lectures on Revealed Religion'.
(Oct)   Marriage to Sara Fricker.
(Dec)   *Conciones ad Populum; The Plot Discovered*.

1796   (March–May)   *The Watchman*.
(June)   Visits William and Dorothy Wordsworth at Racedown in Dorset.
(Sept)   Hartley Coleridge born.

1797   (Nov)   'The Ancient Mariner' begun.

1798   (March)   'The Ancient Mariner' completed.
(spring)   Swiss cantons suppressed: 'Recantation' (later 'France: an Ode'); 'Fears in Solitude'.
(May)   Berkeley Coleridge born.
(Sept)   *Lyrical Ballads* published; to Germany with the Wordsworths.

1799   Attends lectures on literature, biblical criticism and physiology at Göttingen.
(April)   News of death of Berkeley.
(July)   Return to England.
(autumn)   Friendship with Humphry Davy begins.
(Oct–Nov)   Visits Lakes; meets Sara Hutchinson.
(Nov)   In London writing for *Morning Post* to April 1800.
(Dec)   'On the French Constitution'.

1800   (Sept)   Derwent Coleridge born.

1801   (Mar–Nov)   Severe domestic discord.

	(Nov) In London writing for *Morning Post* to March 1802.
1802	(Sept–Nov) In London writing for the *Morning Post.*
	(Oct) Verse-letter of April to Sara Hutchinson published in new form as 'Dejection'.
	(Dec) Sara Coleridge born.
1803	(summer) Scottish tour with Wordsworths.
1804	(Jan–Mar) In London, writing for *The Courier.*
1804–6	In Malta and Sicily, first as under-secretary to Alexander Ball, British High Commissioner. Drafts 'Observations on Egypt'.
1805	(Jan) Acting Public Secretary in Malta.
1806	(Jan) In Rome: meets Washington Allston, the Humboldts, L. Tieck, and Schlegel.
	(Aug) Return to England.
	(Nov) Keswick, determined on separation from Mrs C.
1807	(Mar) Slave trade abolished.
1808	(Jan–June) First literary lectures in London.
	(July) Review of Clarkson, *History of the Abolition of the Slave Trade.*
	(Nov) First prospectus of *The Friend.*
1809	(June) First number of *The Friend.*
1810	(Mar) Last number of *The Friend*; Sara Hutchinson leaves Grasmere for Wales.
	(Oct) To London; quarrel with Wordsworth.
1812	Second edition of *The Friend.*
1813	*Remorse* opens at Drury Lane.
1813–14	In Bath and Bristol; spiritual crisis; lectures on Shakespeare, education, French Revolution and Napoleon.
	(Sept to Dec) 'Letters to Mr Justice Fletcher' in *The Courier.*
1815	(June) Waterloo.
	(July–Sept) Dictating *Biographia Literaria.*
1816	(April) Accepted as house-mate by Gillmans at Highgate.
	(May) 'Christabel', 'Kubla Khan' and 'The Pains of Sleep' published.
	(Dec) *The Statesman's Manual.*
1817	(Jan) *A Lay Sermon.*
	(July) *Biographia Literaria* and *Sibylline Leaves.*
	(Nov) *Zapolya.*
1818	(Jan) 'Treatise on Method' in *Encyclopaedia Metropolitana.*
	(April) Pamphlets supporting Peel against child labour.
	(Nov) New edition ('*rifaccimento*') of *The Friend.*

Introduction

The orientation of Coleridge's religious beliefs changed over the years. Once he began to question the orthodoxy in which he had been brought up, he was strongly attracted by the radical and Unitarian beliefs followed by many young people of his time. When these in turn came to seem facile—particularly in view of the violence displayed in the French Revolution—he was more drawn to those who shared his disillusionment, yet still hoped that human beings might find a better way of expressing their potential for good. For a time his ideas were dominated by his relationship with William and Dorothy Wordsworth, and more especially by the feeling for the 'one Life' which developed during their period together in north Somerset. His quest at that time was for a religious position that would take account of that. The possibility that a probing of the deepest places of the human mind would throw light on the truths of religion also led to some of his most interesting and suggestive investigations during the period immediately following, the results of which sometimes appear in letters but are most commonly to be traced in his notebook entries.

During the same years political developments in Europe, especially the rise of Napoleon, forced on the two poets the need for a more public stance in defence of traditional values. The emphasis on 'principles', which their collaboration produced in the second part of the decade, reflected this, while the turmoil that surrounded Coleridge's subsequent alienation from his friend resulted in a more urgent consideration of his own religious position. In the next few years his experience of spiritual crisis prompted an intensified devotion to orthodox Christianity and a revived allegiance to the Anglican Church.

The seeds of this new position had been germinating for several years, as Coleridge became convinced that a major flaw in Unitarianism was

1

its unwillingness to accept the need for a redeemer and that the other need of the time was for a refreshed idea of the Reason which was generally agreed to be a primary human faculty. The 'Reason' that the age was crying out for, in his view, was not the mechanical engine of much contemporary thinking but something closer to the enlightened views of the seventeenth-century divines—notably those who had come to be called the Cambridge Platonists.

In the latter part of his life he spent much time studying—and often annotating—these and other religious writers. A prominent figure for him was the Scottish bishop Robert Leighton, whose example of simple and holy living and writing eventually provided inspiration for his own work, *Aids to Reflection*. Other writers with whom he engaged at length included Martin Luther, Richard Hooker and Jeremy Taylor. His accounts of them were admiring yet also on occasion critical, as was his attitude to the various leading religious persuasions of his time. In one of his notebook entries he deplored the fact that there was no religious denomination to which he could give unconditional support. The persons with whom he felt most at home were often, in fact, those who tended to be dismissed as 'mystics', ranging from Jacob Boehme, whose writings had enthralled him in youth, to Roman Catholic figures such as St Teresa or Madame de Guyon. The strong imaginative element in their writings appealed to his poetic instincts and raised the hope of establishing a religious literature that would appeal as much to the feelings as to the mind. His various comments show that while he inclined to write defensively about them in his public statements, he found the company of these diverse individuals the nearest to a religious community that he had discovered during his pilgrimage of 62 years.

In later conversations with inquirers and visitors he would revert continually to his convictions concerning Unitarianism and attempt to persuade his interlocutors (some of them prominent theologians, but also writers such as Ralph Waldo Emerson) of its errors. His certainties were cross-hatched with uncertainty, however. He remained confident that he was master of a system that was superior to all others by including each one of them, while demonstrating both its virtues and its shortcomings; yet in his notebooks he was often at pains to stress that his animadversions had no more than provisional status, being the work of a seeker after truth rather than final affirmations. Many readers, indeed, find among such impromptu notes some of his most important and challenging contributions to religious debate.

1
The Early Intellectual Quest

Even in childhood Coleridge was made to feel that he was a person of unusual gifts. Cut off from free intercourse with children of his own age, his position as the youngest child of an elderly clergyman gave him a special status in the Devonshire town where he spent his first years. As he remembered his childhood, '...because I could read & spell, & had, I may truly say, a memory & understanding forced into almost an unnatural ripeness, I was flattered & wondered at by all the old women. ...and before I was eight years old I was a *character* – sensibility, imagination, sloth, & feelings of deep & bitter contempt for almost all who traversed the orbit of my understanding, were even then prominent & manifest.'[1]

After leaving Christ's Hospital in London, where he was sent to school following the death of his father, he was admitted to Jesus College, Cambridge, from which he was initially expected to follow in his father's footsteps by emerging as a candidate for the Anglican priesthood. (He signed himself on one occasion 'Reverend in the future tense and Scholar of Jesus College in the present tense.'[2]) According to a memoir from an unsympathetic commentator, however, even before his undergraduate years his wayward behaviour at Cambridge had become an occasion of comment:

> Some of these youths were sadly corrupted in the *metropolis*, and initiated into the mysteries of Theophilanthropism, when scholars at that excellent seminary, Christ's Hospital. C——dge was nominated to an Exhibition at Cambridge, and the Vice Master (soon after his admission) sent to him, on account of his non-attendance at chapel. This illuminated gentleman affected astonishment that any criminality could attach to him for his non-performance of religious worship,

the trickery of Priestcraft, but if his presence was required, *pro forma*, as at a muster roll, he had no great objection to attend. To the disgrace of discipline, and a Christian University, this avowed Deist was not expelled for such sin.[3]

Whatever the truth of such observations Coleridge was becoming at the very least eccentric in his beliefs. During his undergraduate years he was finding his feet, intellectually, in a contemporary society that had been profoundly stirred by the French Revolution. Under the stimulus of its events he moved aside from the tradition in which he had been brought up, with its bearings from Anglicanism and political conservatism, and was drawn to the dissenting thinking that had been brought to his notice as he came to know William Frend at Jesus College and his circle. This new Coleridge became in due course not only a contributor to Unitarian pulpits but the poet of his 'Religious Musings', reaching for a kind of sublimity that would be suited to the times. So far from leading to a position of certitude, however, the cross-currents of these different trends provoked more and more questions, until for a time, as he later remembered, all was confusion. Impulses to accept the scientific view of the world that was emerging, particularly in the great industrial and manufacturing areas of England, and which invited the cultivation of an impersonal philosophy devoted to human improvement of the kind that would in fact characterize many of the Unitarian contributions to English culture in the nineteenth century, struggled against a binding back of himself into the more personally based religion of Christianity which had been an integral part of English civilization during previous centuries. After the culmination of his Cambridge career in his enlistment as a dragoon, his subsequent discharge with the help of his brothers, his brief readmission and then his permanent withdrawal from the University, he settled in Bristol, where he became intimate with the Unitarians and radical thinkers and delivered a variety of lectures including a series on 'Revealed Religion'. The first of these began with an allegory (to be reproduced in one or two of his later works) in which he expressed his sense that human truth, and its relation to contemporary thought, were of such a nature that in his own age at least, simple statement of it in simple terms would result in one being dismissed as a madman. Yet he also maintained that the argument for the existence of God from the existence of design was irresistible. It seemed as if it was only the loss of ancient wisdom that had blinded human beings to such clear truths – a point he was often to reiterate in the years to come.

Not long after the lectures were given there was a moment when the young Coleridge could be seen in the full strength and confidence of his powers. In December 1796 he wrote a letter to John Thelwall, defending his own position as a Christian[4] and attacking his criticisms of Christianity – particularly his contention that it was a religion fit for slobberers and its morals 'for the Magdalen & Botany Bay'. (In addition to the adultery of Mary Magdalen, Thelwall may have had in mind Christ's pardoning of the thieves on the cross.) As will be seen from his spirited reply, Coleridge not only condemned the inhumanity of such comments but went on to question Thelwall's stated preference for the classics over Christianity: 'can you seriously think that Mercury from Jove equals in poetic sublimity the mighty Angel that came down from heaven, whose face was as it were the Sun, and his feet as pillars of fire?'

For all the vigour of his defence, however, some of Thelwall's shafts were probably forceful enough to penetrate the armour of his certitude. At all events, he was to look back on the subsequent period not as a time of consolidation but of increasing dubiety concerning his own position. He was later to describe how he found himself 'all afloat' in an account in his *Biographia*, the importance of which can hardly be over-estimated, for it sets out the terms of intellectual conflicts that were to dog him for the rest of his life.

In spite of such uncertainties, nevertheless, he was fast becoming known as an effective preacher in the locality, promulgating religious beliefs which at the time contained a strong social element. He went so far as to consider becoming a Unitarian minister. In 1798 the young Hazlitt, whose father, himself a minister in that denomination, was entertaining Coleridge in Shropshire with that very end in view, was drawn to rise before daybreak and walk 'ten miles in the mud' to hear him preach at the chapel in Shrewsbury, where he responded with delight to the pacifist element in the preacher's message.

Never, the longest day I have to live, shall I have such another walk as this cold, raw, comfortless one, in the winter of the year 1798. When I got there, the organ was playing the 100th Psalm, and when it was done, Mr. Coleridge rose and gave out his text, 'And he went up into the mountain to pray, HIMSELF, ALONE.' As he gave out this text, his voice 'rose like a steam of rich distilled perfumes', and when he came to the two last words, which he pronounced loud, deep, and distinct, it seemed to me, who was then young, as if the sounds had echoed from the bottom of the human heart, and as if that prayer might have floated in solemn silence through the universe. The idea of St. John came into my mind, 'of one crying in the wilderness, who had his loins girt about, and whose food was locusts and wild honey.' The preacher then launched into his subject, like an eagle dallying with the wind. The sermon was upon peace and war; upon church and state—not their alliance but their separation—on the spirit of the world and the spirit of Christianity, not as the same, but as opposed to one another. He talked of those who had 'inscribed the cross of Christ on banners dripping with human gore.' He made a poetical and pastoral excursion—and to show the fatal effects of war, drew a striking contrast between the simple shepherd-boy, driving his team afield, or sitting under the hawthorn, piping to his flock, 'as though he should never be old,' and the same poor country lad crimped, kidnapped, brought into town, made drunk at an alehouse, turned into a wretched drummer-boy, with his hair sticking on end with powder and pomatum, a long cue at his back, and tricked out in the loathsome finery of the profession of blood:

'Such were the notes our once-loved poet sung.'

And for myself, I could not have been more delighted if I had heard the music of the spheres. Poetry and Philosophy had met together. Truth and Genius had embraced, under the eye and with the sanction of Religion. This was even beyond my hopes. I returned home well satisfied.[5]

Shortly afterwards, Coleridge's enthusiasm for Unitarianism began to wane. He declined the Shrewsbury appointment in the face of an offer from the Wedgwoods to provide him with financial support unconditionally—which gave him even greater intellectual freedom. He had been attracted by the idea of reanimating current Christianity by a movement away from what he saw as the dead mechanical philosophy of the eighteenth century and towards one which took its cue more readily from those who were responding positively to the new ideas that had recently been current in France, before and after the Revolution—in particular those that concentrated attention on phenomena of life and animation.[6] As he tried to resolve his current intellectual uncertainties, his growing friendship with William and Dorothy Wordsworth would lead him, in the following few years, to be more preoccupied by such ideas as they related to human beings in their relationship with nature than by orthodox or dissenting religion as such.

In his early poetry Coleridge tries to achieve a vehicle for religious instruction, combining serious exposition with imaginative power. The first version of his 'Religious Musings' opens with a vision of the Creation as sublime, followed by a picture of Christ as the personification of the Love which will raise human nature to perception of its centrality.[1]

> This is the time, when most divine to hear,
> As with a Cherub's 'loud uplifted' trump
> The voice of Adoration my thrill'd heart
> Rouses! And with the rushing noise of wings
> Transports my spirit to the favor'd fields
> Of Bethlehem, there in shepherd's guise to sit
> Sublime of extacy, and mark entranc'd
> The glory-streaming VISION throng the night.
> Ah not more radiant, nor loud harmonies
> Hymning more unimaginably sweet
> With choral songs around th' ETERNAL MIND,
> The constellated company of WORLDS
> Danc'd jubilant: what time the startling East
> Saw from her dark womb leap her flamy Child!
> Glory to God in the Highest! PEACE on Earth!
>
> Yet thou more bright than all that Angel Blaze,
> Despised GALILÆAN! Man of Woes!
> For chiefly in the oppressed Good Man's face
> The Great Invisible (by symbols seen)
> Shines with peculiar and concentred light,
> When all of Self regardless the scourg'd Saint
> Mourns for th' oppressor. O thou meekest Man!
> Meek Man and lowliest of the Sons of Men!
> Who thee beheld thy imag'd Father saw.

In 'The Destiny of Nations' he tries his hand at presenting religious arguments about science in verse.[2]

> For what is Freedom, but the unfettered use
> Of all the powers which God for use had given?
> But chiefly this, him First, him Last to view
> Through meaner powers and secondary things

Effulgent, as through clouds that veil his blaze.
For all that meets the bodily sense I deem
Symbolical, one almighty alphabet
For infant minds; and we in this low world
Placed with our backs to bright Reality,
That we may learn with young unwounded ken
The substance from its shadow. Infinite Love,
Whose latence is the plenitude of All,
Thou with retracted beams, and self-eclipse
Veiling, revealest thine eternal Sun.

But some there are who deem themselves most free
When they within this gross and visible sphere
Chain down the wingéd thought, scoffing ascent,
Proud in their meanness: and themselves they cheat
With noisy emptiness of learnéd phrase,
Their subtle fluids, impacts, essences,
Self-working tools, uncaused effects, and all
Those blind Omniscients, those Almighty Slaves,
Untenanting creation of its God.

But Properties are God: the naked mass
(If mass there be, fantastic guess or ghost)
Acts only by its inactivity.
Here we pause humbly. Others boldlier think
That as one body seems the aggregate
Of atoms numberless, each organized;
So by a strange and dim similitude
Infinite myriads of self-conscious minds
Are one all-conscious Spirit, which informs
With absolute ubiquity of thought
(His one eternal self-affirming act!)
All his involvéd Monads, that yet seem
With various province and apt agency
Each to pursue its own self-centering end.

Establishing himself as a lecturer in Bristol, Coleridge embarks on an allegory to help define his own position by showing the absurdity of attending exclusively to Nature.[3]

It was towards Morning when the Brain begins to reassume its waking state, and our dreams approach to the regular trains of Reality, that I found myself in a vast Plain, which I immediately knew to be the Valley of Life. It possessed a great diversity of soils and here was a sunny spot and there a dark one just such a mixture of sunshine and shade as we may have observed on the Hills in an April Day when the thin broken Clouds are scattered over the heaven. Almost in the very entrance of the Valley stood a large and gloomy pile into which I seemed constrained to enter—every part of the building was crowded with tawdry ornament and fantastic deformity—on every window was pourtrayed [in] inelegant and glaring colours some horrible tale or preternatural action—so that not a ray of light could enter untinged by the medium through which it passed. The Place was full of People some of them dancing about in strange ceremonies and antic merriment while others seemed convulsed with horror or pining in mad Melancholy—intermingled with all these I observed a great number of men in Black Robes who appeared now marshalling the various Groups & now collecting with scrupulous care the Tenths of every Thing that grew within their reach. I stood wondering a while what these Things might be when one of these men approached me & with a reproachful Look bade me uncover my Head for that the Place into which I had entered was the Temple of *Religion*—in the holier recesses of which the great Goddess resided. Awestruck by the name I bowed before the Priest and entreated him to conduct me into her Presence—he assented—offerings he took from me, with mystic sprinklings of Water he purified me and then led me through many a dark and winding alley the dew damps of which chilled and its hollow echoes beneath my feet affrighted me till at last we entered a large Hall where not even a Lamp glimmered. Around its walls I observed a number of phosphoric Inscriptions—each one of the words separately I seemed to understand but when I read them in sentences they were riddles incomprehensible and contradictory. Read and believe said my Guide—These are mysteries. In the middle of the Hall the Goddess was placed—her features blended with darkness rose to my view terrible yet vacant. I prostrated myself before her and then retired with my guide wond'ring and dissatisfied. As I reentered the body of the Temple I heard a deep Buz as of discontent, a few whose Eyes were piercing, and whose Foreheads spoke Thought, amid a much larger number who were enraged by the severity of the Priests in exacting their Tenths, had collected in a group, and exclaiming. This is the Temple of Superstition, after much contumely & much maltreatment they rushed out of it. I joined them—we travelled from the Temple with hasty steps and had now nearly gone round half the Valley when we were addressed by a Woman clad in white garments of simplest Texture   Her Air was mild yet majestic, and her Countenance displayed deep Reflection animated by ardent Feelings. We enquired her name. My name is Religion she said The greater part of our Company affrighted by the sound and sore from recent impostures hurried onwards and examined no farther. A few struck by the difference of her form & manners agreed to follow her although with cautious circumspection. She led us to an Eminence in the midst of the Valley, on the Top of which we could command the whole Plain, and observe the Relation of its different Parts, each one to the other. She then gave us an optic Glass which assisted without contradicting our natural vision and enabled us to see far beyond the Valley—and now, with the rapid Transition of a Dream I had overtaken and rejoined the more numerous party, who had abruptly left us, indignant at the very name of religion. Some remained in the Temple of Superstition and went to sleep in its darkest cloisters—but there were many however who lost not the impression of Hatred towards their oppressors and never looking back had in their eagerness to recede from Superstition completed almost the whole of the Circle, and were already in the Precincts of the Temple when they abruptly entered a Vast and dusky Cave. At the mouth of it sate two Figures the first, a female whom by her dress & gestures I knew to be Sensuality the second from the fierceness of his Demeanor and the brutal Scornfulness of his Looks declared himself to be the Monster Blasphemy—he uttered big words, yet ever and anon I observed that he turned pale at his own courage. We entered—the climate of the place was unnaturally cold   in the midst was an old dim eyed Man poring with a microscope over the Torso of a statue, which had neither basis, nor feet, nor head . . . but on its breast . . . was written—NATURE! To this the old Man was continually applying his microscope, and seemed greatly delighted in counting the Irregularities which were made visible by it on the polished surface of the marble! He spoke in diverse Tongues and unfolded many Mysteries, and among other strange Things he talked much about an infinite Series of Causes—which he explained to be—a string of blind men of which the last caught hold of the skirt of the one before him, he of the next, and so on till they were all out of sight; and that they all walked straight without making one false step. We enquired, Who there is at the head to guide them. He answered No one, but that the string of blind men went on for ever without a beginning for though one blind man could not move without stumbling, yet that infinite Blindness

supplies the want of sight. I burst into Laughter at this strange exposition and awoke—

*He continues by arguing that the argument for God's existence from design is
obvious in its force.*[4]

If it were possible said an ancient Philosopher that I could disbelieve
a God it would be for this, that there exists on Earth that intellectual
Deformity an Atheist. The evident contrivance and fitness of things for
one another which we meet with throughout all parts of the Universe
seems to make the belief of a Deity almost an Axiom. There is no need
of nice or subtle Reasonings on this Subject—a manifest Contrivance
immediately suggests a contriver. It strikes us like a sensation, and artful
Reasonings against it may puzzle us, but never convince. No one for
example that knows the principles of optics and the structure of the eye
can believe that it was formed without skill in that Science, or that the
Ear was formed without knowledge of Sounds, or that the male and
female in animals were not formed for each other and for continuing
the Species. All our accounts of Nature are full of instances of this kind
and the more nicely we examine the relations of Things the more clearly
we perceive their astonishing aptitude. This admirable and beautiful
structure of things that carries irresistible Demonstration of intending
Causality, exalts our idea of the Contriver—the Unity of the Design
shews him to be *one*. Thus the existence of Deity, and his Power and his
Intelligence are manifested, and I could weep for the deadened and
petrified Heart of that Man who could wander among the fields in
a vernal Noon or summer Evening and doubt his Benevolence! The
Omnipotent has unfolded to us the Volume of the World, that there we
may read the Transcript of himself. In Earth or Air the meadow's purple
stores, the Moons mild radiance, or the Virgins form Blooming with
rosy smiles, we see pourtrayed the bright Impressions of the eternal
Mind.

I shall now be obliged to introduce abstruser Reasonings unentertaining
indeed but necessary as the foundation of future systems. We have not
the privilege of the Architect which conceals the heavy and inelegant
foundation while the beautiful and sublime superstructure attracts only
admiration. With the Metaphysical Reasoner every fact must be
brought forward and the ground must be well & carefully examined
where the system is to be erected—The sportive sneer of Malignity and
the empassioned tone of Declamation suit not with the Metaphysical

reason—Accuracy & perspicuity are his essential qualifications and to these everything must be sacrificed—On these subjects necessarily introduced I cannot expect to amuse. Let me however hope to gain attention—

In all nations and in all ages these causes have operated and the belief of an intelligent first Cause has been only not universal. In all nations and in all ages however great selfwilledness joining with great coldness of Affections has produced in a few the principles of: Atheism. Their arguments are reducible to two heads. That the very idea of a God implies Contradictions and that the Phaenomena of Nature are explicable without Deity—on the first their Reasonings run thus—Deity is either immaterial or material. If immaterial, how can he act on matter? if he be material and finite how can he act everywhere? If he be material and omnipresent how is there room for any thing else in the Universe? These men think by this Argument that they have incontrovertibly proved the impossibility of Divine Existence, when in reality they have demonstrated the limited nature of the human Intellect—for let us apply the same argument in the same words to the Cause of Gravitation, or of Magnetism. The Cause of Gravitation is either immaterial or material, if the former how can it act on Matter? but if it be material and situate in the centre of Bodies it acts where it is not, if it be material and diffused over the whole sphere of its operation, how is there room for any thing else? Would it not be absurd from these reasonings to conclude that the Stone fell to the Earth and the planets revolved round the Sun from no cause, simply because the Cause is incomprehensible to us? Our nature is adapted for the observation of Effects only and from the Effects we deduce the Existence and attributes of Causes but their immediate Essence is in all other cases as well as Deity hidden from us. But the Phaenomena of Nature (they assert) are explicable without a Deity. Here atheism splits itself into two parties—the first attempt to explain the formation of the Universe from the accidental play of Atoms acting according to mere mechanical Laws, and derived the astonishing aptitude and ineffable Beauty of Things from a lucky hit in the Blind Uproar—even as you may easily suppose a vast number of Gold & Brass Particles accidentally commoved by the Wind would after infinite Trials form themselves into a polished and accurate Watch or Timepiece! Of this Absurdity later Atheists have been ashamed, and have therefore substituted certain plastic Natures as inherent in each particle of Matter—certain inconceivable Essences that are, as it were, the unthinking Souls of each atom! But how these Unthinking Essences came to agree among each other so as by their different & opposite operations to form one Whole is a Mystery into which the pious Disciples of Atheism deem it irreverent to inquire. The argument may be thus explained. The Unthinking Essences of a great number of Iron particles agree to go partners in making One Printers Type—by a miracle of good Luck, the Essences of innumerable other particles agree to do the same, but with great variation of shape. After which these Unthinking Essences place themselves and their subject particles to each others side in a Compositors Form, which said Form the Essences of wooden particles agreed to make at the very same Time and thus by the friendly cooperation of these and some unthinking Essences you no doubt, can easily conceive that Miltons Paradise Lost might be produced or Euclid's Elements. These are the blind Almighties, that forever act most wisely most benevolently yet never know what they are doing——this is the Unintelligent Intelligence, these are the ignorant Omniscients to make place for whom we are exhorted by modern sages to exclude our God and Untenant the Universe. Late natural Philosophers have uniformly agreed that at some Period or other more or less distant the Earth either from Water or more probably Heat must have been in a state of Fluidity, so as to have rendered the existence of Man impossible. The atheistic Philosophers suppose, that in this uncommon state of Nature the Elements might concur unthinkingly to produce Man—self-conscious, intelligent Man! Suppose him thus formed—Will these Elements give him innate Ideas? A considerable Length of Time is necessary to teach the use of Motion: but before he could have learnt this, he must have perished from want of Food. Or suppose what is impossible that without innate Ideas he should be produced with a knowledge of the use of motion, or rather that as he lay helpless on the bosom of his unconscious Mother his Food luckily grew up around him. Who was present to teach him that the Pains which he felt proceeded from the want of Food or that opening his Mouth & chewing were the means of rendering useful what by accidentally stretching out his hand he had acquired   There being no innate Ideas, I am unable to conceive how these Phaenomena are explicable without Deity—

A Difficulty is not to be urged against a Demonstration. The origin of Evil is thought to be a difficulty, by some to be an unanswerable one—By Deity we mean a creative or at least an organizing Intelligence. This Deity is either indifferent or malignant or benevolent or a mixture of both. An indifferent Deity is a contradiction in terms, or rather another word for No Deity. He that created must have created with some view or other. A malignant Deity the experience of all our senses shews to be an Absurdity—he must be therefore either benevolent or a mixture of the two Principles—If these two principles are unequally met in all powerful Beings, the strongest must overpower the weaker. Deity would therefore become either totally one or totally the other. But if equally met he could not act at all. Nothing therefore remains but the hypothesis of total Benevolence—Reasoning strictly and with logical Accuracy I should deny the existence of any Evil, inasmuch as the end determines the nature of the means and I have been able to discover nothing of which the end is not good. Instead of evil, a disputable word, let us use Pain—and two Questions will suggest themselves. Is the *Pain* the *designed* or the accidental Effect of our organization? Is not good the final result even of accidental Pain? We thus answer. The Teeth sometimes ake, but surely that we may eat not that they may ache is the great and evidently designed end of Teeth. This aching does it not proceed from uncleanliness or scorbutic Diseases? Are not these immediately or remotely the Effect of Moral Evil? But the greatest possible Evil is Moral Evil. Those Pains therefore that rouse us to the removal of it become Good. So we shall find through all Nature that Pain is intended as a stimulus to Man in order that he may remove moral Evil. Activity is the proper Happiness of rational Beings—and we cannot conceive a man active without a motive . . . the only conceivable motive by which Nature can and does prompt to Activity is by making Inexertion imme-diately unpleasant & the source of future Pain. The narrow Limits of this Lecture make it inconvenient, or I should not despair of proving that there is not one Pain but which is somehow or other the effect of moral Evil. But whence proceeds this moral Evil? Why was not Man formed without the capability of it? To this it may be answered that in morals as in Science our Wisdom is the effect of repeated Errors. Innocence implies the Absence of Vice from the absence of Temptation. Virtue the Absence of Vice from the knowledge of its Consequences. It was therefore necessary that Man should run through the Course of Vice & Mischief since by Experience alone his Virtue & Happiness can acquire Permanence & Security. From the whole circle of Nature we collect Proofs that the Omnipotent operates in a process from the Slip to the full-blown Rose, from the embryo to the full-grown Man how vast & various the Changes! And this is a new proof of Wisdom & Benevolence—We find that independently of the Pleasures to which we change, every act of changing is itself a pleasure—so that the Sum of Happiness is twice as great to a Being who has arrived at a certain point by gradual progressiveness as it would be to him who was placed there in the first step of his Existence. As for example in Knowledge—Our pleasures are not only derived from our having access to any new object but likewise from comparing our present attainments with our past ignorance ... in short, it is impossible for us to conceive Happiness that does not result from Progressiveness

True! it has been objected—according to the present nature of Things, but why did not God make them otherwise; in other words, why did not the God of all power do those things which are the objects of no Power? Surely it is not irreverent or impious to deny what Descartes, a concealed Atheist was fond of asserting that God if he chose might change a Tree into a Syllogism! A school boy finding his Sum not answer by one figure might complain—Why did not God make two and two 5. If you should convince him that upon the whole it is better that two and two should make four, he might answer. Why were not two and two made to be either four or five ad arbitrium so that I might take that number which occasion made most convenient. But God himself cannot make Contradictions to be true at the same time—and the certain part of human knowledge what is it but an imparted ray of divine omniscience?

We may safely therefore conclude that the existence of moral evil does not impeach the divine power or benevolence. But by the effect of Error the World may be so sunk as to resist all the Impressions of natural Wisdom—Would you employ Reasoning? Where are the Reasoners? Would you employ Reasoning? Where are the minds susceptible of it? There is a state of depravity from which it seems impossible to recall mankind except by impressing on them worthy notions of Supreme Being, and other hopes & other fears than what visible objects supply. But unsusceptible of the effects of Reasoning Understanding so depraved will yield only to the overwhelming of supernatural Intervention. The wisest of the ancient Legislators had recourse to religious Imposture a fact which proves that they felt the necessity of the Revelation which they did not possess. But it has been objected against Miracles that the course of nature is fixed and immutable—that this is evinced by the concurring testimony of all mankind—that therefore the Testimony of a few persons who affirm the contrary cannot be admitted. To this we answer—that each party testifies what it has seen, and why may not the Evidence of both be true? Nothing is more common or constant than the effect of Gravity in making all Bodies upon the surface of our Earth tend to its centre—yet the rare and extraordinary Influences of Magnetism and Electricity can suspend this Tendency. Now before Magnetism & Electricity were discovered and verified by a variety of concurrent facts, there would have been as much reason to disallow the evidence of their particular effects attested by Eyewitnesses, as there is now to disallow the particular Miracles recorded in Scripture. The miracles may have been and I doubt not were worked according to the Laws of Nature—although not by those Laws with which we are as yet acquainted. For the belief of any historical Fact we can require three things only. That the Testimony be numerous & manifestly disinterested—that the Agent be sufficiently powerful and the final Cause sufficiently great. These three Requisites the Scripture Miracles will be found to possess by him who previously believes the existence of a God & his attributes. The World has its Ages as well as Individuals. Its infancy, and its Childhood and its Youth. By what do we most wisely educate our Children? Do we tell them of the beauty of Virtue chiefly or do we tell them to do what is right for its own sake? A child would not understand, and therefore could not be influenced by them. It is with Virtue precisely as it is with money. Originally money is not valued but for its use in the procuring of something else, but in old age, many love and pursue that as an end which at first was only a means. So virtue is first practiced for the pleasures that accompany or the rewards that follow it—and Vice avoided as hateful from the punishment attached. But in length of Time by the magic power of association we transfer our attachment from the Reward to the action rewarded and our fears and hatred from the Punishment to the Vice Punished. Hence it is that gross self-interest rises gradually into pure Benevolence, and appetence of Pleasure into Love of Virtue. Like the air that near the body of the Earths which generate it as gross and heavy, but the farther it recedes from its first principles, the more fine and expansive it becomes till at length it seems to have altered its original Nature and dismissing its former name we call it aether—they who build the house and begin at the Top, they who should regard the Stream only and neglect the Capacity of the Vessel, would be charged with gross Folly—yet not more justly than they who measure divine Revelation by their ideas of God's Perfections and not by the minds that were destined to receive it. The Jews were like the other nations of that Day, comparatively children—nay more so than other nations, as the heavy slavery, they were subjected to in Ægypt must necessarily have bedarkened their Understandings. Like Children therefore they were properly led to Virtue and deterred from Vice by promises of immediate Reward and threats of instant and temporal Punishment They were reasoned with wherever they could be supposed susceptible of reasoning—in other cases, like Children, they were impelled by Authority. In order to take a fair survey of the Mosaic Dispensation we should consider its great Design—The preserving one people free from Idolatry in order that they might be a safe Receptacle

of the necessary precursive Evidences of Christianity! Hence many ordinances which would appear trifling or even injurious if considered as
universal and perpetual, might have been highly useful as preparatory
to such ordinances. If any among us had the legislative Power commit-
ted to us for the next hundred years at the end of which we meant to
introduce a pure Republic or perhaps an abolition of all individual
Property. What a variety of laws should we be obliged to make useful
only as tending to a better form of Things. We are not hastily to conclude
an ordinance or action trifling simply because we at first sight do not
perceive its Uses.

*He develops his point concerning design in more specifically religious terms,
arguing that the progress of the Hebrew religion acted as a providential
preparation for Christianity.*[5]

...we know that our inward feelings are greatly increased and [made]
more permanent as well as more vivid by frequent outward and visible
expressions of them. Now every Age has its peculiar Language. And
Sacrifice unspotted and selected with laborious minuteness of examination was the ordinary Symbol (in the early ages) of dependence and
gratitude and love. This Language therefore which the surrounding
Nations impiously addressed to wood and stone, the Jews were ordered
to pay to the unimaged Creator of all Things.

The argument is made to apply also politically.[6]

...if we...consider the necessity on the account of Christianity for
preserving [the] Israelites themselves, I trust that in the course of these
Lectures I shall be able to prove the final End so vast and benevolent as
to justify any means that were necessary to it. In this view the devas-
tations of the Hebrews were highly useful as rousing against them the
deeply-rooted abhorrence of the surrounding Nations, and thus exciting national antipathy—I might add too that the Belief of one God and
his Perfections were necessary to preserve them a Free State since the
Superstitions that surrounded them disposed the mind to imbecillity
and unmanly Terrors—which would soon bring in political Slavery,
whereas they who accustomed themselves to contemplate the infinite
Love of the true Deity, that by the comparison they do so dwarf the

giant sons of Earth as to become incapable of not yielding Obedience to God by Rebellion to Tyrants—

Prophecies also have their place in the general Design.[7]

[Their] communications [from the Deity] consisted sometimes of Admonitions and moral Precepts, but more frequently contained annunciations of future Events. To determine whether these annunciations were accidental guesses, or imparted Rays of the divine Foreknowledge we must again adopt that mode of reasoning by which we proved the existence of an intelligent First Cause, namely the astonishing fitness of one thing to another not in single and solitary instances which might be attributed to the effects of Chance, but in the combination and Procession of all Nature. And as to the ignorant and unobserving many parts of Animals and of the Universe seem useless or pernicious, in which the Zoologist and Astronomer find the most admirable aptitudes for the most beneficial purposes. So what to the eye of Thomas Paine appears a chaos of Unintelligibles Sir Isaac Newton and John Locke and David Hartley discover to be miraculous Order, and Wisdom more than human.

The fulfilment of prophecies thus serves as a lasting 'moonlight' to replace the more dazzling, but temporary, 'sunlight' of miracles.[8]

At the first Promulgation of a divine Mission Miracles are its best and only Tests. But the full force of such preter-natural Evidence can operate on the Eyewitnesses only. Their influence gradually decreases and becomes more and more faint and then the Accomplishment of predicted Events is substituted and discovers to us the truth of the Revealed Doctrines to us by a sufficient though not so overpowering a Light. So often when yet the Sun is high in heaven we may observe the Moon like a thin white cloud, pale faint and shadowy; but when the sun sets, and the Night comes on, it acquires a gradual increase of Splendor till at length it reigns the presiding Luminary, and the Traveller journeys onward through the illumined Darkness unindangered and rejoicing.

Coleridge points out the singularity of Jesus in speaking to the poor and uneducated, by comparison with the Greek and Roman practice of reserving their instruction in esoteric wisdom for the well-to-do.[9]

in all experience and through all History can any fact be produced that bears any similarity or analogy to this? Should it be answered, that this Character may be an imaginary one, and the Gospels a Forgery—this is multiplying miracles not excluding them. Who were these obscure Forgers, these extraordinary Liars, who at one effort could strike out a System that made the Wisdom of Greece and Rome were as Folly—Is it a Miracle that Jesus should be able to effect it? And no Miracle that Matthew or Luke or men of obscurer name should possess the Power? Xenophon excited his whole power of thought and imagination to sketch out a perfect Character in his Cyropædia but he failed, woefully failed. Who then was this wonderful Genius who could with such minuteness of anecdote and such characterizing Traits imagine and execute a character always perfect yet always imitable? The Writers of the Gospels? Certainly not! . . .

The procedures of science can now be invoked.[10]

In natural philosophy we scruple not to adopt that hypothesis as true which solves Phænomena in a simple and easy manner and if no other can be produced, that gives a similar solution, the probability amounts to a moral Certainty. On this principle rests the Truth of the Newtonian System, and the same principle obtains in Arithmetic. A Rule is given and demonstrated to be the true one, if it solves all the cases to which it can be applied. Let us adopt this undeniable Principle in our reasonings on Revealed Religion. . . . If I adopt this account will it solve all the Phænomena that had so puzzled me. If I reject it will all the phænomena remain unaccountable? Should I answer to myself in the affirmative, as a rational being, I must become a Christian on the same principles that I believe the doctrine of Gravitation, and with the same confidence that I do a sum in Addition or Subtraction. In the perusal of History I never doubt the Truth of any action, if the agent were sufficiently powerful to do it—and any motive appeared sufficiently strong, to induce him—But all powerful God *can* work a miracle, and surely no motive stronger or so strong can be even conceived, as the promulgation of a perfect system of morality, and the ascertainment of a future State.

Thus though I had never seen the Old or New Testament, I should become a Christian, if only I sought for Truth with a simple Heart.

He now moves to assertions of what is essential in Christianity, as distinguished from the doctrines that have subsequently accreted to it.[11]

THAT there is one God infinitely wise, powerful and good, and that a future state of Retribution is made certain by the Resurrection of Jesus who is the Messiah—are all the *doctrines* of the Gospel. That Christians must behave towards the majority with loving kindness and submission preserving among themselves a perfect Equality is a Synopsis of its Precepts.

This still leaves the question of sin and of Christ's act in suffering on the cross as a satisfaction for it. This Coleridge takes on trust, but does not at this time accept, as a necessary complement, the need for Trinitarianism, the imposition of which he ascribes to the worldly interests of priests.[12]

... however mysteriously yet a full and adequate Satisfaction has, it seems, been thus made to the divine Justice for all sins that were and are and will be. How then does it happen, that Repentance and good works are necessary? Can this God of Justice, who has been already paid his full price, exact yet more? A mysterious Doctrine is never more keenly ridiculed, than when a man of sense, who professes it from interested motives, endeavours to make it appear consistent with Reason. By the happy chemistry of explanation, so common among men of abilities who think a good Living a more substantial thing than a good Conscience, he volatilizes absurdity into nothingness, and escapes from the charge of self-contradiction by professing a solemn Belief in the great Mystery of—what every man believes without profession or solemnity. Thus have I heard a very vehement Trinitarian explain himself away into a perfect Humanist! and the thrice strange Union of Father, Son and Holy Ghost in one God, each Person full and perfect God transmuted into the simple notion that God is Love, and Intelligence and Life, and that Love, Intelligence and Life are God! a Trinity in Unity equally applicable to Man or Beast! Thus you are told of the wondrous Power of the Cross, yet you find that this wonder working Sacrifice possesses no efficacy unless there be added to it everything that, if God be benevolent, must be sufficient without it. This is the mysterious cookery of the Orthodox—which promises to make Broth out of a Flint, but when you are congratulating yourself on the cheapness of your proposed Diet, requires as necessary ingredients, Beef, Salt and Turnips! But the Layman might say—I can make Broth out of Beef, Salt and Turnips myself. Most true! but the Cook would have no plea for demanding his wages were it not for his merit in dropping in the Flint.

He now moves to his own interpretation of Platonism as expounding a form of Trinitarianism which is nonsensical, yet in a mysterious way closer to the truth than the interpretations proposed by those who, for their own ends, relate it to moral classical precepts.[13]

Plato, the wild-minded Disciple of Socrates who hid Truth in a dazzle of fantastic allegory, and is dark with excess of Brightness had asserted that whatever exists in the visible World, must be in God in an infinite degree. In the visible World we perceive Life or Power, which Plato calls the Spirit and above Life, Intelligence which he calls ὸ Λογος—the same word which St John uses and which in our Version is rendered by the Word—and above Power and Intelligence the principle of Benevolence which employs them to the production of happiness—this he called το εν και αγαθον. The one and the good. These three Principles are equally God, and God is one—a mysterious way of telling a plain Truth, namely that God is a living Spirit, infinitely powerful, wise and benevolent. Again, the same Plato in his quaint Book De Animâ mundi says that Matter, posterior in order of Things but co-eternal in time, was begotten by Wisdom, and that from Wisdom and matter proceeds Nature, or the Spirit of universal Life. From the Gnostics the Christians had learnt the trick of personifying abstract Qualities, and from Plato they learned their Trinity in Unity.

But though Plato dressed Truth in the garb of Nonsense, still it was Truth, and they who would take the Trouble of unveiling her, might discover and distinguish all the Features, but this would not answer the ends of the Priest. What a man understands and can with little trouble do for himself, he will not pay another to do for him. We pay Physicians to heal us because we cannot heal ourselves—we fee Lawyers to plead for us, because we do not understand the Law, but the Gospels are so obvious to the meanest Capacity that he who runs may read. He who knows his letters, may find in them everything necessary for him. Alas! he would learn too much, he would learn the rights of Man and the Imposture of Priests, the sovereignty of God, and the usurpation of unauthorized Vice-gerents—his attention must be kept from that dangerous Book—false Translations and lying Interpreters shall misrepresent and pervert it, and in return for the tenth of his Substance the Poor Man shall listen to some lilly-handed Sermonizer who gives him Seneca and Tully in lieu of Christ and St Paul, and substitutes schoolboy scraps stolen from the vain babbling of Pagan Philosophy for the pure precepts of revealed Wisdom—

After giving an account of the rise of inequality and its ills, Coleridge argues
the need for nevertheless maintaining the status quo as long as human beings
are not redeemed from vice—citing in support the words of Christ concerning
the 'things that are Caesar's'—while also showing from scripture how the
early Christians attempted a scheme of equality which was nevertheless pre-
mature, the growth of the kingdom needing time for its accomplishment.[14]

While I possess anything exclusively mine, the selfish Passions will
have full play, and our Hearts will never learn that great Truth that the
good of the Whole etc. We find in the twelfth of Luke that our Lord
refused to authorize a division of Inheritance, and in the subsequent
verses forbids all property, and orders men to depend for their subsistence upon their Labor. And in Luke the 20th 21. 22. they asked Jesus—
"Is it lawful for us to give Tribute unto Cæsar or no? And he said unto
them—Shew me a penny whose Image and Superscription hath it?
They answered and said Cæsar's And he said unto them—render unto
Cæsar the Things that are Cæsars, and unto God the Things that are
God's." A wise Sentence. That we use money is a proof that we possess
individual property, and Commerce and Manufactures, and while
these evils continue, your own vices will make a government necessary, and it is fit that you maintain that government. Emperor and
King are but the lord lieutenants of conquered Souls—secondaries and
vicegerents who govern not with their own right but with power dele-
gated to them by our Avarice and appetites! Let us exert over our own
hearts a virtuous despotism, and lead our own Passions in triumph,
and then we shall want neither Monarch nor General. If we would
have no Nero without, we must place a Cæsar within us, and that
Cæsar must be Religion! That I have given no fanciful Interpretation of
these passages is evident from hence—that the Apostles and immediate
Converts of Christ understood them in the same manner. In Acts II.
44. 45. we read "And all that believed were together, & had all things
in common—and sold their possessions & goods and parted them to all
men, as every man had need." But this part of the Christian Doctrine,
which is indeed almost the whole of it, soon was corrupted, and that it
would do so was foretold. Luke 13 v. 18. 21. contains two prophetic
similitudes. "It is like a grain of mustard seed and it grew and waxed
a great Tree," and "it is like a very little leaven which a woman took
and hid in three measures of Meal till the whole was leavened!" It is
natural for seeds which at length rise to great Trees to lie long in the
ground before their vegetation is perceptible and to increase very
slowly for a considerable Length of Time—a small Quantity of Leaven

also enclosed within a great bulk of meal must of necessity operate very slowly . . .

Not long after these lectures, having encountered a doughty warrior in the form of John Thelwall, he is spurred into writing a long and detailed letter defending his religious position.[15]

My dear Thelwall! 'It is the principal Felicity of Life, & the Glory of Manhood to speak out fully on all subjects.' I will avail myself of it—I will express *all* my feelings; but will previously take care to make my feelings benevolent. Contempt is Hatred without fear—Anger Hatred accompanied with apprehension. But because Hatred is always evil, Contempt must be always evil—& a good man ought to speak *contemptuously* of nothing. I am sure a wise man will not of opinions which have been held by men, in *other* respects at least, confessedly of more powerful Intellect than himself. 'Tis an assumption of *infallibility*; for if a man were wakefully mindful that what he now thinks foolish, he may himself hereafter think wise, it is not in nature, that he should *despise* those who now believe what it is possible he may himself hereafter believe——& if he deny this possibility, he must *on that point* deem himself infallible & immutable.—Now in your Letter of Yesterday you speak with *contempt* of two things, Old Age & the Christian Religion:—this Religion was believed by Newton, Locke, & Hartley, after intense investigation, which in each had been preceded by unbelief.—This does not *prove* it's truth; but it should save it's followers from *contempt*—even though thro' the infirmities of mortality they should *have lost their teeth*. I call that man a Bigot, Thelwall, whose intemperate Zeal for or against any opinions leads him to contradict himself in the space of half-a-dozen lines. Now this you appear to me to have done.—I will write fully to you now; because I shall never renew the Subject. I shall not be idle in defence of the Religion, I profess; & my books will be the place, not my letters.—You say the Christian is a *mean* Religion: now the Religion, which Christ taught, is simply 1 that there is an Omnipresent Father of infinite power, wisdom, & Goodness, in whom we all of us move, & have our being & 2. That when we appear to men to die, we do not utterly perish; but after this Life shall continue to enjoy or suffer the consequences & [natur]al effects of the Habits, we have formed here, whether good or evil.—This is the Christian *Religion* & all of the Christian *Religion*. That there is *no fancy* in it, I readily grant; but that it is mean, & deficient in *mind*, and *energy*, it were impossible for me to admit, unless I admitted that there *could be* no dignity, intellect, or force in any thing but *atheism*.—But tho' it appeal not, itself, to the fancy, the truths which it teaches, admit the highest exercise of it. Are the 'innumerable multitude of angels & archangels' less splendid beings than the countless Gods & Goddesses of Rome & Greece?—And can you seriously think that Mercury from Jove equals in poetic sublimity 'the mighty Angel that came down from Heaven, whose face was as it were the Sun, and his feet as pillars of fire: Who set his right foot on the sea, and his left upon the earth. And he sent forth a loud voice; and when he had sent it forth, seven Thunders uttered their Voices: and when the seven Thunders had uttered their Voices, the mighty Angel lifted up his hand to Heaven, & sware by Him that liveth for ever & ever, that TIME was no more?' Is not Milton a *sublimer* poet than Homer or Virgil? Are not his Personages more sublimely cloathed? And do you not know, that there is not perhaps *one* page in Milton's Paradise Lost, in which he has not borrowed his imagery from the *Scriptures?*—I allow, and rejoice that *Christ* appealed only to the understanding & the affections; but I affirm that, after reading Isaiah, or St Paul's Epistle to the Hebrews, Homer & Virgil are disgustingly *tame* to me, & Milton himself barely tolerable. You and I are very differently organized, if you think that the following (putting serious belief out of the Question) is a mean flight of impassioned Eloquence; in which the Apostle marks the difference between the Mosaic & Christian Dispensations—'For ye are not come unto the Mount that might be touched' (i.e. a *material* and earthly place) 'and that burned with fire; nor unto Blackness, and Tempest, and the sound of a Trumpet, and the Voice of Words, which voice they who heard it intreated that it should not be spoken to them any more; but ye are come unto Mount Sion, and unto the city of the living God, to an innumerable multitude of Angels, to God the Judge of all, and to the Spirits of just Men made perfect!'——*You* may prefer to all this the Quarrels of Jupiter & Juno, the whimpering of wounded Venus, & the Jokes of the celestials on the lameness of Vulcan—be it so (The difference in our tastes it would not be difficult to account for from the different feelings which we have associated with these ideas)——I shall continue with Milton to say, that

Sion Hill

Delights *me* more, and Siloa's Brook that flow'd
Fast by the oracle of God!

'Visions fit for Slobberers.' If infidelity do not lead to Sensuality, which in every case except your's I have observed it to do, it always takes away all respect for those who become unpleasant from the infirmities of Disease or decaying Nature. Exempli gratiâ—The *Aged* are '*Slobberers*'—The *only* Vision, which Christianity holds forth, is indeed peculiarly adapted to these *Slobberers*—Yes! to these lonely & despised, and perishing SLOBBERERS it proclaims, that their 'Corruptible shall put on *Incorruption*, & their Mortal put on *Immortality*.'

'Morals for the Magdalen & Botany Bay.' Now, Thelwall! I presume that to preach morals to the virtuous is not quite so requisite, as to preach them to the vicious. 'The Sick need a Physician.' Are morals, which would make a Prostitute a Wife, & a Sister; which would restore her to inward peace & purity; are morals, which would make Drunkards sober, the ferocious benevolent, & Thieves honest, *mean morals*? Is it a despicable trait in our Religion, that it's professed object is 'to heal the broken-hearted, and give Wisdom to the Poor Man?'—It preaches *Repentance*—what repentance? Tears, & Sorrow, & a repetition of the same crimes?—No. A 'Repentance unto good works'—a repentance that completely does away all superstitious terrors by teaching, that the *Past* is nothing in itself; that if the Mind *is* good, that it *was* bad, imports nothing. 'It is a religion for Democrats.' It certainly teaches in the most explicit terms the rights of Man, his right to Wisdom, his right to an equal share in all the blessings of Nature; it commands it's disciples to go every where, & every where to preach these rights; it commands them never to use the arm of flesh, to be perfectly non-resistant; yet to hold the promulgation of *Truth* to be a Law above Law, and in the performance of this office to defy 'Wickedness in high places,' and cheerfully to endure ignominy, & wretchedness, & torments, & death, rather than *intermit* the performance of it; yet while enduring ignominy, & wretchedness, & torments & death to feel nothing but sorrow, and pity, and love for those who inflicted them; wishing their Oppressors to be altogether such as they, 'excepting these bonds.'—Here is *truth* in theory; and in practice a union of energetic *action*, and more energetic *Suffering*. For activity amuses; but he, who can *endure* calmly, must possess the seeds of true Greatness. For all his animal spirits will of necessity fail him; and he has only his *Mind* to trust to.——These doubtless are morals for all the Lovers of Mankind, who wish to *act* as well as *speculate*; and that you should allow this, and yet not three lines before call the same *Morals mean*, appears to me a gross self-contradiction, symptomatic of Bigotry.—I write freely, Thelwall! for tho' *personally* unknown, I really love you, and can count but few human beings, whose hand I would welcome with a more hearty Grasp of Friendship. I suspect, Thelwall! that you never read your Testament since your Understanding was matured, without carelessness, & previous contempt, & a somewhat like Hatred—Christianity regards morality as a process—it finds a man vicious and unsusceptible of noble motives; & gradually leads him, at least, desires to lead him, to the height of disinterested Virtue—till in relation & proportion to his faculties & powers, he is perfect 'even as our Father in Heaven is perfect.' There is no resting-place for Morality. Now I will make one other appeal, and have done for ever with the subject.—There is a passage in Scripture which comprizes the whole process, & each component part of Christian Morals. Previously, let me explain the word Faith—by Faith I understand, first, a deduction from experiments in favor of the existence of something not experienced, and secondly, the motives which attend such a deduction. Now motives being selfish are only the beginning & the *foundation*, necessary and of first-rate importance, yet made of vile materials, and hidden beneath the splendid Superstructure.——

'Now giving all diligence, add to your Faith *Fortitude*, and to Fortitude Knowlege, and to Knowlege Purity, and to Purity Patience, and to Patience Godliness, and to Godliness Brotherly-kindness, and to Brotherly-kindness Universal Love.'

I hope, whatever you may think of Godliness, you will like the *note* on it.—I need not tell you, that Godliness is God*like*-ness, and is paraphrased by Peter—'that ye may be partakers of the divine nature.'—i.e. act from a love of order, & happiness, & not from any self-respecting motive—from the *excellency*, into which you have exalted your *nature*, not from the *keenness* of *mere prudence*.——'add to your faith fortitude, and to fortitude knowlege, and to knowlege purity, and to purity patience, and to patience Godliness, and to Godliness brotherly kindness, and to brotherly kindness universal Love.' Now, Thelwall! [Can you after reading this consciously repeat that these words are fit only for Prostitutes & hardened Rogues?—] Putting *Faith* out of the Question, (which by the by is not mentioned as a virtue but as the leader to them) can you mention a virtue which is not here enjoined—& supposing the precepts embodied in the practice of any one human being, would not Perfection be personified?—I write these things not with any expectation of making you a Christian—I should smile at my own folly, if I conceived it even in a friendly day-dream. But [I do wish to see a progression in your *moral* character, & I *hope* to see it—for while you so frequently appeal to the passions of Terror,

& Ill nature & Disgust, in your popular writings, I must be blind not to perceive that you present in your daily & hourly practice the *feelings* of *universal Love.*] 'The ardor of undisciplined Benevolence seduces us into malignity.'—And while you accustom yourself to speak so *contemptuously* of Doctrines you do not accede to, and Persons with whom you do not accord, I must doubt whether even your *brotherly-kindness* might not be made more perfect. That is surely *fit* for a man which his mind after sincere examination approves, which animates his conduct, soothes his sorrows, & heightens his Pleasures. Every good & earnest Christian declares that all this is true of the *visions* (as you please to style them, God knows why) of Christianity——Every earnest Christian therefore is on a level with *slobberers.* Do not charge me with dwelling on *one* expression—these expressions are always indicative of the habit of feeling.—You possess fortitude, and purity, & a large portion of brotherly-kindness & universal Love—drink with unquenchable thirst of the two latter virtues, and *acquire* patience; and then, Thelwall! should *your* System be true, all that can be said, is that (if both our Systems should be found to increase our own & our fellow-creatures' happiness)—Here lie or did lie *the all* of John Thelwall & S. T. Coleridge—they were both humane, & happy, but the former was the more knowing: & if my System should prove true, we, I doubt not, shall both meet in the kingdom of Heaven, and I with transport in my eye shall say—'I *told* you so, my *dear* fellow.' But seriously, the faulty habit of feeling, which I have endeavoured to point out in you, I have detected in at least as great degree in my own practice & am struggling to subdue it.—

Despite the vigour of this defence Coleridge is later to recall the subsequent period as one of considerable religious and philosophical disquiet.[16]

I retired to a cottage in Somersetshire at the foot of Quantock, and devoted my thoughts and studies to the foundations of religion and morals. Here I found myself all afloat. Doubts rushed; broke upon me *"from the fountains of the great deep,"* and fell *"from the windows of heaven."* The fontal truths of natural religion and the books of Revelation alike contributed to the flood; and it was long ere my ark touched on an Ararat, and rested. The *idea* of the Supreme being appeared to me to be as necessarily implied in all particular modes of being as the idea of infinite space in all the geometric figures by which space is limited. I was pleased with the cartesian opinion, that the idea of God is distinguished from all other ideas by involving its *reality*; but I was not wholly satisfied. I began then to ask myself, what proof I had of the outward *existence* of any thing? . . .

2

A Religion of Life?

During the years after he settled in Bristol Coleridge not only busied himself with religious and philosophical studies, but also began to feel his way as a poet of nature. His most successful venture in this field, the poem 'The Eolian Harp', composed at the time of his marriage and celebrating a visit to the honeymoon cottage which he shared with Sara Coleridge, begins with an effective early attempt at nature-description:[1]

> ... most soothing sweet it is
> To sit beside our cot, our cot o'er grown
> With white-flower'd Jasmin, and the broad-leav'd Myrtle,
> (Meet emblems they of Innocence and Love!)
> And watch the clouds, that late were rich with light,
> Slow sad'ning round, and mark the star of eve
> Serenely brilliant (such should Wisdom be)
> Shine opposite! How exquisite the scents
> Snatch'd from yon bean-field! and the world *so* hush'd!
> The stilly murmur of the distant Sea
> Tells us of Silence. And that simplest Lute,
> Plac'd length-ways in the clasping casement, hark!
> How by the desultory breeze caress'd,
> Like some coy Maid half-yielding to her Lover,
> It pours such sweet upbraidings, as must needs
> Tempt to repeat the wrong!

The passage veers interestingly between the sensibility of eighteenth-century poetry, with the use of elements in nature to represent abstract moral qualities such as 'Innocence', 'Love' and 'Wisdom', at one extreme, and an amoral flirting with temptations of the sensuous at the other.

Throughout this early period he was constantly drawn to seek a further significance in nature that bordered at times on pantheism, a possibility which becomes strikingly clear in the next lines when he tentatively figures a model of individual and natural relationships:

> And what if all of animated nature
> Be but organic Harps diversly fram'd,
> That tremble into thought, as o'er them sweeps
> Plastic and vast, one intellectual Breeze,
> At once the Soul of each, and God of all?

Despite his immediate attempt in the poem to retract such speculations as ungodly, he never actually excised the lines and went so far as to add more later, hoping perhaps that a means would be found to reconcile them with a respectable religious position.

Meanwhile many new currents of thought pressed on his mind as he settled among the radical thinkers of Bristol and tried to establish himself as an intellectual journalist. During the tour a few months later to gain subscribers for his new journal *The Watchman*, Coleridge called on Erasmus Darwin, the well-known doctor, poet and radical thinker—as he put it, 'the everything, except the Christian!' He continued,

> Dr. Darwin possesses, perhaps, a greater range of knowledge than any other man in Europe, and is the most inventive of philosophical men. He thinks in a *new* train on all subjects except religion. He bantered me on the subject of religion. I heard all his arguments, and told him that it was infinitely consoling to me, to find that the arguments which so great a man adduced against the existence of a God and the evidences of revealed religion were such as had startled me at fifteen, but had become the objects of my smile at twenty. Not one new objection—not even an ingenious one.[2]

Although Coleridge had reservations about Darwin's success as a poet, and was baffled by his refusal to consider the arguments in favour of Christianity, he could not but be intrigued by his openness and intelligence as a scientist, as shown in his currently published work *Zoonomia*, and seems to have cherished the hope of making good what he considered his deficiencies in the religious field by filling the gap himself.

Soon afterwards his thinking on the subject was further energized by the advent of William and Dorothy Wordsworth, who brought with them a poetic devotion to the detail of natural life. This did not altogether realize his hopes, however, since Wordsworth showed no sign of sharing his religious attitude:

> On one subject we are habitually silent—we found our data dissimiliar, & never renewed the subject / It is his practice & almost his nature to convey all the truth he knows without any attack on what he supposes falsehood, if that falsehood be interwoven with virtues or happiness—he loves & venerates Christ & Christianity—I wish, he did more—but it were wrong indeed, if an incoincidence with one of our wishes altered our respect & affection to a man, whom we are as it were instructed by our great master to say that not being against us he is for us.[3]

In spite of this, the Wordsworths' evident devotion to nature swept Coleridge into their orbit for several years and prompted many observations of his own, tempered only by constant anxiety to ensure that such reverence differed from outright pantheism. One result was a lasting respect for the philosophy of Spinoza—whom he at once venerated and distrusted as an ultimate guide. According to Crabb Robinson in 1812:

> In the course of a few minutes, while standing in the room, Coleridge kissed Spinoza's face at the title-page, said his book was his gospel, and in less than a minute added that his philosophy was, after all, false. Spinoza's philosophy has been demonstrated to be false, but only by that philosophy which has at the same time demonstrated the falsehood of all other philosophies. Did philosophy begin with an IT IS instead of an I AM, Spinoza would be altogether true; and without allowing a breathing-time he parenthetically asserted: 'I, however, believe in all the doctrines of Christianity, even of the Trinity'.[4]

He was fond of comparing Spinoza's philosophy to an adamantine chain—but one set, unfortunately, into a rock of ice.[5] An effect of the dilemma induced by this opposition, and his fear of falling into pantheism, was an increasing tendency to view nature as symbolic of, rather than identifiable with, the divine—an expedient that would serve him particularly well in later years.

In the spring of 1795 Coleridge declares to George Dyer that the power of associationism means that to live amidst natural beauty will ensure the sustaining of morality.[1]

. . . It is melancholy to think, that the best of us are liable to be shaped & coloured by surrounding Objects—and a demonstrative proof, that Man was not made to live in Great Cities! Almost all the physical Evil in the World depends on the existence of moral Evil—and the long-continued contemplation of the latter does not tend to meliorate the human heart.—The pleasures, which we receive from rural beauties, are of little Consequence compared with the Moral Effect of these pleasures—beholding constantly the Best possible we at last become ourselves the best possible. In the country, all around us smile Good and Beauty—and the Images of this divine καλοκάγαθόν [beautiful and good] are miniatured on the mind of the beholder, as a Landscape on a Convex Mirror . . .

God love you, my very dear Sir! I would that we could form a Pantisocracy in England, and that you could be one of us!—The finely-fibred Heart, that like the statue of Memnon, trembles into melody on the sunbeam touch of Benevolence, is most easily jarred into the dissonance of Misanthropy. But you will never suffer your feelings to be benumbed by the torpedo Touch of that Fiend— / I know you—and know that you will drink of every Mourner's sorrows, even while your own Cup is trembling over it's Brink!—

Soon afterwards, he toys with the idea of a universal Spirit at work in Nature, using the image of the Eolian harp to suggest how every individual human sensibility might be replicating in little its universal working.[2]

> . . . many idle flitting phantasies
> Traverse my indolent and passive brain
> As wild and various, as the random gales
> That swell or flutter on this subject Lute!
> And what if all of animated nature
> Be but organic Harps diversly fram'd,
> That tremble into thought, as o'er them sweeps
> Plastic and vast, one intellectual Breeze,
> At once the Soul of each, and God of all?

His religious concerns cause him to reject such extreme speculations, however; indeed, he is shortly to claim that he has withdrawn from political and radical activity altogether. Under the influence of Wordsworth he renews his search for human improvement by way of the elevation provided by contact with nature and the cultivation of human affection.[3]

...I have for some time past withdrawn myself almost totally from the consideration of *immediate* causes, which are infinitely complex & uncertain, to muse on fundamental & general causes—the 'causae causarum [causes of the causes].'—I devote myself to such works as encroach not on the antisocial passions—in poetry, to elevate the imagination & set the affections in right tune by the beauty of the inanimate impregnated, as with a living soul, by the presence of Life—in prose, to the seeking with patience & a slow, very slow mind 'Quid sumus, et quidnam victuri gignimur'—What our faculties are & what they are capable of becoming.—I love fields & woods & mountains with almost a visionary fondness—and because I have found benevolence & quietness growing within me as that fondness has increased, therefore I should wish to be the means of implanting it in others—& to destroy the bad passions not by combating them, but by keeping them in inaction.

> Not useless do I deem
> These shadowy Sympathies with things that hold
> An inarticulate Language: for the Man
> Once taught to love such objects, as excite
> No morbid passions, no disquietude,
> No vengeance & no hatred, needs must feel
> The Joy of that pure principle of Love
> So deeply, that, unsatisfied with aught
> Less pure & exquisite, he cannot chuse
> But seek for objects of a kindred Love
> In fellow-natures, & a kindred Joy.
> Accordingly, he by degrees perceives
> His feelings of aversion softened down,
> A holy tenderness pervade his frame!
> His sanity of reason not impair'd,
> Say rather that his thoughts now flowing clear
> From a clear fountain flowing, he looks round—
> He seeks for Good & finds the Good he seeks.
> Wordsworth.—

The scientific account of a 'glory' is noted and long to be remembered as an analogue of imaginative and spiritual experience.[4]

Vide Description of a Glory, by John Haygarth, Manchester Trans. Vol. 3. p. 463. On the thirteenth of February, 1780, as I was returning to Chester, and ascending, at Rhealt, the mountain which forms the eastern boundary of the Vale of Clwyd,—in the road above me, I was struck with the peculiar appearance of a very white shining cloud, that lay remarkably close to the ground. The Sun was nearly setting but shone extremely bright. I walked up to the cloud, and my shadow was projected into it; the head of my shadow was surrounded at some distance by a circle of various colours whose centre appeared to be near the situation of the eye, and whose circumference extended to the Shoulders. The circle was complete except where the shadow of my body intercepted it—it exhibited the most vivid colors red being outermost—all the colors appeared in the same order & proportion that the rainbow presents to our view—The beautiful colors of the hoarfrost on snow in sun shine—red, green, & blue—in various angles.

Natural scenery is increasingly explored for the light it may shed on the relation between objects and their reflections, realities and shadows.[5]

Now as we return the fog begins to clear off from the Lake, still however leaving straggling Detachments on it—, & clings viscously to the Hill/—all the objects on the opposite Coast are hidden, and all those hidden are reflected in the Lake, Trees, & the Castle, Lyulph's Tower, & the huge Cliff that dwarfs it!— Divine!—The reflection of the huge pyramidal Crag is still hidden, & the image in the water still brighter //but the Lyulph's Tower gleams like a Ghost, dim & shadowy—& the bright Shadow thereof how beautiful it is cut across by that Tongue of *breezy* water—now the Shadow is suddenly gone—and the Tower itself rises emerging out of the mist, two-thirds wholly hidden, the turrets quite clear—& a moment all is snatched away—Realities & Shadows—

Look at Lodore, from our window—it is a painting—mere motionless Color—thro' the Glass, as it acquires magnitude, it gains motion/ motion is therefore *something*, but it requires a given distinctness to be perceived—not magnitude—for an object that through the glass is no larger than Lodore to the naked eye acquire motion in the same way—it must therefore be the vigor of the rays of Light/—motion seems too generally to have been considered as an affection of Places—we ought to begin by considering motion in the same place—as that of a waterfall—even tho' it were true that this could be analysed in a perception of the *change* of *place*—instead of a simple Sensation.

Tuesday, March 17—9⁰ Clock. The Organ stood in the Reflected Room as a black Form, most distinct & sharp in its Lines & Figure, but perfectly transparent—the Clouds, the Moon, and the moonlike Star of Jove seen thro' with undiminished Brilliance—whereas the Reflection of the Cieling appearing like a milky mist seem'd to dim the Stars that twinkled thro' it.

The aspiration to discover 'what we are' *informs his thinking for some years after.*[6]

When this Book is fairly off my hands, I shall, if I live & have sufficient health, set seriously to work—in arranging what I have already written, and in pushing forward my Studies, & my Investigations relative to the omne scibile of human Nature—*what* we *are*, & *how* we *become* what we are; so as to solve the two grand Problems, how, being acted upon, we shall act; how, acting, we shall be acted upon. But between me & this work there may be Death.

Having planned a prefatory essay to a proposed abridgement by Hazlitt of Abraham Tucker's Light of Nature Pursued, *in which he will give the substance of Hartley's philosophy 'defecated from all the corpuscular hypotheses', he proposes to Southey a 'great book of Criticism respecting Poetry and Prose', following this with a radical criticism of Hartley's Associationism.*[7]

Believe me, Southey! a metaphysical Solution, that does not instantly *tell* for something in the Heart, is grievously to be suspected as apocryphal. I almost think, that Ideas *never* recall Ideas, as far as they are Ideas—any more than Leaves in a forest create each other's motion—The Breeze it is that runs thro' them / it is the Soul, the state of Feeling—. If I had said, no *one* Idea ever recalls another, I am confident that I could support the assertion.——

Increasingly, he concentrates on the mode of contemplation which enables one to 'see into the life of things'.[8]

I have not read on an average less than 8 hours a day for the last three years—but all is vanity—I feel it more & more—all is vanity that does not lead to Quietness & Unity of Heart, and to the silent aweful idealess

Watching of that living Spirit, & of that Life within us, which is the motion of that Spirit—that Life, which passeth all understanding.——

There remains a Christian element in this which provokes him to reproach even Wordsworth for his more irreverent attitude.[9]

A most unpleasant Dispute with W. & Hazlitt Wednesday Afternoon, Oct. 26. 1803.—I spoke, I fear too contemptuously—but they spoke so irreverently so malignantly of the Divine Wisdom, that it overset me. Hazlitt how easily roused to Rage & Hatred, self-projected/but who shall find the Force that can drag him up out of the Depth into one expression of Kindness, into the shewing of one Gleam of the Light of Love on his Countenance.— Peace be with *him*!—But *thou*, dearest Wordsworth—and what if Ray, Durham, Paley, have carried the observation of the aptitudes of Things too far, too habitually—into Pedantry?—O how many worse Pedantries! how few so harmless with so much efficient Good!—Dear William, pardon Pedantry in others & avoid it in yourself, instead of scoffing & reviling at Pedantry in good men in a good cause, & *becoming* a Pedant yourself in a bad cause—even by that very act becoming one!—But surely always to look at the superficies of Objects for the purpose of taking Delight in their Beauty, & sympathy with their real or imagined Life, is as deleterious to the Health & manhood of Intellect, as always to be peering & unravelling Contrivances may be to the simplicity of the affections, the grandeur & unity of the Imagination.—O dearest William! Would Ray, or Durham, have spoken of God as you spoke of Nature?

Other remarks in praise of Wordsworth at this time nevertheless show how his veneration for his friend causes him to think of his imagination as acting like that of God himself.[10]

Wordsworth is a Poet, a most original Poet—he no more resembles Milton than Milton resembles Shakespere—no more resembles Shakespere than Shakespere resembles Milton—he is himself: and I dare affirm that he will hereafter be admitted as the first & greatest philosophical Poet— the only man who has effected a compleat and constant synthesis of Thought & Feeling and combined them with Poetic Forms, with the music of pleasurable passion and with Imagination or the *modifying* Power in that highest sense of the word in which I have ventured to oppose it to Fancy, or the *aggregating* power—in that sense in which it is a dim Analogue of Creation, not all that we can *believe* but all that we can *conceive* of creation.

Such considerations have led him to reject necessitarianism.[11]

I love & honor you, Poole! for many things—scarcely for any thing more than that, trusting firmly in the Rectitude & simplicity of your own Heart, and listening with faith to it's revealing Voice, you never suffered either my Subtlety or my Eloquence to proselyte you to the pernicious Doctrine of Necessity / all praise to the Great Being who has graciously enabled me to find my way out of that labyrinth-Den of Sophistry, &, I would fain believe, to bring with me a better clue than has hitherto been known, to enable others to do the same. I have convinced Southey—& Wordsworth / & W, you know, was even to Extravagance a Necessitarian—Southey never believed, & abhorred the Doctrine, yet thought the arguments for it unanswerable by human Reason. I have convinced both of them of the sophistry of the arguments, & wherein the Sophism consists—viz. that all have hitherto, both the Necessitarians & their Antagonists, confounded two essentially different Things under one name—& in consequence of *this* Mistake the Victory has been always hollow in favor of the Necessitarians.

The 'analogue' of divine creation can be applied even to himself—however rueful the observation.[12]

Some divines hold, that with God to think & to create are one and the same act—if to think & even to compose had been the same as to write with me, I should have written as much too much as I have now written too little.

These speculations are in line with earlier ones which have given him a lasting belief in the impersonality of God, as he has affirmed to Matthew Coates in December 1803.[13]

Believe me, I have never ceased to think of you with respect & a sort of yearning—you were the first man, from whom I heard that article of my Faith distinctly enunciated, which is the nearest to my Heart, the pure

Fountain of all my moral & religious Feelings & Comforts—I mean, the absolute Impersonality of the Deity. The Many would deem me an Atheist; alas! I know them to be Idolaters.—

Such an affirmation is at one with his lasting respect for Spinoza, about whom he has recently written.[14]

If Spinoza had left the doctrine of Miracles untouched, & had not written so powerfully in support of universal Toleration, his Ethics would never, could never, have brought on him the charge of *Atheism*. His doctrine in this respect is truly & severely orthodox, in the reformed Church/neither do I know that the Church of Rome has authoritatively decided between the Thomists & Scotists in their great controversy on the nature of the Being which Creatures possess.

Earlier he has contemplated writing a poem on Spinoza, concerned among other things with the mystery of perceiving the world as infinitely variegated yet at the same time as unity.[15]

If I begin a poem of Spinoza, thus it should begin/
    I would make a pilgrimage to the burning sands of Arabia, or &c &c to find the Man who could explain to me there can be *one*ness, there being infinite Perceptions—yet there must be a *one*ness, not an intense Union but an Absolute Unity . . .

A considered account of Spinoza's strength—and of his weaknesses—is entered in a notebook some years later.[16]

Paradox as it assuredly is, I am convinced that Spinoza's Innocence and Virtue, guarded and matured into invincible Habit of Being by a Life of constant Meditation and of intellectual pursuit, were the conditions, or temptations, sine queis non of his forming & maintaining a system subversive of all Virtue. He saw so clearly the *folly* and *absurdity* of Wickedness, and felt so weakly & languidly the passions tempting to it, that he concluded nothing was wanting to a course of well-doing but clear conceptions and the fortitudo intellectualis [intellectual strength]/ while his very modesty, a prominent feature in his character, rendered him, as it did Hartley, less averse to the system of Necessity.—Add to these causes his profound admiration of pure Mathematics, and the vast progress made in it so unspeakably beneficial to mankind, bodies as well as souls, & souls as well as bodies—the reflection that the essence of mathematical science consists in discovering the absolute properties of Forms and Proportions, and how pernicious a bewilderment was produced in this sublime Science by the wild attempt of the Platonists, especially the later (tho' Plato himself is far from blameless in this respect) to explain the *final cause* of mathematical figures, and of numbers, so as to subordinate them to a *principle* of origination out of themselves—and the further comparison of the progress of SCIENCE (pura mathesis) which excludes all consideration of final Causes with the unequal and equivocal progress of those Branches of Literature which rest on or refer to final causes—& that ~~its~~ the uncertainty, & mixture with error, appeared in proportion to such reference—And if I mistake not we shall have the most important parts of the history of Spinoza's mind. It is a duty, which we owe to Truth, to distinguish Spinoza from the Voltaires, Humes, and the whole mob of *popular* Infidels—to make manifest, how precious a thing is the sincere Thirst of Truth for the sake of Truth, undebased by Vanity, Appetite, and the Ambition of forming a sect of *acquiescents* & trumpeters—& that it is capable to a wonderful degree of rendering innoxious the poisonous fangs of vast errors—nay, Heaven educing good out of the very evil, the important advantages that have been derived from such men, wise & good men would never have seen the true basis & bulwark of ~~their~~ right cause, if they had not been made to know & understand the whole weight & possible force of the wrong cause—nor would have ever purified their own systems from those admissions, on which the whole of Spinozism is built—& which admissions were common to all parties & therefore fairly belonging to Spinoza/Now I affirm, that none, but an eminently pure & benevolent mind could have constructed & perfected such a system as that of the Ethics of Spinoza. Bad-hearted men always *hate* the religion & morality which they attack—but hatred dims & *inturbidates* the logical faculties. There is likewise a sort of lurking terror in such a heart, which renders it far far too painful to keep a steady gaze on the Being of God & the existence of Immortality—they dare only attack it as Tartars, a pot-valiant Inroad, & then they scour off again/ equally painful is self-examination—for if the wretch be *callous*, the *facts* of psychology will not present themselves—if not, who could go on year after year in a perpetual process of deliberate self-torture & Shame? The very torment of the process would furnish facts subversive of the system, for which the process was instituted—The mind would at

length be unable to disguise from itself the unequivocal *fact* of its
own Shame & Remorse—& this once felt, & distinctly acknowleged,
Spinozism is blown up as by a mine.

*Spinoza remains an ambiguous figure for him to the end. In 1832 he
declares*[17]

If you admit Spinoza's premiss, it is in vain to attack his conclusions.
His logic is an adamantine chain!

*The fact that despite his admiration for Spinoza he finds a flaw in Spinozism
as a whole leads him increasingly to develop the association with Nature as a
symbol of the Divine made already in his poetry and to offer it as a promised
blessing to his child.*[18]

> so shalt thou see and hear
> The lovely shapes and sounds intelligible
> Of that eternal language, which thy God
> Utters who from eternity doth teach
> Himself in all, and all things in himself.
> Great universal Teacher! He shall mould
> Thy spirit, and by giving make it ask.

This symbolism of Nature begins with natural human love.[19]

The best, the truly lovely, in each & all is God. Therefore the truly
Beloved is the symbol of God to whomever it is truly beloved by!—but
it may become perfect & maintained lovely by the function of the two/
The Lover worships in his Beloved that final consummation ⟨of itself
which is⟩ produced in his own soul by the action of the Soul of the
Beloved upon it, and that final perfection of the Soul of the Beloved,
which is in part the consequence of the reaction of his (so ammeli-
orated & regenerated) Soul upon the Soul of his Beloved/till each contemplates the Soul of the other as involving his own, both in its givings
and its receivings, and thus still keeping alive its *outness*, its *self-oblivion*
united with *Self-warmth*, & still approximates to God! Where shall I find
an image for this sublime Symbol which ever involving the presence
of Deity, yet tends towards it ever!—Shall it be in the attractive powers

of the different surfaces of the earth?—Each attraction the *vice-gerent &
representative* of the central attraction, and yet *being* no other than that
attraction itself.—By some such feeling as this I can easily believe the
mind of Fenelon & Madame Guyon to have coloured its faith in the
Worship of Saints—but that was most dangerous/it was not idolatry in
them; but it encouraged Idolatry in others/—Now the pure Love of
a good man to a good woman does not involve this Evil, but multiplies,
intensifies the Good.

*The search for such a 'symbol of God' results in his seeing the moon as a subtle
image of the creative principle: not so much God himself as the Logos or
Word, containing in itself the principle of development.*[20]

In looking at objects of Nature while I am thinking, as at yonder moon
dim-glimmering thro' the dewy window-pane, I seem rather to be seeking, as it were *asking*, a symbolical language for something within me
that already and forever exists, than observing any thing new. Even
when that latter is the case, yet still I have always an obscure feeling as
if that new phænomenon were the dim Awaking of a forgotten or hidden Truth of my inner Nature/It is still interesting as a Word, a Symbol!
It is Λογος, the Creator! and the Evolver! . . .

*In this way the association of ideas can still provide a link between the beauties
of nature and therapy for the spirit.*[21]

The Love of Nature is ever returned double to us—not only the
Delighter in our Delight, but by linking our sweetest but of themselves perishable feelings to distinct & vivid images, which we ourselves at times & which a thousand casual associations will often
recall to our memory. She is the preserver, the Treasuress of our Joys—
even in Sickness & nervous Diseases she has peopled our Imaginations
with lovely Forms which have sometimes overpowered the inward
pain & brought with them their old sensations—and even when all
men have seemed to desert us, & the Friend of our heart has passed
on with one glance from his "cold disliking eye", yet even then the
blue Heaven spreads it out & bends over us, & the little Tree still shel-
ters us under its plumage, as a second Cope, a domestic Firmament,
and the low creeping Gale will sigh in the Heath-plant & sooth us as
by a sound of Sympathy, till the lulled Grief loses itself in fixed gaze

on the purple Heath-blossom, till the present beauty becomes
a Vision of Memory—

*This points to the fact that all human feeling for works of Nature emblematizes
the longing of humanity for a world of spirit beyond itself.*[22]

We are born in the mountains, in the Alps—and when we hire ourselves
out to the Princes of the Lower Lands, sooner or later we feel an incur-
able Home-sickness—& every Tune that recalls our native Heights,
brings on a relapse of the Sickness.—I seem to myself like a Butterfly
who having foolishly torn or bedaubed his wings, is obliged to crawl
like a Caterpillar with all the restless Instincts of the Butterfly.

Our Eye rests in an horizon—still moving indeed as we move—yet
still there is an Horizon & there the Eye rests—but our Hands can only
pluck the Fruit a yard from us—there is no Horizon for the *Hand*—and
the Hand is the symbol of earthly realities, the Eye of our Hope & Faith.
And what is Faith?—it is to the Spirit of Man the same Instinct, which
impels the chrysalis of the horned fly to build its involucrum as long
again as itself to make room for the Antennæ, which are to come, tho'
they never yet have been—O the *Potential* works *in* us even as the
Present mood works *on* us!—

Love with Virtue have almost an actual Present—tho' for moments
and tho' for few—but in general, we have no present unless we are
brutalized—the Present belongs to the two extremes, Beast & Angel—
We in youth have Hope, the Rainbow of the Morning in the West—in
age, we have recollections of Hope, the Evening Rainbow in the East!—
In short, all the organs of Sense are framed for a corresponding World
of Sense: and we have it. All the organs of Spirit are framed for a correspondent World of Spirit: & we cannot but believe it.

*Another version is to see such processes as emancipating human beings from
the world of sense.*[23]

The Heimweh [homesickness] of the Mountain-born—Lie on our
Nurse's bosom (the Earth) and hear tales of our great Father not yet
seen/—but the effect of the Sky—how purely intellectual—

The Rainbow of our Morning in the West before us—of our Evening in
the East behind us—The eye reaches to Heaven, the Hands but the Fruit
of the Soul—Why this?—the Eye & Ear first emancipating themselves

from the Thier-dienst [brute-servitude] & became Organs, Glasses that shelter & admit Light, into the inner World of our Nature—but even as the Images of our sensuous Memory prove an correspondent outward World—so does the inward ideal World in us prove a correspondent World, in which ideal & real are one & the same/—

The unsensualized Mind like the Sojourner in Greenland in the sixteen days before the ascent of the Sun above the Horizon—It is refracted and *appears* before it really *is* there/

Stasis and movement seem supreme enigmas.[24]

Rest, Motion!—O ye strange Locks of intricate Simplicity, who shall find the Key? He shall throw wide open the Portals of the Palace of Sensuous or Symbolical Truth; and the Holy of Holies will he find in the Adyta. Rest = Enjoyment, and Death! Motion = Enjoyment and Life! O the depth of the Proverb, Extremes meet!

The Break of the Morning—& from Inaction a nation starts up into Motion & wide fellow-consciousness!—The Trumpet of the Archangel, and a World with all its Troops & Companies of Generations starts up into an hundredfold Expansion, Power multiplied into itself, cubically, by the number of all its possible Acts—all the Potential springing into Power!—Conceive a Bliss from Self-conscience, combining with Bliss from increase of Action, the first dreaming, the latter dead-asleep, in a grain of Gunpowder—conceive a huge Magazine of Gunpowder, & a Flash of Lightning awakes the Whole at once!—What an Image of the Resurrection, grand from its very Inadequacy. Yet again, conceive the living moving Ocean—its bed sinks away from under, and the whole World of Waters falls in at once on a thousand times vaster Mass of intensest Fire—& the whole prior Orbit of the Planet's successive Revolutions *is possessed by it at once* (Potentia fit Actus [Potency becomes Act]) amid the Thunder of Rapture.—

The quest for a visionary symbolism culminates in his seeing the sun suspended in the ether above the sea at Malta as a true image of Being.[25]

The Sky, o rather say, the Æther, at Malta, with the Sun apparently suspended in it, the Eye seeming to pierce beyond, & as it were, behind it—and below the ætherial Sea, so blue, so a zerflossenes Eins [suffused oneness], the substantial Image, and fixed real Reflection of the Sky—O

I could annihilate in a deep moment all possibility of the needlepoint pinshead System of the *Atomists* by one submissive Gaze! Λογος ab *Ente* [Word from Being]—at once the ~~essential~~ existent Reflexion, and the Reflex Act—at once actual and real & therefore, filiation not creation/ Thought *formed not fixed*—the molten *Being* never cooled into a *Thing*, tho' begotten into the vast adequate Thought . . . seu αγιον πνευμα [or Holy Spirit], which being transelemented into we are mystically united with the *Am*— Ειμ ι—.

In the end, the intuitions to be derived from the study of Life turn out to be efficacious in guarding against the emergence of a mechanically based view of the divine.[26]

"The inducement of a Form on a pre-existing material"—is this a true definition of Generation? Wherein then would Generation differ from Fabrication, or a child from a Statue or Picture? It is surely the inducement of a Form on ~~a~~ pre-existing materials in consequence of the transmission of a *Life*, according to the kind of the living Transmitter, this principle of Life so transmitted being both the principle of the induction of the Form, and of the adduction of the pre-existing materials—. The difference therefore between Fabrication and Generation becomes clearly indicable/the Form of the latter is ab intra, *evolved*, the other ab extra, *impressed*—the latter is representative always of something not itself, and the more disparate that something is, the more admirable is the Form, (as in Painting it is more admirable than in solid Wax—in Iron or Bronze rather than Wax/⟨supposing the forms to be⟩ forms of Flesh—&c)—but the former is representative of its own cause within itself, i.e. its causative self—and resembles, not represents, ~~its~~ any thing without Life and a Fluid are incompatible ideas; tho' it is easy to believe, that what we think fluid, may in truth be solid/i.e. have a form of itself and from itself, permanent and organic, tho' its visible *mass* may depend for its visible shapes wholly on outward pressure or motion/as water in a bottle,—& blood in a bottle/quoad form, both to the eye the same while at least the blood is warm, in the one the microscope can, in the other cannot discover organization. The text to this note is from Horsley's Charge, and is not the only passage proving the laxity of the Bishop's Logic: tho' I doubt not that on the whole he would have the Advantage over Priestley/None but a thorough *Theologist* can combat successfully with a *Christologist*—to shew the inanity of Jehovah, Christ, and the Dove admit the adorable Tri-unity of Being,

Intellect, and Spiritual Action, as the Father, Son, and co-eternal Procedent, that these are God (i.e. not mere general Terms, or abstract ideas) and ⟨that they are⟩ one God (i.e. a real, eternal, and necessary Distinction in the divine nature, distinguishable Triplicity in the indivisible Unity.)

3
Self-Examinings

Coleridge was a notable heir to that element in the Protestant tradition which called on its followers to subject themselves to minute scrutiny of their own conduct and motives. As the effects of such searchings could be to produce acute insights into the workings of one's own mind, one result was to encourage the development of psychological enquiry, including psychological novels. Coleridge himself sometimes produced memorable fictions, as in his great poems of the supernatural, but though he once or twice projected a longer work of the kind he never extended his activities so far as to embark on a full-blown novel. Instead, he concentrated on what was to be discovered through direct mental exploration.

An effect of his introspective tendency is to be traced even when his intelligence seems most positively engaged in other pursuits. In 'The Eolian Harp' for instance, the speculation mentioned in the previous section is checked summarily by a lapse into the religious mode:[1]

> But thy more serious eye a mild reproof
> Darts, O beloved Woman! nor such thoughts
> Dim and unhallow'd dost thou not reject,
> And biddest me walk humbly with my God.
>
> Meek Daughter in the Family of Christ,
> Well hast thou said and holily disprais'd
> These shapings of the unregenerate mind,
> Bubbles that glitter as they rise and break
> On vain Philosophy's aye-babbling spring.
> For never guiltless may I speak of Him,
> Th' INCOMPREHENSIBLE! save when with awe

I praise him, and with Faith that inly *feels*;
Who with his saving mercies healed me,
A sinful and most miserable man,
Wilder'd and dark, and gave me to possess
PEACE, and this COT, and THEE, heart-honor'd Maid!

This was not just a poetic change of tack. Its different mode of address amounts to a withdrawal from freely ranging intellectual inquiry in deference to a perceived need for self-abasement before religious imperatives. All his life he remained acutely sensitive to possible criticisms of his behaviour, particularly when weaknesses of some kind were involved, and the practice intensified with the years. In his youth he wrote several autobiographical memoirs in the form of letters recording remembered facts and stories; one of which concluded with the death of his father and a tribute to his simple and guileless religion. Throughout his life, moreover, he was always ready to express remorse for his failings, either to intimate friends or, more privately, to his own notebooks. His accounts range from bitter self-accusations to his brother after his disastrous Cambridge conduct and enlistment as a dragoon, to qualifications in the midst of more assured accounts of his development such as the one in *Biographia Literaria*. In later years such reflections were confined increasingly to his private notebooks as he tried to trace his own spiritual development and evaluate it—whether self-accusingly or defensively. The final result was to include in the composite picture of a spiritual and religious quest that had lasted through a lifetime a permanent dimension of humility, with frequent falterings of self-worth. In a strange coming of the wheel full circle he would eventually revert fully to the Anglican faith of his childhood, even accepting the sacrament: 'Thirty-three years absent from my master's table!' he would exclaim in his notebook. Or, if one prefers Carlyle's more sardonic scrutiny, he showed that he

> could still, after Hume and Voltaire had done their best and worst to him, profess himself an orthodox Christian, and say and print to the Church of England, with its singular old rubrics and surplices at Allhallowtide, *Esto perpetua* [may she remain for ever].[2]

While in the process of being rescued by his brothers from the results of his impulsive enlistment as a dragoon Coleridge falls into penitence and remorse.[1]

My more than Brother What shall I say—what shall I write to you? Shall I profess an abhorrence of my past conduct? Ah me—too well do I know it's Iniquity—but to abhor! this feeble & exhausted heart supplies not so strong an Emotion. O my wayward Soul! I have been a fool even to madness. What shall I dare to promise? My mind is illegible to myself— I am lost in the labyrinth, the trackless wilderness of my own bosom. Truly may I say—I am wearied of being saved. My frame is chill and torpid—the Ebb and Flow of my hopes & fears has stagnated into recklessness—one wish only can I read distinctly in my heart—that it were possible for me to be forgotten as tho' I never had been! The shame and sorrow of those who loved me—the anguish of him, who protected me from my childhood upwards—the sore travail of her who bore me—intolerable Images of horror! They haunt my sleep—they enfever my Dreams! O that the shadow of Death were on my Eyelids! That I were like the loathsome form, by which I now sit! O that without guilt I might ask of my Maker Annihilation! My Brother—my Brother— pray for me—comfort me, my Brother! I am very wretched—and tho' my complaint be bitter, my stroke is heavier than my groaning.—

The note is renewed three days later.[2]

What my future Life may produce, I dare not anticipate.—Pray for me my Brother.—I will pray nightly to the Almighty Dispenser of good and evil, that his Chastisements may not have harrowed up my heart in vain!—Scepticism had mildewed my hope in the Saviour—I was far from disbelieving the Truth of revealed Religion, but still farther from a steady Faith.—True and active Faith, the 'Comforter that should have relieved my Soul', was far from me—

By the time his discharge is complete six weeks later he is able to give a more reasoned account of his beliefs.[3]

I long ago theoretically and in a less degree experimentally knew the necessity of Faith in order to regular Virtues—nor did I ever seriously disbelieve the existence of a future State—In short, my religious Creed bore and perhaps bears a correspondence with my mind and heart— I had too much Vanity to be altogether a Christian—too much tenderness of Nature to be utterly an Infidel. Fond of the dazzle of Wit, fond of subtlety of Argument, I could not read without some degree of pleasure the levities of Voltaire, or the reasonings of Helvetius—but tremblingly alive to the feelings of humanity, and susceptible of the charms of Truth my Heart forced me to admire the beauty of Holiness in the Gospel, forced me to *love* the Jesus, whom my Reason (or perhaps my *reasonings*) would not permit me to *worship*—My Faith therefore was made up of the Evangelists and the Deistic Philosophy—a kind of *religious Twilight*—I said—*perhaps bears*—Yes! my Brother—for who can say—*Now* I'll be a Christian—Faith is neither altogether voluntary, or involuntary—We cannot believe what we choose—but we can certainly cultivate such habits of thinking and acting, as will give force and effective Energy to the Arguments on either side—.

If I receive my discharge by Thursday, I will be—God pleased—in Cambridge on Sunday—Farewell! my Brother—believe me your severities only wound me as they awake the *Voice within* to speak ah! how more harshly! I feel gratitude and love towards you, even when I shrink and shiver——

Nearly ten years later the increasing hold of opium revives his sense of help-lessness and need for mercy as he sails to the Mediterranean in search of a remedy for his poor health.[4]

—O dear God! give me strength of Soul to make one thorough Trial— if I land at Malta/spite of all horrors to go through one month of unstimulated Nature—yielding to nothing but manifest Danger of Life!—O great God! Grant me grace truly to look into myself, & to begin the serious work of Self-amendment—accounting to Conscience for the Hours of every Day. Let me live in *Truth*—manifesting that alone which *is*, even as it *is*, & striving to be that which only Reason shews to be lovely—that which my Imagination would delight to manifest!—I am loving & kind-hearted & cannot do wrong with impunity, but o! I am very, very weak—from my infancy have been so—& I exist for the moment!—Have mercy on me, have mercy on me, Father & God! omni-present, incomprehensible, who with undeviating Laws eternal yet carest for the falling of the feather from the Sparrow's Wing.—Sunday Midnight, May 13th, 1804.

His searchings of conscience extend even to his persisting love of nature, so that a vision of the sky as a symbol of the divine is shot through with a sense of his total unworthiness.[5]

Friday—Saturday 12—1° clock/What a sky, the not yet orbed moon, the spotted oval, blue at one edge from the deep utter Blue of the Sky, a *mass* of *pearl*-white Cloud below, distant, and travelling to the Horizon, but all the upper part of the Ascent, and all the Height, such *profound* Blue, *deep* as a deep river, and deep in color, & those two ⟨depths⟩ so entirely *one*, as to give the meaning and explanation of the two different significations of the epithet (here so far from divided they were scarcely *distinct*) scattered over with thin pearl-white Cloudlets, hands, & fingers, the largest not larger than a floating Veil/Unconsciously I stretched forth my arms as to embrace the Sky, and in a trance I had worshipped God in the Moon/the Spirit not the Form/I felt in how innocent a feeling Sabeism might have begun/O not only the Moon, but the depth of Sky!—the Moon was the *Idea*; but deep Sky is of all visual impressions the nearest akin to a Feeling/it is more a Feeling than a Sight/or rather it is the melting away and entire union of Feeling & Sight/And did I not groan at my unworthiness, & be miserable at my state of Health, its effects, and effect-trebling Causes? O yes!—Me miserable! O yes!—Have Mercy on me, O something *out* of me! For there is no *power*, (and if that *can* be, less *strength*) in aught *within* me! Mercy! Mercy!

Returning from Malta he finds his sense of guilt exacerbated by his inability to control his addiction. He is haunted by the dreadful thought that examination of our own lives cannot begin to approach those of the all-seeing, all-knowing God, and that subjection to such a remorseless scrutiny after death may be the worst punishment of all.[6]

The omniscience of the supreme Being has always appeared to me among the most tremendous thoughts, of which an imperfect rational Being is capable; and to the very best of men one of the most awful attributes of God is, the Searcher of Hearts. As he knows us, we are not capable of knowing ourselves—it is not impossible, that this perfect (as far as in a creature can be) Self-knowlege may be among the spiritual punishments of the abandoned, as among the joys of the redeemed Spirits.

A year later he laments the paralysis of his own heart.[7]

Alas! my Heart seems of very truth palsy-stricken/It is dead-alive, yet trembles ceaselessly. O mercy! O for the *power* to cry out for mercy from the inmost/That would be Redemption! Now I understand, now I feel the anguish of not feeling savingly the prayer—I believe! Lord help my unbelief!

The spiritual crisis through which he passes at the end of 1813 turns his thoughts back to the necessity of redemption.[8]

. . . You have no conception of what my sufferings have been, forced to struggle and struggle in order not to desire a death for which I am not prepared.—I have scarcely known what sleep is, but like a leopard in its den have been drawn up and down the room by extreme pain, and restlessness, worse than pain itself.

O how I have prayed even to loud agony only to be able to pray! O how I have felt the impossibility of any real *good will* not born anew from the Word and the Spirit! O I have seen far, far deeper and clearer than I ever saw before the ground of pernicious errors! O I have seen, I have felt that the worst offences are those against our own souls! That our souls are infinite in depth, and therefore our sins are infinite, and redeemable only by an infinitely higher infinity; that of the Love of God in Christ Jesus. I have called my soul infinite, but O infinite in the depth of darkness, an infinite craving, an infinite capacity of pain and weakness, and excellent only as being passively capacious of the light from above. Should I recover I will—no—no may God grant me power to struggle to become *not another* but a *better man*—O that I had been a partaker with you of the discourse of Mr Robt Hall! But it pleased the Redeemer to appoint for me a sterner, fearfuller, and even more eloquent preacher, if to be impressive is to be eloquent. O God save me—save me from myself. . . .

Writing to Joseph Cottle in 1814 he takes up the sense of his own worthlessness again, dwelling on the irony inherent in a desire to pray that is coupled with an inability to do so.[9]

You have no conception of the dreadful Hell of my mind & conscience & body. You bid me, pray. O I do pray inwardly to be able to *pray*; but indeed to pray, to pray with the faith to which Blessing is promised, this is the reward of Faith, this is the Gift of God to the Elect. O if to feel how infinitely worthless I am, how poor a wretch, with just free will enough to be deserving of wrath, & of my own contempt, & of none to merit a moment's peace, can make a part of a Christian's creed; so far I am a Christian—

Reading Leighton's Commentary on the 1st Epistle of St Peter in the same month he is appalled at the picture of himself that he immediately recognizes in it. To Leighton's comment 'If any one's Head or Tongue should grow apace, and all the rest stand at a Stay, it would certainly make him a Monster; and they are no other, that are knowing and discoursing Christians, and grow daily in that, but not at all in Holiness of Heart and Life, which is the proper Growth of the Children of God' he responds:[10]

Father in Heaven have mercy on me! Christ, Lamb of God have mercy on me! Save me Lord! Or I perish. Alas, I am perishing.

To Leighton's subsequent assurance, 'A well furnished Table may please a Man, while he hath Health and Appetite; but offer it to him in the Height of a Fever, how unpleasant would it be then? Though never so richly decked, 'tis not only then useless, but hateful to him: But the Kindness and Love of God is then as seasonable and refreshing to him, as in Health, and possibly more; he can find Sweetness in that, even on his Sick bed', his response is equally desolate:[11]

To the regenerate; but to the conscious Sinner a Source of Terrors insupportable. S. T. C. i.e. Sinful, tormented Culprit.

Nine years later, it occurs to him to make a record of his own mental battles as introduction to a fiction concerning the problems of a search for truth.[12]

Mental Revolutions & Moral Epochs: or—the Sceptic's Pilgrimage: or the mental revolutions and moral epochs in the Life of a Seeker after Truth.
1. Birth & childhood. 2. Boyhood in a Metropolitan public School ⟨moral Perplexities⟩ Innocence Loss of—. Early Infidelity by force of the Ludicrous & Apparently absurd, with the charm of new knowlege— from Voltaire's Philosophical Dictionary—Cato's Letters: & Necessity.— 3. Youth/—Paley—Arianism/Despise Voltaire—strong hold of the Morality of the Gospel—but all Morality made to consist in Sensibility, generosity, and abhorrence of Meanness & baseness, with vindictive Indignation at all real or supposed Oppression/Negative Democracy— i.e. Intolerance of Lords, and Kings; but far more of rich men—& hence

a purely *Ideal* Politician—So far good that it preserved the link between politics & religion.—/4. University—platonizing Socinianism/ &cc 5. Early Manhood—/ henceforward the facts & characters fictitious/

The first of his fictitious episodes evidently reflects his own problem in having become enslaved to a drug—[13]

A Conversation to a young man of great susceptibility and *heart*, and fine Imagination who had been railing, reasoning & laughing at the notion of the *Spirits*—A lively picture of the various Vices or Habits, foreseen as too likely to befall *him*, drawn out poetically as so many possessions of evil Spirits, under all the wildest yet truest forms of Thought. Ex. gr.—In health seemingly—eye clear, pulse regular, the delight of all who heard him/in one moment the evil Spirit comes/*Opium*. He had sold himself to *Death* to escape Pain—& the Spirit comes regularly to *dun* him—
 So of the others.

In an episode of his own, two years later, remorse is renewed as he recalls the consolation offered by a friend and his feelings of unworthiness.[14]

Poor—embarrassed—sick—unpatronized, unread—/ But (replied the soft consoling Friend) *innocent.*—I felt only as one that recoils—& sinful dust and ashes that I am—groaning under self-reproached inproaches!— *I* innocent?—.—Be thankful still! (repeated the same so sweet Voice) you are an *innocent* man—Again I draw back but as a little child from a *kind* Stranger, but without letting go of the Stranger's hand/—"You have the child-like Heart.["]—Ah but even in boyhood there was a cold hollow spot, an aching in that heart, when I said my prayers—that prevented my entire union with God—that I could not *give up*, or that would not give *me* up—as if a snake had wreathed around my heart, and at this one spot its Mouth touched at & inbreathed a weak incapability of willing it away—/—Never did I more sadly & sinkingly prostrate myself in sense of my worthlessness—and yet, after all, it was a *comfort* to me—/My innocency was a comfort—a something, for which that was the name, there were which I would *not* resign for Wealth—Strength— Health—Reputation—Glory—/—Hence I learnt—that a sinful Being may *have* an innocence/I learnt, that the Skirt of Christ is nearer to a Man than his own Skin! For that *spot* in my heart even my ⟨remaining &⟩

unleavened *Self*—all else the Love of Christ in and thro' Christ's Love of me!

S. T. C.

In a final memoir, two years before his death, he surveys his early years once again, including his religious errings, to the point where his poor health led to the ill-starred experiments with opium that delivered him into the fatal addiction.[15]

Retrospect, fragments of.

1. Early Childhood. The last child, the youngest Child of Ten by the same Mother, viz. John, William, who died in infancy—James, William, Edward, George, Luke, Anne, Francis, and myself, Samuel Taylor Coleridge, beneficially abridged Esteese = S. T. C., and the 13th, taking in three Sisters by my dear Father's first Wife, ~~Elizabeth~~ Mary (afterwards Mrs Bradley) Sarah, who married a Sea-man & is lately dead. I forget the name—and Elizabeth (afterwards, Mrs Philips) who alone was bred up with us after my birth, & whom alone of the three I was wont to think of, as a Sister—tho' not exactly, yet I did not know why, the same sort of Sister as my Sister Nancy—

The youngest Child, possibly inheriting the commencing decay of musculo-arterial Power in my Father who died in his 62nd year when I had not yet reached my 7th—possibly therefore, in part, from a constitutional overbalance of the Sensibility, the cerebro-nervous System, over the Irritability, better called the Instinctivity, or the Musculo-Arterial System—and a consequent predisposition of the Productivity, or Venoglandular & Capillary System, to the affections of sensitive Astheny, tho' it never positively put on the type of Scrophula—

And certainly, from the Jealousy of Old Nolly, my Brother's Frank's dotingly-fond Nurse. And if ever Child by beauty & liveliness deserved to be doted on, my Brother Francis was that child/and by the infusions of her Jealousy into my Brother's mind, I was in earliest childhood lifted away from the enjoyments of muscular activity—from Play—to take refuge at my mother's side on my little stool, to read my little books and to listen to the Talk of my Elders—I was driven from Life in Motion to Life in thought and sensation. I never played except by myself, & then only acting over what I had been reading or fancying, or half one, half the other, with a stick, cutting down the Weeds & Nettles, as one of the Seven Champions of Christendom—/Alas! I had all the simplicity, all the docility of a little child; but none of the Child's Habits—I never thought as a Child; never had the language of a Child.—

I forget whether it was in my 5th or 6th year, but I believe the latter, in consequence of some quarrel between me and my Brother, it was in the first week of October, I ran away—from fear of being whipt and passed the whole night, a night of rain and storm, on the bleak side of a Hill on the River Otter, & was found, alive but without the power of my limbs, at day-break about six yards from the naked banks of the River— The consequence, a remittent, and then a rheumatic fever—

In my Seventh year, about the same time if not the very same, i.e. Octob^r 4, my most dear, most revered Father, the Revd John Coleridge, died suddenly—O that I might so pass away, if like him, I were an Israelite without guile. The Image of my Father, my revered kind simple-hearted Father, is a Religion to me!

2. Boyhood.—I was sent for by Judge Buller—and placed in Christ's Hospital. O what a change!—Deprest, moping, friendless poor Orphan, half-starved/at that time the portion of food given to the Blue-coats was cruelly insufficient, for those who had no friends to supply them—from 8 to 14 I was a playless Day-dreamer, an Helluo Librorum, my appetite for which was indulged by a singular Incident, a stranger who struck by my conversation made me free of a ~~lib~~ great Circulating Library in King's Street, Cheapside—& I read thro the whole Catalogue, folios and all—whether I understood them or did not understand them—running all risks, in skulking out, to get the two Volumes which I was entitled to have daily—Conceive what I must have been at 14—I had never played—I was in a continued low fever—my whole Being was with eyes closed to every object of present sense—to crumple myself up in a sunny Corner, and read, read, read—~~th~~ finding myself in Rob. Crusoe's Island, finding a Mountain of Plum Cake, and eating out a room for myself, and then eating it into the shapes of Chairs & Tables—Hunger and Fancy—

3. Ladhood. My talents, and superiority—even in the routine I was at the head, tho' utterly without the desire to be so—without a spark of ambition—and as to Emulation, it had no meaning for me—but the difference between me & any form-fellows in our Lessons & Exercises bore no proportion to the measureless difference between me & them in the wide, wild wilderness of useless, unarranged Book knowlege, and book-thoughts—Thank Heaven! it was not the age, or the fashion, of getting up prodigies. But at 14 or at 12 I should have made as pretty a juvenile Prodigy as was ever emasculated & ruined by fond and idle wonderment. Thank Heaven! I was flogged instead of flattered—However as I climbed upward in the School, my lot was somewhat alleviated— against my will. I was ~~B~~ chosen by Mr B. as one of those destined for the

University—and about this time, my Brother Luke, or the Doctor, so called from his infancy because being the 7th Son he had from infancy been dedicated to the medical profession, came to town, to walk the London Hospital under (Blizard—)   Dr Saumarez, Brother of the Admiral, Lord Saumarez, was his continual Friend—/Every Saturday, that I could make or obtain leave—to the London Hospital trudged I—O the bliss if I were permitted to hold the plaister, or to attend the dressings—30 years afterwards Mr Saumarez retained the liveliest recollections of the extra-ordinary enthusiastic Blue-coat Boy, and was exceedingly affected in identifying me with that Boy. I became wild to be apprenticed to a Surgeon—English, Latin, yea, Greek Books of Medicine read I incessantly—Blanchard's Latin Medical Dictionary I had almost by heart—Briefly, it was a wild dream—which gradually blending with gradually gave way to a rage for Metaphysics, occasioned by the Essays on Liberty & Necessity in Cato's Letters—and then by Theology, after I read Voltaire's Philosophical Dictionary—I sported infidel! for which Boyer flogged me soundly—and I determined out of spite to be more infidelical—but that night my heart smote me, & I <u>prayed</u>—/My infidel vanity (it never touched my heart) was but of a mock nature. Afterwards I became Sabellian then Arian, then (tho' much later) Socinian, even to my 25th year—But only in these few months, in the enjoyment of the supposed new light given me by Voltaire, and the pride of courage in them, have I ever even with my lips (with my heart I never did) abandon the name of Christ/—

In my 16th year I had made friends—a Widow Lady, who had a Son, whom I as upper Boy had protected, took to me & taught me what it was to have a Mother. I loved her as such—she had three daughters—& I, of course, fell in love—& with the eldest—& from this time to my 19th when I quitted School for Jesus, Cambridge, was the æra of poetry & love—

But from the exuberance of my animal Spirits, when I had burst forth from my misery & mopery, and the indiscretions resulting from these Spirits,—ex. gr. swimming in the New River in my Clothes & remaining in them full half the time—from 17 to 18 was passed in the Sick Ward, Jaundice, and Rheumatic Fever—

Youth & commencing Manhood—

Went to Jesus—for the first term, & as long as Middleton was at Pembroke (afterward Bp of Calcutta) read hard, got the Greek Ode &c— without my intention or knowlege, but thro' pure ignorance, got into debt for the furniture of my rooms, which I had desired the Man ~~to~~ in my simplicity to furnish as he pleased—in fact, I never looked at them enough to know the difference between a deal & mahogany—became miserable—drank bad wine—& volunteered the credit of vices of which I was not guilty—A dreary time of self-reproach, and bewilderment followed—I was in heart & feeling innocent as a child—& my imagination unstained—but in the agitation of mind & its consequences my Constitution assuredly was arrested in its efforts to establish itself—Whatever errors, I or single acts of transgression I may have incurred from 20 to 23—in my 23rd year there was an end—and from my 23rd year I have not knowingly offended, in intemperance or unchastity—

From 1794 to 1800—for N.b. my purpose here is exclusively to give the retrospect of my bodily state & its probable causes—

Much moral, social, intellectual enjoyment—alas! much domestic sorrow & disquiet—& complaining state of health—Subject to bowel complaints—among the least uneasiness of mind was not felt in the mind but in the lesser bowels, or above the regions of the heart—At last, my knees began to swell—& for some months after my return from Germany & my establishment at Greta Hall, Keswick, I had been all but bed-ridden; when my old taste returning, for the study of medical works, having borrowed a load of old Medical Journals from my Medical Attendant, Mr Edmonson, I found—i.e. I fancied I findound a case precisely like my own—in which a marvellous cure had been effected by rubbing in laudanum, at the same time that a dose was administered inwardly—/I tried it—It answered like a charm/in a day I was alive—all alive!—Wretched Delusion!—but I owe it in justice to myself to declare before God, that this,—the curse of and slavery of my life, did not commence in any low craving for sensation, in any desire or wish to stimulate or exhilarate myself—in fact, my nervous spirits and my mental activity was such as never required it—but wholly in rashness, and delusion, and presumptuous Quackery, <and afterwards in pure terror—not lured, but goaded!>—Bad enough as it is—God forgive me— the Penance has been most bitter—

During a dialogue with a friend he once again recalls his early errors but pleads his sincerity and his lack of self-interest.[16]

S. T. C. I would fain hope, that thro' my whole life I have afforded no ground for the suspicion, that I ever professed to be that which I did not at the time believe myself to be.—I trust, in no relation; but assuredly not in religion at the period of commencing Manhood, without a guide, or with bad guides. I had unbeliever [? down] to the

Priestleian Infra-Socinianism: and during little less than two years was, I think (God forgive my errors of Ignorance, and the immaturities of a growing Mind!) was sufficiently loud and open in my avowels of dissent from, and hostility to, the Faith, of all the fundamental Articles of the Faith, of the Established Church: and this to the known, and distinctly foreseen, abandonment of all my worldly prospects—and the alienation of all my nearest and natural Connections. At the close of this period I became unsatisfied with my Unitarian Scheme, as a Creed of Negatives; and having collected in this what I did not believe, applied myself seriously to find out, what I did believe, to make a Creed of Positives—The result was, a final and decisive Return to the doctrines of the Catechism, I had learnt as a child; to a full and avowed Conviction of the Faith of Luther, Melanchthon, and the Fathers and Founders of the Church, in which I was baptized & bred, the Established Protestant Church of England. But I have yet to be informed, first, what I ever gained by this Return, in friends, or in preferment, &c; and what I ever sought to obtain, or put myself in the way of obtaining by it. I made most unwillingly many bitter enemies among the Party, I had left: & till within a very recent period have been regarded by the zealous Churchman, as still belonging to it—or perhaps, worse/

B.A. Forgive me! I do not wonder at your repelling what my words might have been understood to insinuate. But I should have made a better choice, if I had ever thought of any interested views influencing you, or even of their being suspected of you by others—! On the contrary, I am aware, that the charges—circulated in confidential whispers, or in the great Whispering-gallery of the anonymous Press, against you—as a Dreamer, a Visionary, a Supporter of absurd Paradoxes, for the sake of the ability, you can shew off in defending them, &c, have arisen out of the want of any plausible grounds of putting you down either as Fool or Knave.

His return to the Church of England Communion sacrament in 1827 provokes reflections on its efficacy and on his own position.[17]

Christmas day. Received the Sacrament—for the first time since my first year at Jesus College/Christ is gracious even to the Laborer that cometh to his Vineyard at the eleventh hour—33 years absent from my Master's Table/— —Yet I humbly hope, that spiritually I have fed on the Flesh & Blood the Strength and the Life of the Son of God in his divine Humanity, during the latter years—. The administration & Communion Service of our Church is solemn & affecting—& very far to be preferred both to the Romish, which may excite awe & wonder in such as believe the real transmutation of the Bread & Wine, but assuredly no individual comfort or support—and to the few among our Dissenters who practice what to the shame of our Church the great majority of our own Clergymen teach—& cold and flat the ceremonial is—as how can it be otherwise, when the Eucharist is considered as a mere and very forced visual metaphor for the mere purpose of reminding the Partakers of a single event, the sensible crucifixion of Jesus?—and without any connection with that most vital mystery revealed in John VI, of which the Eucharist is at once symbol & instance—Compared with either the Romish or the Dissenting Service our's is a subject of gratitude with me—Yet I cannot but think it capable of great improvement, both for the impression on the affections & for edification in knowlege—and it's being disjoined from the Love-supper, I think a great misfortune/—But this is a necessary consequence of a sterile National Church—i.e. a National Church that is merely such, instead of comprehending a <u>Christian</u> Church in it's inmost concentric circle.

4
Psychological Speculations

If Coleridge's study of the workings of the human mind had connections with the introspective tendencies in current Protestant thinking it also appealed deeply to his own proclivities. In an early poem he referred to himself as a 'subtle-souled psychologist'—even if he went on immediately to accuse himself of a failure in the world of activism. He was particularly drawn to the cult of animal magnetism, or hypnotism, which was much practised in France at the end of the eighteenth century,[1] but also had a considerable fashionable success in London. A young man of his upbringing and interests could hardly be unaware of the excitement around him—or indeed of the connections between the similar enthusiasm in France and the ferment that produced the Revolution. The interest also sought scientific validity by way of certain passages of Newton's *Principia*, where it was supposed that a subtle fluid termed aether pervaded the universe. The theory was popular among the magnetists, who perceived in it a possible medium for magnetic forces; but it provoked discussion and dissent among late eighteenth-century scientists, especially Coleridge's admired Joseph Priestley, whose arguments for materiality precluded him from adopting such an expedient. Coleridge's newfound Unitarianism drew him to the attractions of Priestley's position yet also prompted questions:

> How is it that Dr. Priestley is not an atheist?—He asserts in three different Places, that God not only *does*, but *is*, every thing. But if God *be* every Thing, every Thing is God—: which is all, the Atheists assert—. An eating, drinking, lustful *God*—with no unity of *Consciousness*—these appear to me the unavoidable Inferences from his philosophy . . .[2]

Animal magnetism had a fascination of its own, meanwhile. Coleridge derived from its demonstration that more than one level of consciousness existed in the human mind sustenance for his growing interest in the imaginative powers of human beings, his interest being notably demonstrated, among other things, in the first version of *The Rime of the Ancient Mariner*.[3] His clear reference there to animal magnetism disappeared from the poem after 1798, however, and the reason can hardly have been poetic awkwardness alone. Just as the first *Lyrical Ballads* volume was going through the press, he had set off in the company of the Wordsworths for Germany, where among other things he attended the lectures of one of the most distinguished physiologists of the time, J. F. Blumenbach. If he had hoped to learn more about magnetism there he was destined to be disappointed, since, as he must soon have discovered, Blumenbach was sceptical concerning the very existence and validity of hypnotic phenomena. Although this must have been a strong setback to his thinking it did not put a stop to related speculations concerning the power of the imagination. On the contrary, his interest in what in 1796 he had listed as his chief interests: 'History. Metaphysics, & Poetry, & "Facts of Mind"',[4] extending to the connections between them, was intensified.

Among these the most important connection of all was that which he could be encouraged by scripture and ancient philosophy to trace between the poetic expression and the creative act. God said 'Let there be . . . ' and 'there was'; Apollo played his music and a temple was raised. In the same fashion Coleridge's Kubla Khan decrees a stately pleasure-dome and it is there—as if by magic; more magical still is the pleasure-dome in air dreamed by the poet in the last stanza, built simply by 'music loud and long'. In the same way Coleridge maintained that in human beings the Primary Imagination was 'a repetition in the finite mind of the eternal act of creation in the infinite I AM'. The implications of his statement are intricate and extensive, for they seem to extend from the simple fact of the mysterious processes hidden in the act of creation, by which the thing created often seems to escape from the conscious control of the creator, to an inference that every creative act mirrors the divine.

Many orthodox Christians would regard this as blasphemy, of course, and Coleridge was wary of promulgating such doctrines openly, or pursuing them to their logical conclusions. The old sense of guilt was always lurking, ready to negate such visions and turn them inside out, leaving him no longer a visionary but now a cringing sinner who must reproach himself for having dared to lift up his head in such presumption. But between such extremes of attitude the 'inquiring spirit' was ready to show its face in a restless curiosity concerning the possible significance of unusual psychological states. Throughout his career, for instance,

Coleridge retained a strong interest in nightmare states and conditions of unusual fear. His unusually well-endowed imagination made him especially aware of the aptitude of the human mind for the creation of compelling illusions. His well-known reply to a lady who asked if he believed in ghosts and apparitions, 'No, Madam! I have seen far too many myself',[5] serves him ill if it is taken to belie a deep interest in the subject. His fascination belongs with a longstanding respect for the supernatural—seen, in the words of *The Destiny of Nations*, as

> Wild phantasies! yet wise,
> On the victorious goodness of high God
> Teaching reliance, and medicinal hope,
> Till from Bethabra northward, heavenly Truth
> With gradual steps, winning her difficult way,
> Transfer their rude Faith, perfected and pure.[6]

This is a key passage in assessing the religious significance for him of such fictions. He was evidently feeling his way toward a view of the subconscious which would make it an auxiliary power for the imprinting of religious truth in the minds of those who might not otherwise grasp it.

All such considerations brought him back to the mysterious nature of consciousness itself, and his belief that truth often revealed itself most surely when the rational consciousness was in some way blocked or inhibited. This called for constant attention to the ways of the subconscious, as well as for a necessary awareness of the fact that Consciousness was not necessarily the same as Being. As in the case of nature, the effect was to encourage a cultivation of symbols and correspondences, as providing the means by which the ordinary rational mind could accomplish the leap to a true understanding of the Being that would survive when ordinary mortal consciousness was dissolved in death. The ultimate distinction as far as human minds were concerned lay between those of 'continuous' and 'discontinuous' minds. The former were capable of the 'disjunction conjunctive' inherent in seizing the truth of Being to be elicited from ordinary facts by the exercise of passion and imagination, while the excellence of minds cast in the other nature would be restricted to the 'conjunction disjunctive' characteristic of fine wit. Whatever its qualities and stylishness, it could not in his eyes constitute a true *religious* consciousness.

Coleridge shows an early interest in the abnormal psychology of religious experiences.[1]

She had in her sickness some curious & well-becoming fears respecting
the final state of the soul—but from thence she passed into a deliquium,
or a kind of Trance, and as soon as she came forth of it, as if it had been
a Vision or that she had conversed with an angel, & from his hand had
received a Labell or Scroll of the *Book of Life* & there seen her name
enrolled, she cried out aloud/"Glory be to God on high; now I am sure,
I shall be saved." Concerning which manner of discoursing we are
wholly ignorant what Judgment can be made; but certainly there are
strange things in the other World; and so there are in all the immediate
Preparations to it; & a little *Glimpse* of Heaven, a minute's conversing
with an angel, any ray of God, any communication from the Spirit of
Comfort which God gives to his servants in strange & unknown manners, are infinitely far from Illusions; & they shall then be understood
by us, when we feel them, & when our new & strange needs shall be
refreshed by such unusual Visitations.

*His account of the 'clock-idiot' may be recorded for a possible satire on those
who regard the universe purely as a clock-like mechanism, originally wound
up and set going by its Creator.*[2]

An ideot whose whole amusement consisted in looking at, & talking to
a clock, which he supposed to be alive—/the Clock was removed—/he
supposed that it had walked off—& he went away to seek it—was absent
nine days—at last, they found, almost famish'd in a field—He asked
where it was buried—for he was sure it was dead—/he was brought
home & the clock in its place—his Joy—&c He used to put part of every
thing, he liked, into the clock-case.

*Studying his child Hartley he is struck by the ease with which he moves into
symbolizing process.*[3]

It seems to elucidate the Theory of Language, Hartley, just able to speak
a few words, making a fire-place of stones, with stones for fire.—four
stones—fire-place—two stones—fire—/arbitrary symbols in Imagination/
⟨Hartley walked remarkably soon/& *therefore* learnt to talk rem. late.⟩

*Yet Hartley finds it agonizingly difficult to distinguish between a thing and its
reflection.*[4]

March 17, 1801. Tuesday—Hartley looking out of my study window fixed his eyes steadily & for some time on the opposite prospect, & then said—Will yon Mountains *always* be?—I shewed him the whole magnificent Prospect in a Looking Glass, and held it up, so that the whole was like a Canopy or Ceiling over his head, & he struggled to express himself concerning the Difference between the Thing & the Image almost with convulsive Effort.—I never before saw such an Abstract of *Thinking* as a pure act & energy, of *Thinking* as distinguished from *Thoughts*.

Materialists, by contrast, in the process of dismissing mystery from their universe seem to ignore what is most mysterious about it.[5]

Materialists unwilling to admit the mysterious of our nature make it all mysterious—nothing mysterious in nerves, eyes, &c: but that nerves think &c!!—Stir up the sediment into the transparent water, & so make all opaque.

Yet even in everyday experience there is an observable difference between our conscious life and the subconscious life of feeling which it masks.[6]

> —and the deep power of Joy
> We see into the *Life* of Things—

i.e.—By deep feeling we make our *Ideas dim*—& this is what we mean by our Life—ourselves. I think of the Wall—it is before me, a distinct Image—here. I necessarily think of the *Idea* & the Thinking I as two distinct & opposite Things. Now let me think of *myself*—of the thinking Being—the Idea becomes dim whatever it be—so dim that I know not what it is—but the Feeling is deep & steady—and this I call *I* identifying the Percipient & the Perceived—.

He tries another experiment, and projects more.[7]

Saturday, June   16—$\frac{1}{2}$ of a mile from John Stanley's toward Grasmere, whither I was going to stand Godfather to Wm Wordsworth's first Child—put the colored Glasses to my eyes as a pair of Spectacles, the red to the left, the yellow Glass to the right eye—saw only thro' the yellow—closed my right eye with my finger, without in the least altering the position of the left eye—& then I instantly saw thro' the red Glass. The right eye manifestly the stronger, tho what is curious, & to be explained by the greater Light of the yellow Glass, when I altered the Glasses, namely the yellow to the left eye, the red to the right, then I saw the Landscape as thro' the yellow—perhaps a very little reddish, while the clouds & skies were now as thro' the red./. These experiments must be tried over again & varied—

These are accompanied by speculations as to the growth of feeling in the infant.[8]

Contact—the womb—the amnion liquor—warmth + touch/—air cold + touch + sensation & action of breathing—contact of the mother's knees + all those contacts of the Breast + taste & wet & sense of swallowing—
    Sense of diminished Contact explains the falling asleep—/this *is* Fear, [?not/and] this produces Fear—
    Eye contact, pressure infinitely diminished, organic Connness (con to ken) proportionately increased.

Observation of dream experience and its relation to buried memory.[9]

Tuesday Night, July 19, 1803—Intensely hot day—left off a waistcoat, & for yarn wore silk stockings—about 9 °clock had unpleasant chilli-nesses—heard a noise which I thought Derwent's in sleep—listened anxiously, found it was a Calf bellowing—instantly came on my mind that night, I slept out at Ottery—& the Calf in the Field across the river whose lowing had so deeply impressed me—Chill + Child + Calf-lowing probably the rivers Greta and Otter.

The comparative effectiveness of reason and anger.[10]

Defence of Aristotle & the Ancients as to their logical metaphysical physics/two ways of giving importance to physics, *magic*, & *psychology*/ to *reason* on them necessary before experiments & yet justify Bacon for his *angry* attacks/anger more practical than Love/God by *Anger* drove out Polytheism/This very important/

The solitariness of the religious subconsciousness.[11]

Without Drawing I feel myself but half invested with Language—Music too is wanting to me.—But yet tho' one should unite Poetry, Draftsman's-ship & Music—the greater & perhaps nobler certainly all the subtler parts of one's nature, must be solitary—Man exists herein to himself & to God alone/—Yea, in how much only to God—how much lies *below* his own Consciousness.

Further notebook entries on the relationship between Things and the work of subconscious thought and feeling.[12]

Print of the Darlington Ox, sprigged with Spots.—Viewed in all moods, consciously, uncons. semiconsc.—with vacant, with swimming eyes—made a Thing of Nature by the repeated action of the Feelings. O Heaven when I think how perishable Things, how imperishable Thoughts seem to be!—For what is Forgetfulness?—Renew the state of affection or bodily Feeling, same or similar—sometimes dimly similar/ and instantly the trains of forgotten Thought rise from their living catacombs!—Old men, & Infancy/and Opium, probably by its narcotic effect on the whole seminal organization, in a large Dose, or after long use, produces the same effect on the *visual*, & *passive* memory.

Nothing affects me much at the moment it happens—it either stupifies me, and I perhaps look at a merry-make & dance the hay of Flies, or listen entirely to the loud Click of the great Clock/or I am simply indifferent, not without some sense of philosophic Self-complacency.—For a Thing at the moment is but a Thing of the moment/it must be taken up into the mind, diffuse itself thro' the whole multitude of Shapes & Thoughts, not one of which it leaves untinged—between W^ch & it some new Thought is not engendered/this a work of Time/but the Body feels it quicken with me—

One may best judge of men by their Pleasures. Who has not known men who have passed the Day in honorable Toil with Honor, & Ability—& at night sought the vilest pleasures in the vilest Society. This is the Man's Self—the other is a trick learnt by heart—for we may even learn the power of extemporaneous elocution & instant action, as an automatic Trick/—but a man's Pleasures—children, Books, Friends, Nature, the Muse/—O these deceive not!—

Frid. Morn. 5°clock—Dosing, dreamt of Hartley as at his Christening—
how as he was asked who redeemed him, & was to say, God the Son/he
went on, humming and hawing, in one hum & haw, like a boy who
knows a thing & will not make the effort to recollect it—so as to irritate
me greatly. Awakening ⟨gradually I found I was able compleatly to
detect, that⟩ it was the Ticking of my Watch which lay in the Pen Place
in my Desk on the round Table close by my Ear, & which in the diseased
State of my Nerves had *fretted* on my Ears—I caught the fact while it
Hartley's Face & moving Lips were yet before my Eyes, & his Hum & Ha,
& the Ticking of the Watch were each the other, as often happens in
the passing off of Sleep—that curious modification of Ideas by each
other, which is the Element of *Bulls.*—I arose instantly, & wrote it
down—it is now 10 minutes past 5.

*His investigations into such conscious and subconscious processes led him to
question whether Kant's arguments about the relationship between reason
and feeling are sufficiently subtle—or indeed match his own intuition of
human dual nature and its religious implications.*[13]

Reverence for the LAW of Reason/now this truly is a *feeling*, but says Kant
it is a self-created, not a received passive Feeling—*it is the Consciousness
of the Subordination of the Will* [*to a Law*].—Examine this: for in Psychology Kant is but suspicious Authority.—As an imposed Necessity it is
Fear, or an Analogon of Fear; but as a Necessity imposed on us by our
own Will it is a species of Inclination/& in this word, as in many others,
Man's double Nature appears, as Man & God. I am fully persuaded, that
all the Dogmas of the Trinity & Incarnation arose from Jesus asserting
them of himself, as man in genere/

*The importance of distinguishing between simple volition and truly free will,
and possible physical reasons.*[14]

Of the intimate connection of Volition, and of the Feeling & Consciousness of Volition, on the state of the Skin, I have noticed long ago in a
former Pocket-book, occasioned by the curious phænomenon experienced the X^tmas of 1801 at Mr Howel's, N° 10, King S^t, Covent Garden,
my Skin deadened, the effect of violent Diarrhœa/My Speculations
thence on double Touch—the generation of the Sense of Reality & Life
out of us, from the Impersonation effected by a certain phantasm of

double Touch, &c &c &c, and thence my Hope of making out a radical distinction between this Volition & Free Will or Arbitrement, & the detection of the Sophistry of the Necessitarians/as having arisen from confounding the two.—Sea sickness, the Eye on the Stomach, the Stomach on the Eye/—Eye + Stomach + Skin—Scratching & ever after in certain affections of the Skin, milder than those which provoke Scratching a restlessness for double Touch/Dalliance, & at its height, necessity of Fruition.—Fruition the intensest single Touch, &c &c &c; but I am bound to trace the Ministery of the Lowest to the Highest, of all things to Good/and the presence of a certain Abstract or Generical Idea, in the Top, Bottom, & Middle of each Genus. Λιβιδινοσιτᾶτ των Ιδιωτων [the Libidinousness of Idiots]—this must be explained in the first instance—then of brutal men. ⟨Sensatio urioræ [the sensation of urinating], when gratified at any pressing want, wherein it differs &c⟩ Rutting-time of Brutes &c &c &c &c &c &c &c—An Ocean.

Inquiry into the reasons for failing to perform what is seen as a duty, even when pleasurable.[15]

All this evening, indeed all this day (Monday, Jan. 9) I ought to have [been] reading & filling the Margins of Malthus—I had begun & found it pleasant/why did I neglect it?—Because, I OUGHT not to have done this.—The same in reading & writing Letters, Essays, &c &c—surely this is well worth a serious Analysis, that understanding I may attempt to heal/for it is a deep & wide disease in my moral Nature, at once Elm-and-Oak-rooted.—Love of Liberty, Pleasure of Spontaneity, &c &c, these all express, not explain, the Fact.

Tuesd. Morn. Jan. 10. 1804.—After I had got into bed last night, I said to myself, that I had been pompously enunciating, as a difficulty, a problem of easy & common solution/viz. that it was the effect of Association, we from Infancy up to Manhood under Parents, Schoolmasters, Tutors, Inspectors, &c having had our pleasures & pleasant self-chosen Pursuits (self-chosen because pleasant, and not *originally* pleasant because self-chosen) interrupted, & we forced into dull unintelligible Rudiments or painful Labor/—*Now,* all Duty is felt as a *command,* commands *most often,* & therefore by Laws of Association felt as if *always,* from without & consequently, calling up the Sensations &c of the pains endured from Parents', Schoolmasters', &c &c—commands from without.—But I awoke with gouty suffocation this morning, $\frac{1}{2}$ past one/& as soon as Disease permitted me to think at all, the shallowness & falsity of this Solution flashed on me at once/I saw, that the phænomenon occurred far far too early—in early Infancy, 2 & 3 months old, I have observed it/& have seen it in Hartley, turned up & lay'd bare to the unarmed Eye of merest common sense. That *Interruption* of itself is painful because & as far as it acts as Disruption/& then, without any reference to or distinct recollection of my former theory, I saw great Reason to attribute the effect wholly to the streamy nature of the associating Faculty and especially as it is evident that *they most* labor under this defect who are most reverie-ish & streamy—Hartley, for instance & myself/This seems to me no common corroboration of my former Thought on the origin of moral Evil in general.

Observation of the behaviour of sailors at sea confirms his view of superstition as displaced anger.[16]

... Vexation, which in a Sailor's mind is always linked on to Reproach and Anger, makes the Superstitious seek out an Object of his Superstition, that can feel his anger—Else the Star, that dogged the Crescent or my "Cursed by the last Look of the waning moon," were the better— What an extensive subject would not superstition form taken in its philos. and most comprehen. sense for that mood of Thought & Feeling which arises out of the having placed our summum bonum (what we think so, I mean) in an absolute Dependence on Powers & Events, over which we have no Controll. While the Essayist treated of Sailors, Savages, Fishermen, rustic Lovers, Farmers, Gamesters & the poor Gamblers at Lottery Insurances/in short, with all those who have no established Church, or at least, a known Meeting-house of Superstition who Cloath it in acknowleged & conventional Formulæs & Practices, attached to the Traditional Part of Revealed Religion or dimly borrowed of an old Idolatry, all would go on, the Essayist being a man of right feeling, fleetly and fairly—in a current of interesting narration. The difficulty & the power of the work would begin with the Superstition of those, who have no religion or only what is called an entirely rational one, & who from infancy have been taught to derive a self-importance from Contempt of & ⟨supposed⟩ Insight into all the common forms & conventional Outlets of Superstition; & yet *are* superstitious, i.e. according to the definition. To trace out & detect its subtle Incarnations & Epiphanies & to prove the sameness of the Genus. Hic Labor hic Opus est [This is the labour, this the task].

The distinction between the image of a person and the feeling associated with that person again suggests a relation between the ordinary consciousness and the religious subconscious.[17]

Remember my repeated Memoranda—Dorothy, myself, &c in my Red Cottle Book. Does not this establish the existence of *a Feeling* of a Person quite distinct at all times, & at certain times *perfectly separable* from, the Image of the Person? And that this Feeling forms a most important Link of Associations—& may be combined with the whole Story of a long Dream just as well as with one particular Form no way resembling the true Image? I seem to see, tho' darkly, that the Inferences hence are many & important/Madness—Bulls—Self—God—Past Life + Present; or Conscience, &c—

Similarly, the perfunctory killing of a hawk is a reminder of the effect when feeling is disjoined from thought.[18]

Hawk with ruffled Feathers resting on the Bowsprit—Now shot at & yet did not move—how fatigued—a third time it made a gyre, a short circuit, & returned again/5 times it was thus shot at/left the Vessel/flew to another/& I heard firing, now here, now there/& nobody shot it/but probably it perished from fatigue, & the attempt to rest upon the wave!—Poor Hawk! O Strange Lust of Murder in Man!—It is not cruelty/ it is mere non-feeling from non-thinking.

A long attempt to explain nightmare in similar terms as relating extreme terror to past experience by invoking the creative subconscious imagination.[19]

Elucidation of my all-zermalming [overwhelming] argument on the subject of ghosts & apparitions by what occurred last night in my sleep—I drew up my legs suddenly: for a great pig was leaping out direct against them. No!—a great pig appeared to leap out against me because by a fear-engendering disease of the stomach, affecting the circulation of the Blood or nervous powers my Legs were suddenly twitched up.

Night-mair is, I think, always—even when it occurs in the midst of Sleep, and not as it more commonly does after a waking Interval, a state not of Sleep but of Stupor of the outward organs of Sense, not in words indeed but yet in fact distinguishable from the suspended power of the senses in true Sleep; while the volitions of *Reason* i.e. comparing &c, are awake, tho' disturbed. This stupor seems occasioned by some painful sensation, of unknown locality, most often, I believe, in the lower Gut, tho' not seldom in the Stomach, which withdrawing the attention to itself from its sense of other realities present makes us asleep to them indeed but otherwise awake—and when ever this derangement occasions an interruption in the circulation, aided perhaps by pressure, awkward position, &c, the part deadened—as the hand, or his arm, or the foot & leg, on this side, transmits ~~single~~ double Touch as ~~double~~ single Touch: to which the Imagination therefore, the true inward Creatrix, instantly out of the chaos of the elements ⟨or shattered fragments⟩ of Memory puts together some form to fit it—which derives an over-powering sense of Reality from the circumstance, that the power of Reason being in good measure awake, most generally presents to us all the accompanying images very nearly as they existed the moment before, when we fell out of anxious wakefulness into this *Reverie*—ex. gr. the bed, the curtains, the Room, & its furniture, the knowlege of who lies in the next room &c—

Last night before awaking or rather delivery from the night-mair, in which a claw-like talon-nailed Hand grasped hold of me, interposed between the curtains, I ha~~ve~~d just before with my foot felt some thing seeming to move against it (—for in my foot it commenced)—I detected it, I say, by my excessive Terror, and dreadful Trembling of my whole body, Trunk & Limbs—& by my piercing out-cries—Good Heaven! (reasoned I) were this real, I never should or could be, in such an agony of Terror—

In short, this Night-mair is not properly *a Dream*; but a species of Reverie, akin to Somnambul~~ance~~ism, during which the Understanding & Moral Sense are awake tho' more or less confused, and over the Terrors of which the Reason can exert no influence ~~that~~ because it is not true Terror: i.e. apprehension of Danger, but a sensation as much as the Tooth-ache, a Cramp—I.e. the Terror does not *arise* out of a painful Sensation, but is itself a specific sensation = terror corporeus sive materialis.—To explain & classify these strange sensations, the organic material Analogons (Ideas materiales ⟨intermedias,⟩ as the Cartesians say) of Fear, Hope, Rage, Shame, & (strongest of all) Remorse, forms at present the most difficult & at the same time the most interesting Problem of Psychology, and intimately connected with prudential morals (= the science of morals in its relation, not the ground & Law of Duty, but to the empirical hindrances & fumbulations in the realizing of the Law by the human Being)—. The solution of this Problem would, perhaps, throw great doubt on this present dogma, that the Forms & Feelings of Sleep are always the reflections & confused Echoes of our waking Thoughts, & Experiences.—

Apparitions are similarly to be explained by the mind's effort to make sense of experiences of terror while its involvement in time and space bars it from any ability to appreciate eternity and infinity.[20]

Apparitions—The story of the Young woman from Birmingham/—My converse with Faringdon/
The mind never perhaps wholly uninformed of the circumstantia in Sleep—by means of the feeling, the temperature/&c.—Persons will awake by removing Lights—how does sensation produce corresponding images?—My Father's dream—frequent cause of the terror struck by apparitions is that in the first feeling the terror (as a bodily sensation) is the cause of the *Image*/not vice versâ—This illustrated & brought as a confutation of the reality of apparitions—"You are alive."—
2. Eternity, Infinitity, ever negative, contemplated under the relations of Time/the contradiction & consequent perplexity/Hence the terrors of Conscience—
3. Lastly, and an overpowering answer to those who think Religion aided by Dæmonology, an apparent removal from God's protection, which is *for us* one with an established order of Cause and Effects—in Mechanism—and when the mind expands, Law in dynamics—: but Free Will to Powers ab extra [from outside], not subject to *human Love*— & supposed in rebellion to divine Law—would necessarily shelter itself in *Polytheism*—i.e. make the things themselves be sources of the Law/

A long attempt to explain and classify the different forms of dream-experience.[21]

Language of Dreams.—The language of the Dream = Night is ⋈ that of Waking = the Day. It is a language of Images and Sensations, the various dialects of which are far less different from each other, than the various Day-Languages of Nations. Proved even by the Dream Books of different Countries & ages.
2. The images either direct, as when a Letter reminds me of itself, or symbolic—as Darkness for Calamity. Again, either anticipation or reminiscence.
3. These latter either grounded on some analogy, as to see a friend passing over a broad & deep water = Death, or seemingly arbitrary, as in the signification of Colors, different animals &c.
4. Frequently ironical: as if the fortunes of the Ego diurnus appeared exceedingly droll and ridiculous to the Ego nocturnus—Dung = Gold &c. So in Nature, Man, Baboon, Horse, Ass. Cats' Love & Rage &c.

5. Probably, a still deeper Dream, or Ὑπερονειρος [Hyperdream], of which there remains only an imageless but profound Presentiment or Boding...

6. The Prophets, and the Laws of Moses, the most majestic Instances.—

7. Prophetic combinations, *if* there be such, = the instincts previous to the use and to the organ. Bull-calf *buts*—and to the preparation of organs in a lower class for the higher—as rudiments of eyes useless to A but perfected in B.—

8. Beasts of Concord and Independence ending in the Elephant—Beasts of Discord and Dependence——the Lion.

Man and the beasts drawn into his Circle—Dog, Ox. Man—a mystery in this.

9 The Conscience—the Unity of Day and Night—Q^y Are there two Consciences, the earthly and the Spiritual?—

10. The sensuous Nature a Lexicon raisonné of Words, treating of, not being, ⟨αυτα τα πραγματα⟩ [things themselves] spiritual things—Our Fall at once implied and produced a resistance, this a more or less confused Echo, and this a secondary Echo &c—And thus deeming the Echo to be the Words, the Words became Things—Ειδωλολατρεῖα [Idolatry]. On this principle is the system of Emanuel Swedenborg grounded: and may be true, tho' the particular Translations should be found arbitrary or fantastic.

10 [*a*]. Let them be compared with the views that might be presented by the physiologic Ideas of Reil, Bichat, Autenrieth, & the better disciples of the Natur-philosophy.—First, the Cerebral System—⊁ the Ganglionic, and at once ÷ and ≈ the Sympathic and its vocal nerves. The importance of the Gastric and especially the hepatic—and the paramouncy of the Ganglionic over the Cerebral in Sleep. The Liver, and lower Abdomen—the Engastrimuthi [Ventriloquists], and the prophetic Power of *diseased* Life in the ancient Oracles, hard by Streams & Caverns of deleterious influences—these numerous in early Paganism, then decreased & with them the Oracles. Plutarch knew but of 3 or 4 remaining.—⟨Curious Phrase of St Basil, that Ezra totum το βιβλιον *eructavit* [disgorged the whole book].⟩

11. Liver—&c. The passions of the Day as often originate in the Dream, as the Images of the Dream in the Day. Guilt, Falsehood, traced to the Gastric Life. See my *Pains* of Sleep, & a curious Passage in G. Fox's Journal.

12. The good side of this—i.e. ganglionic—System. As all Passions, and Feelings, so Love roots therein. The process of the action of Inspiration

in the Prophets, as well as in the Sibyls.—The autobiographies of the New-born—the Durch-bruch of the Herrnhüter ['Awakening' of the Moravians]—&c. Whatever part be the source of the Disease, into that must the medicine first enter. In this way only can it be Specific.

The opposite of nightmare is the release of volition without any such stimulation, which can produce a sensation of flying.[22]

Flying or rather self-shooting in dreams, with me the accompaniment or rather <u>translation</u> of a slight pain and restlessness in the Bowels, just above, or below, or across the umbilical Line—that at least is what I commonly find on awaking. What is it?—Imperfect awakening of the Volition, with sense of the nascent activity of the voluntary muscles— In short, Motion without *Touch*, but with sense of *effort*, all corrupt in a continued series (= awaking & relaxing Volition) seems to solve the phænomenon. Hence, you never fly in a night-mair—for then the sensation of *Touch* or of being touched is called up.

An account of the ability of the subconscious to act more readily when the upper conscious is inhibited, as in the recollection of a buried name.[23]

I feel that there is a mystery in the sudden by-act-of-will-unaided, nay, more than that frustrated, recollection of a Name. I was trying to recollect the name of a Bristol Friend, who had attended me in my Illness at Mr Wade's—I began with the Letters of the Alphabet—A B C &c—& I know not why, felt convinced that it began with H. I ran thro' all the vowels, a e i o u y, & with all the consonants to each—Hab, Heb, Hib, Hob, Hub & so on—in vain—I then began other Letters—all in vain— Three minutes afterwards, having completely given it up, the name, Daniel, at once started up, perfectly insulated, without any the dimmest antecedent connection, as far as my consciousness extended.—There is no explanation, ὡς ἐμοίγε δοκεῖ [as it seems to me, at least] of this fact but by a full sharp distinction of Mind from Consciousness—the Consciousness being the narrow <u>Neck</u> of the Bottle. The name, Daniel, must have been a living <u>Atom</u>-thought in my mind, whose uneasy motions were the craving to recollect it—but the very craving led the mind to a search which at each successive disappointment (= a tiny pain) tended to contract the orifice or <u>outlet</u> into Consciousness. Well—it is given up—& all is quiet—the Nerves are asleep, or off their guard—& then the Name pops up, makes it way, & there it is!—not assisted by any association, but the very contrary—by the suspension & <u>sedation</u> of all associations.

Table-talking in April 1830, Coleridge reveals how much he himself fears the expression of 'lower or bestial states of Life' through their irruptions via the subconscious at the expense of Reason.[24]

Madness is not simply a bodily disease. It is the sleep of the Spirit with certain conditions of wakefulness; that is, lucid intervals. During this sleep or recession of the Spirit, the lower or bestial states of Life rise up into action and prominence. It is an awful thing to be eternally tempted by the perverted senses; the Reason *may* resist—it *does* resist, for a long time—but too often, at length, it yields for a moment and then the man is mad for ever. An act of the will is in many instances precedent to complete insanity. Bishop Butler said he was all his life struggling against the devilish suggestions of his senses, which would have maddened him, if he had relaxed the stern wakefulness of his Reason for a moment.

Endeavouring to teach his son Hartley the elements of his system Coleridge begins by making a crucial distinction between Consciousness and Being. Just as in the Rabbinical scheme the Aleph is not simply a letter, but the fountain of all letters, or the One can be the fountain of all numbers as well as an individual number, Being can be seen as the fountain of all Beings. A true philosopher must acquire sufficient suppleness of mind to appreciate such subtleties.[25]

We can become CONSCIOUS of *Being* only by means of *Existence*, tho' having thus become conscious thereof, we are in the same moment conscious, that Being must be prior (in thought) to Existence: as without seeing, we should never *know* (i.e. know ourselves to have known) that we had Eyes; but having learnt this, we know that Eyes must be anterior to the act of seeing. With equal evidence we understand that Existence supposes *relation*—for it is, Sisto me *ad extra* [I set myself against what is external], and thereby distinguished from Being. Well then. We know A by B: and B by A. We know, that between A and B there is, first, a something peculiar to each, *that*, namely, by which A is A and *not* B, and B is B and *not* A: and secondly, a something common to them, a one in both; namely, that which is expressed by the copula, *is*: and thirdly, that the latter, = Being, is in order of thought presupposed in the former. What is last in Reflection, is first in the *genesis*, or order of causation, . . . as One can never be *known* but as it is revealed in and by the Many, so neither can the Many be *known* (i.e. reflected on) but by it's relation to a *One*, and ultimately therefore, *Ones* being = Many, only by reference to THE ONE, which includes instead of excluding the Alter. The Aleph, say the Rabbinical Philologists, is no Letter; but that in and with which all Letters are or become. Even so, there is a higher than 1. or the 1. is an equivocal for two most disparate senses: in the nobler of which it is equivalent to the O positive, which is no *thing* because it is the ground and sufficient cause of *all* things, and no *number* because it is the Numerorum omnium Fons et Numerus [the Number and Fountain of all Numbers].—N.B. No man can *be*, or can *understand*, a Philosopher, till he has acquired the power and the habit of attaching to words the *generic* sense purely and unmixed with the accidents of comparative *degrees*. It is this which constitutes the difference between the *proper* Nomenclature of Science and the inevitable language of ordinary life. The latter speaks only of *degrees*. With *quantity* and quality it is familiar; but knows nothing of *quiddity* but as a synonyme for worthless subtleties: and only grins wider and with more intense self-complacency when it hears the former speak of invisible *Light*, the *Heat* of Ice, &c. The *Uno* nel Più of the philosophical Saint & Bishop of Geneva (Francesco Sales) would be as senseless to a common Italian.

Personal identity remains a mystery, suggesting that mind should not be identified with 'I-ness'.[26]

—The definition of Mind by me long adopted & still retained is a Subject that <u>is</u> it's own Object!—but for this reason it may with no less propriety be defined, an object involving it's own Subject— —But this is not the definition of the "I"—/this must be defined, a Subject recognizing itself as a <u>Subject</u>. The "I" therefore cannot be conceived as the WHOLE <u>Mind</u>; and tho' it is indeed the mind itself, of which the Mind is conscious (ni rectius dicetur, <u>scious</u> [it is not properly called, *knowing*]): yet it is not of necessity conscious of it *as* itself. Something more, therefore, seems to be required for the existence of an "I", than mind in the universal idea!—What is this?—Have I not in my former disquisitions fallen into some error, from identifying the definitions of Mind and der *Ichheit* [I-ness]? I must examine—but I suspect, that the aweful subjects of Conscience, on the one hand, and of the Personæ Somnii [of sleep] = Dreamatis Personæ, in which the Subject is recognized as an Object, depend for their solution on this distinction.—The Conscience being the real antitheton of the I—and Dreams the <subjective> antitheton, in the absence of some higher power yet to be determined/ Q^y—Reason = mind exclusively objective? and hence in relation to a Subject = Science relatively to Mind, Conscience relatively to Will.—It is indeed a deep & subtle Investigation; but a most important one!

The problem of consciousness and identity is worked over again: is there a triple 'I-ness'?[27]

I doubt and am inclined to let loose again my stray Thought-Fly—respecting the Consciousness as the Copula of the triple Ichheit. Indeed, to begin with the first, I suspect, that I shall annul the change of my original idea, in which I affirmed only a twofold I—the superior, or the I of the Spirit—and the inferior or the I of the Ground—the latter indeed being the Copula or emaning Unity of the Sense and the Understanding—the vegetive and the lower instinctive Life having properly no *I*, but being merely the Basis, the appropriated Meum of the I, as the correlative Subject of the "Mind of the Flesh,["] as the correspondent Objective.—But waiving this question for the present, I am on meditation more disposed to consider the secondary Consciousness (of which the Recollection or Memory in actu is a species or modification) as exclusively the self-manifestation of the inferior I, the I of the actualizing Ground—and that it's affirmation is, Hoc et illud scio una cum scientia mei, et meorum [This and that I know as one with the knowledge of me, and mine]—And this view is supported by the facts of the variableness and dependency of the Consciousness on the state of the Organs, and it's confusion or total suspension by even slight affections of certain Organs—the Stomach for instance, and the Abdominal Viscera.—And verily, this "I" is the Subjective and the Representative of the Mortal Man. Hence the constant Relation of this Consciousness to Time and Contingency—while the Superior I, the Subjective of the Reason and of the Moral Will, yea, even of the pure Imagination, is ever affirmative of that which is, and even in images of the eternal Form translucent thro' the Image, of the Idea in Idolon—/ The Acts and affirmations are ever timeless. The mystery is in the Shining down of the Light into the Darkness, in the Irradiation of the Mind of the Flesh, by virtue of which it becomes a human Understanding, in the apt phrase of Shakespere "a Discourse of Reason"—a mysterious Fact so sublimely annunciated by the Evangelist John—I.5. "The Light shineth into and in the Darkness: and the Darkness comprehendeth it not"—The Understanding in it's Unity [as opposed to] it's Multëity, (which is the same as the Subjectivity of the Understanding [as opposed to] it's Objectivity) knows the existence of the Light <= Lux> by the co-existence of <the Lumen,> with it's knowlege of itself—yet that the living possession of itself, the Sensation, Empfindung, Self-finding, is raised into "sciousness" and thence by reference to the superior Presence into a Con-sciousness of that presence; *1.* this is itself the effect and potenziation of the Lumen—which the Understanding knows because it knows itself, by virtue of it's co-presence. Yet if we made the Lumen itself the Consciousness, the same consequence would follow for the Lumen cannot be abstracted or separated from the darkness which it's illuminates, i.e. from the Mass, or Materia that reflects it. Subtract either the Lumen or the reflecting Surface—and alike in either Case the Consciousness ceases—just as Water ceases to be, whether you separate the Oxygen from the Hydrogen, or the Hydrogen from the Oxygen. But as, one surface or reflecting or transmitting Body being removed, another of higher reflective or receptive qualities may be substituted—and the Lumen will remain as long as the Lux or lucific Power is and acts—even so, no argument against the survival of the Soul and the Revival of the Consciousness can be legitimately grounded on the fugacity and mutability of our present Consciousness—which is, after all, but as the Lamp or Candle in a well-furnished Chamber, which you may (to aid the Similitude) suppose tenanted by intelligent Mutes who can only converse by the figures & visual signs.—Carry on the parable—and suppose that during the absence of the Taper or Lamp, a certain portion of the least valuable furniture had been removed, and other far nobler articles put in place of them—this would answer to the revival of Consciousness with the superinduction or supereduction of a glorified Body—The Light would be the Con-sciousness of this Body.—The connection of this Consciousness with the Consciousness of the Body previously illumined, and the identity of the Consciousness is another and distinct question. That the sense of the identity is not necessarily dependent on any recollection of the former, is proved by the fact of our own infancy, and <early> child-hood. The only indispensable condition seems to be a continuity, i.e. that the change should be without any saltus [*leap*]. Yet even this must be qualified & explained, before it can be safely affirmed—a mere chasm of Time forms no such destructive saltus—as is proved in

Trances, by profound Sleep, by a long suspension of all memory during certain derangements or oppressions of the Brain, and as I trust will be proved in the awakening from the Sleep of the Grave.—The Imperishability of Thought, the perishability of the Consciousness, and the possible reviviscence of the latter by consequence of the former—these are the three aweful Facts, of deepest interest in for every contemplative Man.—The preceding Remarks are but sparks struck into Tinder—but the time may come when the prepared <u>Match</u> may transfer them kindled into flame to the well-fed wicks of the Golden Lamp, hung from the Roof of the Temple!

P.S. The ground of the intelligibility of the whole is the <u>spirituality</u> of the Hades. The Spirit <u>was</u> Light <u>of</u> Light as long as it abode <u>in</u> the Light—and fell into Darkness, self-precipitated into a blank potentiality, which but for the Absolute Will would have been equal to mere non-essence, and which antecedent to the Condescension of the Spirit, and the lucific Word was equivalent to non-existence—but which by the Word successively <u>actualized</u> is restored from Mass = substantial darkness to dark Warmth; from Warmth to Gloomy, from the Gloomy to Light by reception of Light/. Hence the Light is <u>our</u> Light/. The Darkness becomes Light, is actualized into <u>Light</u>—. The divine Light being the <u>Actualizing</u> Power a <u>Supra</u>—and hence (Nota bene) does the Simile or Analogy conveyed in the terms, the Light = Lumen

A few months later he asserts that his own belief is in a double human identity, antecedent to its unification, which still leaves the mystery of consciousness ultimately unsolved.[28]

Psychologically, Consciousness is the Problem, the solution of which cannot be too variously be re-worded, too manifoldly be illustrated. The solution I believe myself to have discovered in the duplicity of the I, the antecedent unific Unit—but in it's <u>application</u> to the facts of our experience, especially to the elucidation of Death, and the nature and degree of the necessary dependence of Consciousness on the Organs, of which Death is the dissolution, almost all is yet to be achieved. If it please the All-wise to prolong my life, humbly & earnestly I implore strength, and grace, so to redeem the time!—

Resuming his correspondence with C.A. Tulk, the Swedenborgian, he reiterates his belief in 'Symbols and Correspondences'.[29]

If I mistake not, one formula would comprize your philosophical faith & mine—namely, that the sensible World is but the evolution of the Truth, Love, and Life, or their opposites, in Man—and that in Nature Man beholds only (to use an Algebraic but close analogy) the integration of Products, the Differentials of which are in, and constitute, his own mind and soul—and consequently that all true science is contained in the Lore of Symbols & Correspondences.—

The supremacy of 'continuous' minds.[30]

In the men of continuous and discontinuous minds explain & demonstrate the vast difference between the disjunction conjunctive of the sudden Images *seized* on from external Contingents by Passion & Imagination (which is Passion eagle-eyed)— The Breeze I see, is in the Tree—It comes to cool my Babe and me.—which is the property & prerogative of continuous minds of the highest order, & the conjunction disjunctive of Wit—

> And like a lobster boil'd the Morn
> From black to red began to turn,

which is the excellence of men of discontinuous minds—
    Arrange & classify the men of continuous minds—the pseudo-continuous, or *juxta-ponent* mind/metaphysician not a poet—poet not a metaphysician?—poet + metaphysician/—*the faithful* in Love &c—

Recognizing the difficulty of expressing adequately the continuity of the underlying primary consciousness with more familiar modes, he pays tribute to the strenuousness and heroism of those who have wrestled with the problem.[31]

Speaking of the original unific Consciousness, the primary Perception, & its extreme difficulty, to take occation to draw a lively picture of the energies, self-denials, sacrifices, toils, trembling knees, & sweat-drops on the Brow, of a philosopher who has really been sounding the depths of our being—& to compare it with the greatest & most perseverant Labors of Travellers, Soldiers, and whomever else Men honor & admire—how trifling the latter! And yet how cold our gratitude to the former—Say not, that they were vainly employed—compare the mind & motives of a vulgar Sensualist, or wild Savage with the mind of a Plato or an Epictetus—& then say if you dare that there is any more comparison between the *effects* of the toils of the Philosopher & the Worldling, than there is between the intensity of the toils themselves.

5
The Existence and Nature of God

Coleridge's initial acquaintance with Unitarianism may well have taken place during his Cambridge days through his acquaintance with William Frend, the Fellow of his college who was well known for his controversial views. 'Mr Frend's company is by no means invidious,' he wrote to his brother in January 1793, three months after his arrival in Cambridge, adding, however, ' ... Though I am not an *Alderman*, I have yet *prudence* enough to *respect* that *gluttony of faith* waggishly yclept Orthodoxy.'[1] But when in the following year Frend was tried and banished from the University after being found guilty of violating the statutes of the University by publishing a pamphlet considered as subversive, Coleridge, sitting among the undergraduates who attended the trial in the Senate House, was reputedly vociferous in his support of the heretic.

He was attracted to other Unitarians and when writing to Lamb's and his own friend George Dyer in London early in 1795 he promised to present Southey to him 'right orthodox in the heterodoxy of Unitarianism'.[2] In Bristol he was soon friendly with the minister J.P. Estlin, who seems to have commended him to various West Country colleagues: according to his later recollection he was thought of as the 'rising star' of the denomination and, as has already been related, almost became the minister at Shrewsbury. Although he believed that the undemanding few doctrinal requirements of the sect would leave him largely free to 'play off my intellect ad libitum',[3] the central tenet concerning the unity of God would trouble him for the rest of his life. While his growing interest in the possibility of developing a religion of nature attracted him increasingly, this, as we have seen, led logically to the pantheism of Spinoza and to a God who must be impersonal. In the end he could not forsake allegiance to the idea of a personal God, or for that matter to the Christ of the Christian faith.

To believe in the divinity of Christ, however, involved the acceptance of the Father also, and so a divinity which was also a relationship, which meant turning away from the central belief of Unitarianism. At the same time it did not in itself entail the acceptance of Trinitarianism, which came later. His recognition that a dilemma was nevertheless involved is evident from a notebook entry of these years: 'As we recede from anthropomorphitism we must go either to the Trinity or to a Pantheism—The Fathers who were Unitarians, were Anthropomorphites.'[4] A key clue to the further development of his religious ideas is to be found in a further notebook entry, this time from 1805,[5] which suggests the turmoil of his mind as he wrestled with his continuing scepticism concerning certain aspects of the Gospel record and his belief in the impersonality of God, yet his persistent sense of the importance of a personal figure who could be worshipped as divine. In a retrospective passage in *Biographia Literaria* he described himself as having been earlier a 'Trinitarian' of a Platonic kind, presumably following the lines of the 1795 lecture quoted from above, where he had evidently been toying with the idea that the significance of Jesus was to have been not a redeemer from sin but an exemplar of living. By 1806, when he was asked for guidance from his wife's brother, he was groping his way towards a fuller acceptance of the Trinity. His formulation then was to think of them in terms of 'the Deity, the redemption, and the thereto necessary assumption of humanity by the Word'.[6]

Henceforth he would spend much time seeking a true formulation of such a doctrine while castigating believers in his former faith. In 1812 he would cause indignation and rebuttal from his old Unitarian friend J.P. Estlin when he commented in the course of a lecture that Milton, in *Paradise Regained*, had presented Satan as a 'scoffing Socinian'— presumably on the strength of assertions such as he made in tempting Jesus: 'All Men are sons of God . . .'[7] (There may also have been a hidden element of self-castigation in the remark, if one recalls his earlier benediction to Davy: 'May God & all his Sons love you as I do.'[8])

In letters and notebook entries he set out formula after formula, of which one or two are recorded here (often in the form of mathematical diagrams), as he tried to reach one that was fully satisfactory. At times he moved from a triad to a fourfold tetractys as his model, a conclusion which, according to J.R. Barth, his early editor W.G.T. Shedd questioned on the grounds of his 'assumption of an aboriginal Unity existing primarily by itself, and in the order of nature, *before* a Trinity—of a *ground* for the Trinity . . . which is not in its own nature either triune or personal, but is merely the impersonal base from which the Trinity proper is evolved.'[9] Coleridge himself, on the other hand, saw the failure to grasp this 'all-truths-including truth of the Tetractys eternally manifested in the Triad' as 'the ground and cause of all the main heresies from Semi-Arianism, recalled by Dr. Samuel Clarke, to the last setting ray of departing faith in the necessitarian Psilanthropism of Dr. Priestley.'[10] The continuing assertion suggests the degree to which, despite his insistence on the personality of God, Coleridge was still moved by an urge to reconcile it with the need to find a place for the impersonal in his account of the divine, which he tried to resolve by calling on his term 'personëity'.[11]

The existence of these and other perplexities induces doubts as to whether he found a position on the necessity of a Trinity that might command general assent. This is not to say, however, that he ever gave up the quest, as will become evident: he was firmly reasserting his position concerning the nature of the godhead even on his deathbed.

In Biographia Literaria *Coleridge looks back to his days as a Unitarian and tries to justify his earlier beliefs as the common-sense views of a young man who had not yet thought sufficiently deeply.*[1]

... I was, at that time and long after, though a Trinitarian (i.e. ad normam Platonis [on the Platonic pattern]) in philosophy, yet a zealous Unitarian in Religion; more accurately, I was a *psilanthropist*, one of those who believe our Lord to have been the real son of Joseph, and who lay the main stress on the resurrection rather than on the crucifixion. O! never can I remember those days with either shame or regret. For I was most sincere, most disinterested! My opinions were indeed in many and most important points erroneous; but my heart was single. Wealth, rank, life itself then seemed cheap to me, compared with the interests of (what I believed to be) the truth, and the will of my maker. I cannot even accuse myself of having been actuated by vanity; for in the expansion of my enthusiasm I did not think of *myself* at all.

At the end of his life, Coleridge again traces his course through Socinianism, and suggests why at the time he found it acceptable.[2]

Socinus worshipped Jesus Christ, and said that God had given him the power of being omnipresent. David, with a little more acuteness, suggested that mere audition or presence in a creature could not justify worship from men;—that a man, however glorified, was no nearer God in essence than a common scoundrel. Prayer, therefore, was inapplicable. And how could a man be mediator between God and man? How could a man with sins himself offer any compensation for or expiation of sin? unless the most arbitrary caprice were admitted into the counsels of God? Then at last it was discovered that there was no such thing as sin.

Priestley was the author of the modern Unitarianism. I owe, under God, my return to the faith to my having gone much further than the Unitarians, and so came round to the other extreme. I never falsified the Scripture. I always told them that their interpretations of the Scripture were intolerable; and that if they were to affect to construe the will of their neighbour as they did that of their Maker, they would be scouted out of society. I said then plainly and openly, that it was clear enough that John and Paul were not Unitarians: But at that time I had a strong sense of the repugnancy of the doctrine of vicarious atonement to the moral being, and I thought nothing could counterbalance that. "What care I," I said, "for the Platonisms of John or the Rabbinisms of Paul? My conscience revolts."

Always believing in the government of God, I was an optimist; but as I could not but see that the *present* state of things was not the *best*, I was necessarily led to look to a future state.

He also regards it as a very natural course for a young man.[3]

I dare avow—& hope, I shall give no offence to serious Believers—that it appears to me scarcely possible, that a young man of ingenuous dispositions, warm sensibility, and an enquiring mind should avoid Socinianism—educated as we all are—1. The grounds are—the application of common Logic, i.e. the law of incongruity (regula contradictionis) to premises abstracted from Matter, & falsely applied to Spirit—. Thus in the word *one*—Logic in short applied without any previous analysis of the faculties of the mind, and the seat or source of different notions— thus, time & space/—cause and effect—are all applied to Duty & to human Soul in the same sense & with the same confidence as to the phænomena of the Senses/—2. The custom so inveterate of disputing a Religion by Texts—Text marshalled against Text—the consequence of which must necessarily be, that one class of Texts appearing to contradict the other, the preference will—& indeed ought to be given to that sense which is the most congruous with Reason—3. Young men ignorant of the corruption & weakness of their own hearts, & therefore always prone to substitute the glorious *Ideal* of human nature for the existing reality—This may be most affectingly shewn by the fervent friendships & bitter quarrels of young men, each expecting the other to be an Angel, & taking their generous wishes in their most generous moods for Virtue—/Hence no need is felt of Redemption—.—4. a subtler & abstruser ground—why young men are inclined to necessitarianism, in addition to the pleasure from clear & distinct notions, which those must needs be which are but in truth material Images by a sophism of metathesis passed off for operations of mind—in addition to this, strange as it may appear, yet it is true, that we least value & think of that which we enjoy in the highest degree—this free-agency, the unsettled state of Habit not yet Tyranny—we begin to think of, & intellectually to know, our freedom when we have been made to feel its imperfections, & its loss—From these causes I explain & justify the fact of the Trinity not being taught to young Christians, to the catechumens—And this is a glorious proof that to *acquiesce* in a doctrine was, by no means, all that the Christian Church required—till Christianity had already done part of its work, in turning the mind in upon itself, & leading it gradually to a deep faith in its free-agency in *posse*, the Trinity could not be understood or believed, in the Christian sense of the word *belief*. Therefore, it was not taught—This is a most important fact—and places or shews the true corner stone, or foundation of Christian Faith, which is not κατανοεῖν το προσωπον εν εσοπτρῳ [to hold one's face in a glass], but παρακυψαι εις νομον τελειον τον της Ελευθεριας [to look into the perfect law of liberty]—This is the great fundamental Article of Christian Faith.—The last ground, I have now to mention, in addition to all said in another Memorandum Book is—the Chillingsworthian Touch, that the whole Religion of Protestants not only is in the Bible, but is capable of being demonstrated from it, without assistance of Tradition, or the writings of the Fathers—/—Prove that this is not the orthodox Faith of the Church of England, & its dangerous Consequences—/

In a contemporary notebook of 1805 he records the steps by which he has come to the need for an acknowledgement of the Trinity.[4]

Thinking during my perusal of Horsley's Letters in Rep[ly] to D[r] P[riestley's] objections to the Trinity on the part of Jews, Mahometans, and Infidels, it burst upon me at once as an awful Truth what 7 or 8 years ago I thought of proving with a *hollow Faith* and for an *ambiguous purpose*, my mind then wavering in its necessary passage from Unitarianism (which as I have often said is the Religion of a man, whose Reason would make him an Atheist but whose Heart and Common sense will not permit him to be so) thro' Spinosism into Plato and St John/No Christ, No God!—This I now feel with all its needful evidence, of the Understanding: would to God, my spirit were made conform thereto—that No Trinity, no God.—That Unitarianism in all its Forms is Idolatry, and that the remark of Horsley is most accurate, that Dr Priestley's mode of converting the Jews & Turks is in the great essential of religious Faith to give the name of Christianity to their present Idolatry—truly the trick of Mahomet, who finding that the Mountain would not come to *him* went to the Mountain. O that this Conviction may work upon me and in me/and that my mind may be made up as to the character of Jesus, and of historical Christianity, as clearly as it is of the Logos and intellectual or spiritual Christianity—that I may be made to know either their especial and peculiar Union, or their absolute disunion in any peculiar Sense.

In a letter to his wife's brother, written in 1806, after his return from Malta and Italy, Coleridge explains the reasons for his retreat from Unitarianism. His failure to find true love in his marriage, coupled with poor health and other ills has caused him to find that faith too optimistic and shallow.[5]

My dear young friend,

I am sorry that you should have felt any delicacy in disclosing to me your religious feelings, as rendering it inconsistent with your tranquillity of mind to spend the Sunday evening with me. Though I do not find in that book, which we both equally revere, any command, either express, or which I can infer, which leads me to attach any criminality to cheerful and innocent social intercourse on the Lord's day; though I do not find that it was in the least degree forbidden to the Jews on their Sabbath; and though I have been taught by Luther, and the great founders of the Church of England, that the Sabbath was a part of the ceremonial and transitory parts of the law given by heaven to Moses; and that our Sunday is binding on our consciences, chiefly from its manifest and most awful usefulness, and indeed moral necessity; yet I highly commend your firmness in what you think right, and assure you solemnly, that I esteem you greatly for it. I would much rather that you should have too much, than an atom too little. I am far from surprised that, having seen what you have seen, and suffered what you have suffered, you should have opened your soul to a sense of our fallen nature; and the incapability of man to heal himself. My opinions may not be in all points the same as yours; but I have experienced a similar alteration. I was for many years a Socinian; and at times almost a Naturalist, but sorrow, and ill health, and disappointment in the only deep wish I had ever cherished, forced me to look into myself; I read the New Testament again, and I became fully convinced, that Socinianism was not only not the doctrine of the New Testament, but that it scarcely deserved the name of a religion in any sense. An extract from a letter which I wrote a few months ago to a sceptical friend, who had been a Socinian, and of course rested all the evidences of Christianity on miracles, to the exclusion of grace and inward faith, will perhaps surprise you, as showing you how much nearer our opinions are than what you must have supposed. 'I fear that the mode of defending Christianity, adopted by Grotius first; and latterly, among many others, by Dr. Paley, has increased the number of infidels;—never could it have been so great, if thinking men had been habitually led to look into their own souls, instead of always looking out, both of themselves, and of their nature. If to curb attack, such as yours on miracles, it had been answered:—Well, brother! but granting these miracles to have been in part the growth of delusion at the time, and of exaggeration afterward, yet still all the doctrines will remain untouched by this circumstance, and binding on thee. Still must thou repent and be regenerated, and be crucified to the flesh; and this not by thy own mere power; but by a mysterious action of the moral Governor on thee; of the Ordo-ordinians [ordering order], the Logos, or Word. Still will the eternal filiation, or Sonship of the Word from the Father; still will the Trinity of the Deity, the redemption, and the thereto necessary assumption of humanity by the Word, "who is with God, and is God," remain truths: and still will the vital head-and-heart FAITH in these truths, be the living and only fountain of all true virtue. Believe all these, and with the grace of the spirit consult your own heart, in quietness and humility, they will furnish you with proofs, that surpass all understanding, because they are felt and known; believe all these I say, so as that thy faith shall be not merely real in the acquiescence of the intellect; but actual, in the thereto assimilated affections; then shalt thou KNOW from God, whether or not Christ be of God. But take notice, I only say, the miracles are extra essential; I by no means deny their importance, much less hold them useless, or superfluous. Even as Christ did, so would I teach; that is, build the miracle on the faith, not the faith on the miracle.'

May heaven bless you, my dear George, and | Your affectionate friend,

S. T. C.

A postscript five days later:[6]

I fear, you rather misunderstood one part of my Letter. I by no means gave that extract, as containing the whole of my Christian Faith; but as comprising such doctrines, as a clear Head & honest Heart assisted by divine Grace might in part discover by self-examination and the light of natural conscience, & which *efficiently* and *practically* believed would prepare the way for the *peculiar Doctrine* of Christianity, namely, Salvation by the Cross of Christ. I meant these doctrines as the Skeleton, to which the death & Mediation of Christ with the supervention of the Holy Ghost were to add the Flesh, and Blood, Muscles, nerves, & vitality.—— God of his goodness grant, that I may arrive at a more living Faith in these last, than I now feel. What I now feel is only a very strong *presentiment* of their Truth and Importance aided by a thorough conviction of the hollowness of all other Systems. Alas! my moral being is too untranquil, too deeply possessed by one lingering passion after an earthly good withheld—& probably withheld by divine goodness—from me, to be capable of being that, which it's own 'still small voice' tells me, even in my dreams, that it ought to be, yet of itself cannot be.

A year later he expands his thoughts when writing to Thomas Clarkson.[7]

My dear Sir

You have proposed to me questions not more awful than difficult of Solution. What metaphysically the Spirit of God *is*? What the Soul? What the difference between the Reason, and the Understanding (νοῦς καὶ ἐπιστήμη: Vernunft, und Verstand) and how metaphysically we may explain St Paul's assertion, that the Spirit of God bears witness to the Spirit of man?—In the first place I must reduce the two first questions to the *form* of the 3rd and fourth. What the Spirit of God *is*, and what the Soul *is*, I dare not suppose myself capable of *conceiving*: according to my religious and philosophical creed they are *known* by those, to whom they are revealed, even (tho' in a higher and deeper degree) as color (blue for instance); or motion; or the difference between the Spirals of the Hop-plant and the Scarlet Bean. *Datur*, non intelligitur [it is *given*, not comprehended]. They can only be explained by images, that themselves require the same explanation, as in the latter Instance, that the one turns to the right, the other to the Left, the one is with, the other against the Sun: i.e. by relative & dependent, not positive and fundamental, notions. The only reasonable form of question appears to me to be, under what connection of ideas we may so conceive and express ourselves concerning them, as that there shall be no inconsistency to be detected in our definitions, and no falsehood felt during their enunciation, which might war with our internal sense of their actuality. And in this sense these definitions are not without their use—they remove the stumbling-block out of the way of honest Infidels, that we are either Enthusiasts or Fanatics, that is, that our faith is built wholly either on blind bodily feelings arising in ourselves, or caught contagiously by sympathy with the agitations of a supersti[ti]ous crowd around the Fanes. (*Fanatici*.) And further, Seraphs and purified Spirits may burn unextinguishably in the pure elementary fire of direct knowlege, which has it's life and all the conditions of it's power in itself—but our Faith resembles sublunary Fire, that needs the Fuel of congruous, tho' perhaps perishable, notions to call it into actuality, and maintain it in clearness and the flame that rises heaven-ward, thus raising and glorifying the thick Vapor of our earthly Being. This premised, I venture—(most unfeignedly not without trembling and religious awe—) to proceed in an attempt to answer your first question:

First, then what is the difference or distinction between THING and THOUGHT? (or between those two experiences of our nature, which in the unphilosophical jargon of Mr Hume and his Followers, in *opposition* say rather, in direct contrariety, to the original and natural sense of the words, it is now fashionable to misname, IMPRESSIONS and IDEAS—) In other words, what do we mean by REALITY?—I answer—that there exist a class of notices which have all a ratio of vividness each with the other, so that tho' the one may be more vivid than the other, yet in the sane and ordinary course of our nature, they are all alike contra-distinguishable to another class of notices, which are felt and conceived as dependent on the former, and to be to them in some sort as a stamp on paper is to a seal sharp-cut in hard Stone. The first class we call *Things & Realities*; and find in them—not indeed absolutely, but in a sense which we all *understand*—(and I am not now disputing with a quibbler in mock-logic, but addressing myself to a Reasoner, who *seeks* to understand, and looks into himself for a sense, which my words may excite in him, not *to* my words for a sense, which they must against his own will *force* on him) we find, I say, in this first class a *permanency*, and *expectability* so great, as to be capable of being contra-distinguished both by these, and by their *vividness* to the second class, that is our Thoughts, which therefore as appearing posterior & faint we deem the Images & imperfect Shadows of the former. Language seems to mark this process of our minds / *Res—Reor*. So Thought is the participle of the Past: *Thing*, derived from the

Participle present, or actuality in full and immediate action.—Consequently, all *our* Thoughts are in the language of the old Logicians
inadequate: i.e. no *thought*, which I have, of any *thing* comprizes the
whole of that Thing. I have a distinct Thought of a Rose-Tree; but what
countless properties and goings-on of that plant are there, not included
in my *Thought* of it?—But the Thoughts of God, in the strict nomenclature of Plato, are all IDEAS, archetypal, and anterior to all but himself
alone: therefore consummately *adequate*: and therefore according to our
common habits of conception and expression, incomparably more *real*
than all things besides, & which do all depend on and proceed from
them in some sort perhaps as our Thoughts from those *Things*; but in a
more philosophical language we dare with less hesitation to say, that
they are more intensely *actual* / inasmuch as the human understanding
never took an higher or more honorable flight, than when it defined
the Deity to be—Actus purissimus sine *potentialitate* [the purest Act
without *potentiality*]: and Eternity, the incommunicable Attribute, and
may we not say, the Synonime of God, to be the simultaneous possession of all equally.——These considerations, my dear Sir! appear to me
absolutely necessary, as pioneers, to cut a way thro' to the direct solution
of your first Question—What is (i.e. what can we without detectible
incongruity conceive of) the Spirit of God? Answer.—God's Thoughts
are all consummately adequate Ideas, which are all incomparably more
real than what we call *Things*. God is the sole self-comprehending Being,
i.e. he has an Idea of himself, and that Idea is consummately adequate,
& superlatively real—or as great men have said in the throes and striv-
ings of deep and holy meditation, not only substantial or essential, but
super-substantial, super-essential. This Idea therefore from all eternity
co-existing with, & yet filiated, by the absolute Being (for as OUR purest
Thoughts are *conceived*, so are God's not first conceived, but *begotten*:
& thence is he verily and eminently *the* FATHER) is the same, as the
Father in all things, but the impossible one, of self-origination. He is the
substantial Image of God, in whom the Father beholds well-pleased his
whole Being—and being substantial (ὁμοούσιος) he of divine and
permanent Will, and a necessity which is the absolute opposite of compulsion, as delightedly & with as intense LOVE contemplates the Father
in the Father, and the Father in himself, and himself in the Father. But
all the actions of the Deity are intensely real or substantial / therefore
the action of Love, by which the Father contemplates the Son, and the
Son the Father, is equally real with the Father and the Son; & proceeds
co-eternally both from the Father and the Son—& neither of these
Three *can* be conceived *apart*, nor *confusedly*—so that the Idea of God

involves that of a Tri-unity; and as that Unity or Indivisibility is the intensest, and the Archetype, yea, the very substance and element of all other Unity and Union, so is that Distinction the most manifest, and indestructible of all distinctions—and Being, Intellect, and Action, which in their absoluteness are the Father, the Word, and the Spirit will and must for ever be and remain the 'genera generalissima' of all knowlege. Unitarianism in it's immediate intelligential (the Spirit of Love forbid, that I should say or think, in it's intentional and actual) consequences, is Atheism or Spinosism—God becomes a mere power in darkness, even as Gravitation, and instead of a moral Religion of practical Influence we shall have only a physical Theory to gratify ideal curiosity—no Sun, no Light with vivifying Warmth, but a cold and dull moonshine, or rather star-light, which shews itself but shews nothing else—Hence too, the Heresy of the Greek Church in affirming, that the Holy Spirit proceeds only from the Father, renders the thrice sacred doctrine of the Tri-unity not only above, but against, Reason. Hence too, the doctrine of the Creation assumes it's intelligibility—for the Deity in all it's three distinctions being absolutely perfect, neither susceptible of addition or diminution, the Father *in* his Son as the Image of himself surveying the Possibility of all things possible, and *with* that Love, which is the Spirit of holy Action (τὸ ἅγιον πνεῦμα [the holy spirit], as the air + motion = a wind) exerted that Love *in* that Intelligence, & that Intelligence *with* that Love, (as nothing new could be affected on the divine Nature, in it's whole Self) therefore in giving to all possible Things contemplated in and thro' the Son that degree of Reality, of which it's nature was susceptible.

He now comes to see Unitarianism as a kind of retreat from belief, in which successive possibilities are abandoned through the processes of logic.[8]

Unitarianism, as a scheme of Religion, never could have entered into any man's head ab initio—it is the last remainder of a segment or fraction of Belief, from which bit after bit had been *chipped off*, by the stern chissel of necessary *Consequence*—viz.—but if A, then by parity of reason B—if B, then by p. of r. C. & so on—. The History of this Tartar Creed (consisting in articles of Disbelief, the one or two positive Credos being only the Heft and wooden Handle of the Ax—laid to the root & trunk of Xtnty) from ⟨the⟩ Socinian who denied the proper Godhead of the Redeemer & asserted the perfect freedom of the human Will to Priestley & Belchum who denied Redemption, and all guilt or *responsible* evil, and not only the free will but any *Will* at all, might almost seem to have been invented for the purpose of shewing by fictious example the force & coercive propulsion of logical consequence from Error A–Z to Error Z–A, or rather from A–Z to –Z + –ZA.

In correspondence with Cottle at the time of his Bristol visit in 1814, he embarks on a long exposition of his views on the Trinity.[9]

. . . You ask me my views of the *Trinity*. I accept the doctrine, not as deduced from human reason, in its grovelling capacity for comprehending spiritual things, but as the clear revelation of Scripture. But perhaps it may be said, the *Socinians* do not admit this doctrine as being taught in the bible. I know enough of their shifts and quibbles, with their dexterity at explaining away all they dislike, (and that is not a little) but though beguiled once by them, I happily, for my own peace of mind, escaped from their sophistries, and now, hesitate not to affirm, that Socinians would lose all character for honesty, if they were to explain their neighbour's will with the same latitude of interpretation, which they do the Scriptures.

I have in my head some floating ideas on the *Logos*, which I hope, hereafter, to mould into a consistent form; but it is a gross perversion of the truth, in *Socinians*, to declare that we believe in *Three Gods*, and they know it to be false. They might, with equal justice affirm that we believe in *three suns*. The meanest peasant, who has acquired the first rudiments of christianity, would shrink back from a thought so monstrous. Still the Trinity has its difficulties. It would be strange if otherwise. A *Revelation* that revealed nothing, not within the grasp of human reason!—no religation, no binding over again, as before said: but these difficulties are shadows, contrasted with the substantive and insurmountable obstacles with which they contend who admit the *Divine authority of Scripture*, with the *superlative excellence of Christ*, and yet undertake to prove that these Scriptures teach, and that Christ taught, his own *pure humanity*!

If Jesus Christ was merely a Man,—if he was not God as well as Man, be it considered, he could not have been even a *good man*. There is no medium. The SAVIOUR *in that case* was absolutely *a deceiver*! one, transcendently *unrighteous*! in advancing pretensions to miracles, by the 'Finger of God,' which he never performed; and by asserting claims, (as a man) in the most aggravated sense, blasphemous! These consequences, Socinians, to be consistent, must allow, and which impious arrogation of Divinity in Christ, (according to their faith,) as well as his false assumption of a community of 'glory' with the Father, 'before the world was,' even they will be necessitated to admit, completely exonerated the Jews, according to their law, in crucifying one, who 'being a man,' 'made himself God!' But in the Christian, rather than in the *Socinian*, or *Pharisaic* view, all these objections vanish, and harmony succeeds to inexplicable confusion. If Socinians hesitate in ascribing *unrighteousness* to Christ, the inevitable result of their principles, they tremble, as well they might, at their avowed creed, and virtually renounce what they profess to uphold.

The Trinity, as Bishop Leighton has well remarked, is 'a doctrine of faith, not of demonstration,' except in a *moral* sense. If the New Testament declare it, not in an insulated passage, but through the whole breadth of its pages, rendering, with any other admission, the Book, which is the christian's anchor-hold of hope, dark and contradictory, then it is not to be rejected, but on a penalty that reduces to an atom, all the sufferings this earth can inflict.

Let the grand question be determined: Is, or is not the Bible *inspired*? No one Book has ever been subjected to so rigid an investigation as the Bible, by minds the most capacious, and, in the result, which has so triumphantly repelled all the assaults of Infidels. In the extensive intercourse which I have had with this class of men, I have seen their prejudices surpassed only by their ignorance. This I found conspicuously the case in Dr. D[arwin], the prince of their fraternity. Without, therefore, stopping to contend on what all dispassionate men must deem undebatable ground, I may assume inspiration as admitted; and, equally so, that it would be an insult to man's understanding, to suppose any other Revelation from God than the christian Scriptures. If these Scriptures, impregnable in their strength, sustained in their pretensions by undeniable prophecies and miracles, and by the experience of the *inner man*, in all ages, as well as by a concatenation of arguments, all bearing upon one point, and extending, with miraculous consistency, through a series of fifteen hundred years; if all this combined proof does not establish their validity, nothing can be proved under the sun; but the world and man must be abandoned, with all its consequences to one universal scepticism! Under such sanctions, therefore, if these Scriptures, as a fundamental truth, *do* inculcate the doctrine of the *Trinity*, however surpassing human comprehension, then I say, we are bound to admit it on the strength of *moral demonstration*.

The supreme Governor of the world, and the Father of our spirits, has seen fit to disclose to us much of his will, and the whole of his natural and moral perfections. In some instances he has given his *word* only, and demanded our *faith*; while on other momentous subjects, instead of bestowing a full revelation, like the *Via Lactea*, he has furnished a glimpse only, through either the medium of inspiration, or by the exercise of those rational faculties with which he has endowed us. I consider the Trinity as substantially resting on the first proposition, yet deriving support from the last.

I recollect when I stood on the summit of Etna, and darted my gaze down the crater; the immediate vicinity was discernible, till, lower down, obscurity gradually terminated in total darkness. Such figures exemplify many truths revealed in the Bible. We pursue them, until, from the imperfection of our faculties, we are lost in impenetrable night. All truths, however, that are essential to faith, *honestly* interpreted, all that are important to human conduct, under every diversity of circumstance, are manifest as a blazing star. The promises also of felicity to the righteous in the future world, though the precise nature of that felicity may not be defined, are illustrated by every image that can swell the imagination; while the misery of the *lost*, in its unutterable intensity, though the language that describes it is all necessarily figurative, is there exhibited as resulting chiefly, if not wholly, from the withdrawment of the *light of God's countenance*, and a banishment from his *presence*!—best comprehended in this world by reflecting on the desolations which would instantly follow the loss of the sun's vivifying and universally diffused *warmth*.

You, or rather *all*, should remember that some truths, from their nature, surpass the scope of man's limited powers, and stand as the criteria of *faith*, determining, by their rejection, or admission, who among the sons of men can confide in the veracity of heaven. Those more ethereal truths, of which the Trinity is conspicuously the chief, without being circumstantially explained, may be faintly illustrated by material objects.—The eye of man cannot discern the satellites of Jupiter, nor become sensible of the multitudinous stars, whose rays have never reached our planet, and, consequently, garnish not the canopy of night; yet, are they the less *real*, because their existence lies beyond man's unassisted gaze? The tube of the philosopher, and the *celestial telescope*,—the unclouded visions of heaven will confirm the one class of truths, and irradiate the other.

The *Trinity* is a subject on which analogical reasoning may advantageously be admitted, as furnishing, at least, a glimpse of light, and with this, for the present, we must be satisfied. Infinite Wisdom deemed clearer manifestations inexpedient; and is man to dictate to his Maker?

I may further remark, that where we cannot behold a desirable object distinctly, we must take the best view we can; and I think you, and every candid and enquiring mind, may derive assistance from such reflections as the following.

Notwithstanding the arguments of Spinoza, and Descartes, and other advocates of the *Material system*, (or, in more appropriate language, the *Atheistical system!*) it is admitted by all men, not prejudiced, not biased by sceptical prepossessions, that *mind* is distinct from *matter*. The mind of man, however, is involved in inscrutable darkness, (as the profoundest metaphysicians well know) and is to be estimated (if at all) alone by an inductive process; that is, by its *effects*. Without entering on the question, whether an extremely circumscribed portion of the mental process, surpassing instinct, may, or may not, be extended to quadrupeds, it is universally acknowledged, that the mind of man, alone, regulates all the voluntary actions of his corporeal frame. Mind, therefore, may be regarded as a distinct genus, in the scale ascending above brutes, and including the whole of intellectual existences; advancing from *thought*, (that mysterious thing!) in its lowest form, through all the gradations of sentient and rational beings, till it arrives at a Bacon, a Newton, and then, when unincumbered by matter, extending its illimitable sway through Seraph and Archangel, till we are lost in the GREAT INFINITE!

Is it not deserving of notice, as an especial subject of meditation, that our *limbs*, in all they do or can accomplish, implicitly obey the dictation of the *mind?* that this operating power, whatever its name, under certain limitations, exercises a sovereign dominion, not only over our limbs, but over all our intellectual pursuits? The mind of every man is evidently the fulcrum, the moving force, which alike regulates all his limbs and actions; and in which example, we find a strong illustration of the subordinate nature of mere *matter*. That alone which gives direction to the organic parts of our nature, is wholly *mind*; and one mind, if placed over a thousand limbs, could, with undiminished ease, control and regulate the whole.

This idea is advanced on the supposition, that *one mind* could command an unlimited direction over any given number of *limbs*, provided they were all connected by *joint* and *sinew*. But suppose, through some occult and inconceivable means, these limbs were dis-associated, as to all material connexion; suppose, for instance, one mind with unlimited authority, governed the operations of *two* separate persons, would not this, substantially, be only *one person*, seeing the directing principle was one? If the truth, here contended for, be admitted, that *two persons*, governed by *one mind*, is incontestably *one person*; the same conclusion would be arrived at, and the proposition equally be justified, which affirmed that, *three*, or otherwise, *four* persons, owning also necessary and essential subjection to *one mind*, would only be so many diversities or modifications of that *one mind*, and therefore the component parts virtually collapsing into *one whole*, the person would be *one*. Let any man ask himself, whose understanding can both reason and become the depository of truth, whether, if *one mind* thus regulated with absolute authority, *three*, or otherwise, *four* persons, with all their congeries of material parts, would not these parts, inert in themselves, when subjected to one predominant mind, be, in the most logical sense, *one person*? Are ligament and exterior combination indispensable pre-requisites to the sovereign influence of mind over mind? or mind over matter?

But perhaps it may be said, we have no instance of one mind governing more than one body. This may be, but the argument remains the same. With a proud spirit, that forgets its own contracted range of thought and circumscribed knowledge, who is to limit the sway of Omnipotence? or presumptuously to deny the possibility of *that* Being, who called light out of darkness, so to exalt the dominion of *one mind*, as to give it absolute sway over other dependent minds, or (indifferently) over detached, or combined portions of organized matter? But if this superinduced quality be conferable on any order of created beings, it is blasphemy to limit the power of GOD, and to deny *his* capacity to transfuse *his own* Spirit, when and to whom he will.

This reasoning may now be applied in illustration of the Trinity. We are too much in the habit of viewing our Saviour Jesus Christ, through the medium of his body. 'A body was prepared for him,' but this body was mere matter; as insensible in itself, as every human frame when deserted by the soul. If therefore the Spirit that was in Christ, was the Spirit of the Father; if no thought, no vibration, no spiritual communication, or miraculous display, existed in, or proceeded from Christ, not immediately and consubstantially identified with JEHOVAH, the Great First cause; if all these operating principles were thus derived, in consistency alone with the conjoint divine attributes; if this Spirit of the Father ruled and reigned in Christ as his own manifestation, then, in the strictest sense, Christ exhibited 'the God-head bodily,' and was undeniably '*one* with the Father;' confirmatory of the Saviour's words: 'Of myself,' (my body) 'I can do nothing, the Father that dwelleth in me, he doeth the works.'

But though I speak of the body as inert in itself, and necessarily allied to matter, yet this declaration must not be understood as militating against the christian doctrine of the *resurrection of the body*. In its grosser form, the thought is not to be admitted, for 'flesh and blood cannot inherit the kingdom of God,' but that the body, without losing its consciousness and individuality, may be subjected, by the illimitable power of Omnipotence, to a sublimating process, so as to be rendered compatible with spiritual association, is not opposed to reason, in its severe abstract exercises, while in attestation of this *exhilarating belief*, there are many remote analogies in nature exemplifying the same truth, while it is in the strictest accordance with that final dispensation, which must, as christians, regulate all our speculations. I proceed now to say, that:

If the postulate be thus admitted, that one mind influencing two bodies would only involve a diversity of operations, but in reality be one in essence; or otherwise, (as an hypothetical argument, illustrative of truth) if one pre-eminent mind, or spiritual subsistence, unconnected with matter, possessed an undivided and sovereign dominion over two or more disembodied minds, so as to become the exclusive source of all their subtlest volitions and exercises, the *unity*, however complex the modus of its manifestation, would be fully established; and this principle extends to DEITY itself, and shows the true sense, as I conceive, in which Christ and the Father are one.

In continuation of this reasoning, if God who is light, the Sun of the Moral World, should in his union of Infinite Wisdom, Power, and Goodness, and from all Eternity, have ordained that an emanation from himself (for aught we know, an essential emanation, as light is inseparable from the luminary of day) should not only have existed in his Son, in the fulness of time to be united to a mortal body, but that a like emanation from himself (also perhaps essential) should have constituted the Holy Spirit, who, without losing his ubiquity, was more especially sent to this lower earth, *by* the Son, *at* the impulse of the Father, then, in the most comprehensive sense, God, and his Son, Jesus Christ, and the Holy Ghost, are ONE—'Three Persons in one God,' and thus form the true Trinity in Unity.

To suppose that more than ONE Independent Power, or Governing mind, exists in the whole universe, is absolute Polytheism, against which the denunciations of all the Jewish and Christian Canonical books were directed. And if there be but ONE directing MIND, that Mind is GOD!—operating, however, in Three Persons, according to the direct and uniform declarations of that inspiration which 'brought life and immortality to light.' Yet this divine doctrine of the Trinity is to be received, not because it is or can be clear to finite apprehension, but, (in reiteration of the argument) because the Scriptures, in their unsophisticated interpretation expressly state it. The Trinity, therefore, from its important aspects, and Biblical prominence, is the grand article of faith, and the foundation of the whole christian system.

Who can say, as Christ and the Holy Ghost proceeded from, and are still one with the Father, and as all the disciples of Christ derive their fulness from him, and, in spirit, are inviolately united to him as a branch is to the vine, who can say, but that in one view, what was once mysteriously separated, may, as mysteriously, be recombined, and (without interfering with the everlasting Trinity, and the individuality of the spiritual and seraphic orders) the Son, at the consummation of all things, deliver up his mediatorial kingdom to the Father, and God, in some peculiar and infinitely sublime sense, become All *in* All!

A year later he is drawing a subtle analysis between the writer making a whole out of narrative and the creative mind of God himself.[10]

The common end of all *narrative*, nay, of *all*, Poems is to convert a *series* into a *Whole*: to make those events, which in real or imagined History move on in a *strait* Line, assume to our Understandings a *circular* motion—the snake with it's Tail in it's Mouth. Hence indeed the almost flattering and yet appropriate Term, Poesy—i.e. poiēsis = *making*. Doubtless, to *his* eye, which alone comprehends all Past and all Future in one eternal Present, what to our short sight appears strait is but a part of the great Cycle—just as the calm Sea to us *appears* level, tho' it be indeed only a part of a *globe*. Now what the Globe is in Geography, *miniaturing* in order to *manifest* the Truth, such is a Poem to that Image of God, which we were created into, and which still seeks that Unity, or Revelation of the *One* in and by the *Many*, which reminds it, that tho' in order to be an individual Being it must go forth *from* God, yet as the *receding from him* is to *proceed* towards Nothingness and Privation, it must still at every step turn back toward him in order to *be* at all—Now a straight Line, continuously retracted forms of necessity a circular orbit. Now God's Will and Word CANNOT be frustrated. His aweful *Fiat* was with ineffable awefulness applied to Man, when all things and all living Things, Man himself (as a mere animal) included, were called forth by the Universal—*Let there be*—and then the Breath of the Eternal superadded to make an *immortal* Spirit—immortality being, as the author of the 'Wisdom of Solomon' profoundly expresses it, the only possible Reflex or Image of Eternity. The Immortal Finite is the contracted Shadow of the Eternal Infinite.—Therefore *nothingness* or *Death*, to which we move as we recede from God & the Word, *cannot* be nothing; but that tremendous Medium between Nothing and true Being, which Scripture & inmost Reason present as most, most horrible!

To Mr Pryce at the same time he argues the case for such a Christian philosophy.[11]

I give you my word, as a Gentleman, that *I* could conscientiously subscribe to all the Articles of *Faith*, (discipline, church-government, & the article on Baptism not included) of our church in their national interpretation.

1. The πρῶτον ψεῦδος [first lie] of Spinoza is not his first definition; but one in which all his Antagonists were as deeply immerged as himself. He alone had the philosophic courage to be *consequent*. We need only correct the convenient *clinamina* of the Theistic Philosophers to reduce all their systems into Spinosism. The πρῶτον ψεῦδος consists in the assumed Idea of a pure independent *Object*—in assuming a Substance beyond the I; of which therefore the I *could* only be a modification.—The argumentum in circulo, the magic Circle of Anti-logic, within which all human Logic is confined by necessity of our finiteness, as reflecting not creative Minds, is, that the Ego presupposes the Non-ego (Percipiens rem perceptam [perceiving the thing perceived]) as it's Opposite; while again the Non-ego can have no existence for the Ego except as an Act of the Ego—*See my literary Life, & opinions, Vol. I.*

2. Make yourself thoroughly, intuitively, master of the exceeding difficulties of admitting a one Ground of the Universe (which however *must* be admitted) and yet finding *room* for any thing else. If A have all power, infinite activity, for B. can remain only infinite passivity: if in A *all* Being be, to B. nothing remains but τὸ μὴ ὄν [the non-existent].— Does not Intellect as necessarily imply Limit (cogitatio infinita quoad infinita non potest finiri [infinite thinking inasmuch as infinite cannot come to an end]) as on a geometrical figure?—Spatium infinitum quoad infinitum haud figurabile [infinite space as infinite cannot be figured].

3. Does not personality necessarily suppose a *ground* distinct from the Person . . . ? . . . The *Me* in the objective case is clearly distinct from the *Ego*.—I was so exclusively attentive to the music, that I lost myself. On the oversight of this distinction Paley's whole system is founded: and the *possibility* of the Irishman's *Bull*, 'I was a Christian child till you changed me,' arises out of this distinction. I mean, that without this no mind could have so blundered. The only possible mode of conceiving

God as at once infinite and yet personal, is that of assuming that in the former sense it is God, as τὸ θεῖον [the god], in the latter sense only Ὁ Θεός [God]: that these are bonâ fide distinct—and the contra-distinction of God from all finite Beings consists in God's having the *ground* of his existence in himself, whereas all other Beings have their *ground* in another. Therefore God alone is a self-comprehending Spirit; and in this incommunicable *Adequate* Idea of himself (Λόγος [Word]) his Personality is contained—πρὸς τὸν Θεόν (very ill translated by the pre-position, with) καὶ Θεός [with God . . . and God].—Philo has asserted the same, and anxiously guards against the misconception that the Logos is an Attribute or Personification or generic or abstract term.—*Est* enim, et est Deus alter et idem [for he *is* and is God, the other and the same].— St John effects the same by interposing the account of *John*, a concrete, a man, and then adds—*He* was not the Logos. Can any thing be con-ceived more absurd than to affirm that John was not one of God's *Properties*?—In the beginning of this Mahogany Table was redness; and this Redness was in indivisible approximity to this Table, and was the Table—There was likewise a Looking-glass in the same Parlour—But this Looking-glass was not the Redness, of which I am speaking—&c.—Now Philo & John were Contemporaries—either therefore Philo learnt the doctrine from the Christians, of which there is no proof or probability— or (of which there are many proofs) he wrote long before John wrote the Gospel. In the latter case John could not have used words so familiar to all the Hellenistic Jews for whom his Gospel was written, in a sense utterly different, and without giving them the least hint of this change, without intentional delusion. Rationally or irrationally, the Logos in his time meant a personal Being—.

4. The Trinity is not the doctrine; but one of the explanations of it— that which after 300 years' experience the Church found to be the only tenable explanation.—Above all things, read Waterland's Letters to a country gentleman in two volumes, Octavo—You may often meet with them in Catalogues of old books, more often each volume separ-ately—Then read Bull de fide Nicenâ.—The doctrine is involved in the fact—that language & attributes are attributed to Christ both by himself & his Disciples which admit but of two explanations, either that he was a blaspheming Fanatic like James Nayler, or that he was God. I and my Father will come: & *we* will dwell in you.—Likewise, the Doctrine of Redemption implies the divinity—And without it, the Redemption, what is Xtnity? Remove from it, first, all it's peculiar doctrines as held in common by all Churches but those of the Unitarians—& 2nd all that it has in common with the Old Testament and the Greek & Roman

Ethical writers—and what remains?—The resurrection?—No. For I have as much right to believe in the resurrection of the Dead man who touched the Bones of the Prophet, the ditto of the Widow's Son &c, as that of Jesus. But what man in his senses would found the belief of the future conscious personality of the whole human Race on either? on an *anecdote*! Who ever did? Mankind take it for granted—So says St Paul— he represents the belief as a previous condition of Xtnty.—

Renewed correspondence with Tulk induces further comments on his agreements and disagreements—notably on the question of the Trinity.[12]

Of the too limited time, which my Ill-health and the exigences of the To Day leave in my power, I have given the larger portion to the works of Swedenborg, particularly to the 'Univer. Theol. of the New Church'.— I find very few & even those but *doubtful* instances, of tenets, in which I am conscious of any substantial difference of opinion with the enlightened Author; but many, in which fully coinciding with his statements of the main Christian truths & his interpretation of the Scriptural Doctrine, I could nevertheless use & actually have been accustomed to use the words & terms, to which, & to those who so express themselves, he attaches and attributes notions very different, and which equally with himself I regard & should deprecate as more than erroneous—as *pernicious* errors. The probable explanation of this may be: that I, herein imitating Leibnitz, have been in the habit of considering what the meaning of the *words*, rightly & scripturally defined, *might* be; while Swedenborg, more gifted and more accustomed to distinguish the spirits of men, attended principally to the Meaning of the Users, the sense in which such words were in fact understood and employed by the majority of those who had adopted them for their *standard*, as the motto for their sectarian *Coat of Arms*, the heraldic scroll of their peculiar Guild.—Thus, in Swedenborg's definition of the term, Faith, I subscribe with my whole heart and spirit to his doctrine respecting Solifidianism, and I find a paragraph in one of my Memorandum Books, which I had written 15 or 16 years ago, in which I declared Faith in *this* sense, taken as meritorious or the source of merit, to be the Queen Bee in the Hive of theological Error.—But I have been accustomed to give a far other definition of that Term—& have lately written a short essay or tract on the true nature of Faith, the result of which is in perfect harmony with Swedenborg; & to it's completion it needs only what I am about to add, a collation of all the passages in the Old & New Testament in which the word occurs, with proof that the senses differ only as the same tree in different stages of it's growth & developement. So again with regard to the Tri-unity. As far as respects the *Christian* Dispensation, the first record of which is in my belief the first Chapter of Genesis, I hold the same conviction as is so admirably unfolded and enforced in the Univ. Theol.—& had long held it as the literal and only defensible sense of St John, i. 18, Θεὸν οὐδεὶς ἑώρακε πώποτε ὁ μονογενὴς υἱός, ὁ ὢν εἰς τὸν κόλπον τοῦ πατρός, ἐκεῖνος ἐξηγήσατο [no man hath seen God at any time; the only begotten son, which is in the bosom of the father, he hath declared him].—But I do not see that this precludes the *philosophical* idea of an essential Trinity which God is: (i.e. *esse*ntial as essentially *self-exist*ential) tho' I am ready to acknowlege, that the former alone is an article of Faith. The pseudo-athanasian Creed I reject as of no authority in the first place, as intemperate in the next, then as most inconveniently worded, and lastly as at once superfluous and defective—tautologically superfluous in the point of the co-equality, & dangerously defective in that of the subordination. Altogether I apply to it in increased measure what Hilary says against Creeds in general, not sparing even the Nicene.—But yet I doubt, whether the authorized use of the term, person, was not posterior to the Council of Nice—& if I recollect aright, the words, οὐσία and ὑπόστασις, were, about that time, so little appropriated, that sometimes the οὐσία was used to signify that which was afterwards called πρόσωπον or person, and ὑπόστασις for subsistence & sometimes vice versâ. But I am pretty confident that this inappropriate term, Person (what indeed could be other than inappropriate to a subject absolutely unique?) was *at first* intended to convey the contrary to the crude εἴδωλον [idol], into which it has since then been too often perverted. Assuredly, the etymon of the word, Persona, sive forma, per quam sonat aliquis [or the form, through which it sounds to some] (& you may be certain, I do not like the word the better for it's having been borrowed from the Greek Drama) suggests as the properest sense, that in and by which God manifests himself to us.—In the article of the Holy Ghost, which relies on the Baptismal Form for it's only plausible scripture-authority, I seem to detect clearly the *origin* of the common notions or rather notionless dicta of the Trinity in the confusion of the philosophical *Idea* of Deity with the Christian *Fact* of the incarnate Jehovah, God manifest in the Flesh.

He believes that the functions of Platonism and neoPlatonism, as part of the way in which the whole world was preparing in diverse ways for the Christian revelation, may still be legitimately and usefully studied as a supplement to Old Testament preparations.[13]

Of the ungenerous fears of modern Christians, cowed by the railing of the Socinians, concerning the connection of the Christian Doctrine with those of Plato & the East—which is more sublime, their present confinement of the Evangelic Preparation to Judæa, or to believe as of old, that the whole world, barbarians & Greeks, were all ripening & preparing the way for, this last greatest Epiphany—To set this forth with what majesty & grandeur I may be enabled to command, by an aggregation & superstruction of the particulars—The necessary union of Phil[osophy]. & Christ—& the as necessary subordination of the former to the latter

These philosophies can serve as a useful and attractive preparation, even for modern intellects.[14]

Tho' the dependence of all theologic speculation on the practical Reason & its moral postulates will always preserve the religious faith of a true philosopher within the modesty of the Gospel; yet it would not be amiss if our belle esprits had made part of their intellectual voyages in the groves & enchanted Islands of Plato, Plotin. & even Proclus—rendering the mind lofty and generous & *abile* by splendid Imaginations that receive the beauty of form by the proportions of Science/Fancy moulded in Science, & thence no unbecoming Symbols—Counters at least—of moral Truth/holding to truth the same ascetic & preparatory relations as the Game of Chess to War.

A good example of this at the most complex can be found in the way that the philosophy of Plotinus throws light on the opening of St John's Gospel, and so on the doctrine of the Trinity.[15]

...the Soul is conscious of an intellectual κινησις [motion], it moves from this to that, tho' it attributes the motion to its own imperfection, and strives to express its subjective act and the Objective Verity, which it is contemplating, negativing for the latter what it declares of the former, by the term *Co-inherence*—/(a similar struggle we have even in expression the diversity of chemical introsusception from Solution or mechanical juxta-position)—on the other hand, in meditating on the absolute Unity, the eternal προπατηρ [prefather], all *act* is suspended or reabsorbed into the identity of *agere* et pati—tota agit, tota patitur [acting and suffering—it acts all, it suffers all]—and on this Plotinus discourses divinely. Ennead VI. L. IX. c. 6.—

———

The Socinian Syllogism—

Deus est Ens [God is Being] absolutely *simplex*—excellently confuted *ad hominem*/the Socinian professing to believe God an infinite intelligence, & in this sense receiving the *first* of John// by Plotinus who assuming the same position carried it to its legitimate consequence— ουδε νοησις ινα μη ετεροτης [there is no intelligence where there is no otherness]—and in this consists the diversity (of endless importance) between the Trinity of Plotinus and the Athanasian Tri-unity—under which form alone can ⟨we support⟩ the Intelligence & Self-consciousness or Self-knowlege of God, which Plotinus directly denies of his To Εν—or Τ'Αγαθον—έν δε ον συνον αυτω, ου δεῖται νοησεως εαυτου.— [The One— or The Good—being one and in union with itself it does not need thought of itself]

With this all personality too—we are not to conceive him as *Thinking* as a *Thinker*, but as *Thought* itself—I.e. Plotinus takes infinite pains & exerts the finest dialectic ingenuity to demonstrate that his Superessential *One* is an *Abstraction* & not an Idea

P.S. The only even partially successful attempt for the revivifying the Pagan Idolatry built on this Plotinism, the 1 v. of John may fitly be deemed *prophetic*, *pre*clusive/

Turning to the Platonic fathers, he sees their alternative version of the Trinity as containing an equivalent Truth.[16]

The Platonic Fathers, instead of the Πατηρ, Υιος and Αγιον Πνενμα, [The Father, the Son and the Holy Ghost] used Του Θεου, και του Λογου αυτου, και της Σοφιας αυτου [God, his Word and his Wisdom].—Θεος, Λογος, Σοφια, Ανθρωπος. Theophil. as quoted by Horsley.—and this seems as precise and true as human words can be applied to so recondite a subject. 1. Being, the eternal evermore I am = Deity, or eternal Life, or as we well say the Supreme Being (which word Supreme is most often most grossly apprehended, as synonimous to the Sublimest or Sovran, whereas it is equivalent to *the Absolutest*)—2. Reason, Proportion, communicable Intelligibility intelligent and communicant, the WORD—which last expression strikes me as the profoundest and most comprehensive Energy of the human Mind, if indeed it be not in some distinct sense ενεργημα θεοπαραδοτον [an activity delivered from God]. 3. But holy action, a Spirit of holy Action, to which all holy actions being reducible as to their Sine qua non, is verily the Holy Spirit proceeding ﬀ at once from Life and Reason, and effecting all good gifts, what more appropriate Term is conceivable than *Wisdom*: which in its best & only proper sense, involves action, application, habits and tendencies of realization. "A Bad man may be *intelligent*; but the Good only are *wise*. He may be a clever man, etc; but I am sure, he is not a *wise* man." These common phrases shew the natural meaning of Wisdom; and in this way even now a true Philosopher is something very different from a mere man of Science—*he lived the Life of a Philosopher.*—But why the Son should both create and redeem (for our Catechism seems to have sacrificed Orthodoxy to a rhetorical division & appropriation of offices in making the Father the Creator, not the Son. The Word created all things, being with the Father, and redeemed all things in like manner/& the Father both created and redeemed us by the Son—) is of no very difficult solution, seeing that no ⟨*true*⟩ energies can be attributed to an Ον αλογον [Wordless Being]; the moment we conceive the divine energy, that moment we co-conceive the Λογος [Word]. But tho' this may redeem, i.e. procure for us the *possibility* of salvation, it is only the *Spirit* of *holy Action*, manifested in the *habits of Faith and good works*, (the wings of the brooding Dove) that *sanctifies* us, the Redeemer still co-operating in the completion of that work of which himself is the Corner Stone—in truth, the A and the Ω, seeing that the redeemed & sanctified become finally themselves Words of the *Word*—even as articulate sounds are made by the Reason to represent Forms, in the mind, and Forms are a language of the notions—Verba significant phænomena, phænomena sunt quasi verba noematum (των νουμενων) [Words signify phenomena, phenomena are almost words of the notions]. As he in the Father, even so we in him! The practice in the Church ab initio of giving distinct offices to the Father most pernicious.—

He turns back to the Unitarians, arguing that they can still be properly called Christians.[17]

I make the greatest difference between *ans* and *isms*. I should deal insincerely with you, if I said that I thought Unitarianism was Christianity;— no—it has nothing to do with the religion of Christ Jesus: but God forbid that I should doubt that you and many other Unitarians, as you call yourselves, are very good Christians. We do not win Heaven by Logic.

What do you mean by exclusively assuming the title of Unitarians?—as if Triunitarians were not necessarily Unitarians—as much as an apple-pie must of course be a pie.

If I could contemn any men for their religious tenets, it would be the Unitarians; for they themselves universally call all believers in the orthodox doctrine either fools or knaves; to be sure they were forced to make an exception of me—and it annoyed them that were so forced; but they had flattered me so much as the champion of their cause that they could not pretend that I was not master of all they could say for themselves—and they could not for the life of them make out that I had any sinister or interested motive; so they set me down for a visionary, and fond of a paradox as a theme for display in conversation.

What is probably his final attempt at formulation is made in 1833–4.[18]

IDENTITY

The *absolute* Subjectivity, whose only attribute is the GOOD; whose only definition is, that which is essentially causative of *all* possible true Being—Ground and Cause. = The Absolute WILL: the adorable πρόπρωτον [prior to the first]; i.e. that which, whatever is assumed as the First, must be *pre*sumed as its Antecedent. Θεος [God], without the article; & yet not as an adjective—v. 18th of the first Ch. of the Gosp. of John as differenced from Θεος, v. 1. of Ch. 1. But that which is essentially Causative of *all* Being, must be causative of its own: Causa Sui. ἀυτοπατωρ [self-engendered]. Thence

IPSËITY

The eternally self-affirmant, self-affirmed: The I AM, in that I AM—(in the Hebrew literally, "I shall be that I will to be.["]) The FATHER: the *relatively* Subjective: whose attribute is, the HOLY ONE, whose definition is, the essential Finific in the form of the Infinite. Dat sibi fines [He gives limits to himself]. But the Absolute WILL, the Absolute Good, in the eternal act of Self-affirmation, the Good as the Holy, co-eternally begets the divine

ALTERITY

The Supreme BEING. O οντως ὧν [The real being]. The Supreme Reason—The Jehovah. The Son. The Word. whose *attribute* is the TRUE (The TRUTH, the LIGHT, the Fiat [Let there be]) and whose Definition, the PLEROMA [Fullness] of Being, whose essential poles are Unity and Distinctity; or the *essential* Infinite in the *form* of the Finite: lastly, the relatively OBJECTIVE = Deitas objectiva in relation to the I AM or the Deitas SUBJECTIVA.

The *Objectivity*

The Distinctities in the pleroma are the Eternal IDEAS—the Subsistential Truths, ⟨each⟩ considered in itself an Infinite in the form of the Finite; but all considered as one with the Unity, the Eternal Son, they are the energies of the Finific. John, Chap: I—But with the relatively Subjective, and the relatively Objective, the great Idea needs only for its completion a co-eternal which is both, i.e. relatively Objective to the Subjective, relatively Subjective to the Objective. Hence, the

COMMUNITY

The eternal LIFE, which is LOVE—the Spirit, relatively to the Father, the *Spirit* of Holiness, the Holy *Spirit*: relatively to the Son, the Spirit of Truth whose attribute is Wisdom. Sancta Sophia [Holy Wisdom]. The Good in the reality of the True, in the form of actual Life = Wisdom.

Throughout his career Coleridge has taken an interest in the longstanding 'proofs' of God's existence. In a notebook entry of 1811 he argues for the necessary interim involvement of the mind with what it contemplates and so to the inadequacy of both the idealism and materialist positions.[19]

How got the Atheist his Idea of that God which he denies?—I have always held Des Cartes' Proof the best & tenable. The Materialist is the Idealist of the intelligible World—as the Idealist constrains the realities ab extra into illusions ab intra, so the Mat. the realities *in* us into reflexes and echoes of things without us.—To the one the Universe is but an echo-chamber of the Soul; to the other the Soul is but an empty echo-chamber or Whispering Labyrinth of the World—. Both alike deduce the "Is" from the "Appears", the Substance from the Shadow, the Sound from the Echo—both mistake analysis for preformation—both confound the Genealogist with the Proto-Patriarch.—

By 1816, he sees a flaw in Descartes' argument.[20]

I see the defect of the Cartesian Proof of Deity—the Idea of God is distinct from all other real or possible Ideas by involving in itself Existence as well as Essence—i.e. essential Existence—but no! it does not imply existence; but only the *idea* of existence. If I form such an idea, I form at the same time the Idea of its extra Reality—but then what compels me to form it? Whatever be the answer, removes the ground or Proof from the Idea itself—

Nevertheless the argument can be sustained by attending to the nature of the Idea.[21]

Did you *deduce* your own being? Even that is less absurd than the conceit of *deducing* the Divine Being? Never would you have had the notion had you not had the Idea—rather, had not the Idea worked in you, like the Memory of a Name which we cannot recollect and yet feel that we have, and which reveals its existence in the mind only by a restless anticipation & proves its prior actuality by the almost explosive instantaneity with which it is welcomed & recognized on its re-emersion out of the Cloud, or its re-ascent above the horizon of Consciousness.—

In the last year of his life, however, he argues in conversation that the only true method can be to take the conclusion for granted and work on from there. All other arguments must recognize their own fallibility.[22]

22. Feb. 1834

Assume the existence of God—and then the harmony and fitness of the physical creation may be shown to correspond with and support such an assumption; but to set about *proving* the existence of a God by such means is a mere circle—a delusion. It can be no proof to a good reasoner, unless he presumes his conclusion.

———

Kant once set about proving the existence of God, and a masterly effort it was. But in his later great work the Critique of the Pure Reason, he saw its fallacy—and said of it that *if* the existence *could* be *proved* at all— it must be in the manner indicated by him.

6
Questions of Evil and the Will

For a few years in his youth, and once he had declared his allegiance to the doctrine of necessitarianism, the problem of evil did not trouble Coleridge.[1] Initially, the optimism concerning human benevolence that had prompted the setting up of the Pantisocratic scheme meant that he could set it to one side, confident that given the right associations of ideas in the first participants a steady progress towards human perfection must ensue, which could in time act as a model for the rest of humanity. Even when the scheme failed to materialize, he still believed that contemporary Unitarianism offered a framework for the experimental investigation of such possibilities. In one or two of his early poems, notably *Religious Musings*, he pictured the ideal human society that might still emerge from the troubled world around him. By 1801, however, he was writing to Poole that he had overthrown the doctrine— a part of what he now described as 'all the irreligious metaphysics of modern Infidels'—along with 'Associationism, as taught by Hartley'.[2] Yet the more he investigated the problem of consciousness as a result, the more he found himself facing the question of evil. We have already seen how his intellectual speculations could be checked by a feeling of unworthiness that cast his mind into what seemed like a different mode altogether. How could the two kinds of thinking be reconciled? To his brother George he had written in March 1798 'Of GUILT I say nothing; but I believe most steadfastly in original Sin; that from our mothers' wombs our understandings are darkened...'[3]

As he became disappointed in the behaviour of his fellow human beings, however, his psychological interest increasingly encouraged him to ask whether it was possible to trace in the human mind itself processes that might help to explain the emergence of evil behaviour. From acknowledging that human wills were darkened by the experience of being in the world he was forced to question whether they were not after all *infected* in some way—whether the age-old doctrine of original sin might not after all be the correct one. The enigma increased with the years, particularly as he became aware of his increasing slavery to opium, despite his desperate efforts of will to break himself of the habit. (Since the effects of sudden withdrawal were not properly understood at the time, he was often bewildered by the results of his efforts.) Around 1803 he wrote a number of intricate notes on the subject. If only from his reading of Milton, he was well aware of the problems raised for a Christian thinker by the problem of relating the omniscience of God to the existence of human free will;[4] this now became the subject of some of his most intricate discussions.

While the issue of evil increasingly dogged his mind, it was accompanied by questions concerning the effectiveness of his own will. He believed himself to act from the best of intentions, yet his actions seemed often to go astray. This was particularly true of his growing addiction. A remedy that seemed necessary to relieve his physical pain turned out to have enslaving powers also, until he found that his will was in thrall. He was also mystified by the nature of his dreams, where impulses and urges that he readily disowned in daily conscious life would rise up to find immediate and vivid expression. No psychoanalytic theories were yet available to acknowledge and attempt to account for such things.

In the end, as with the Trinity, he was forced to conclude that the nature of evil was itself a mystery; another example of what was, strictly speaking, *incomprehensible*. This led to the urge to give an explanation of original sin and the need for redemption, where, once again, the attempt to give a rational account must fail. Considering the position of young men who, like himself, had been drawn into Unitarianism by reflecting on the manifest injustice of traditional doctrines on the subject, he would later be drawn to express his sympathy with their bewilderment. His own solution, as set out in his *Aids to Reflection*, would be to maintain that the biblical story of the fall of the first man, entailing a necessary sequence of punishments on all his succeeding progeny for the duration of the world was manifestly unjust and called for a different kind of interpretation, one that did not involve a strictly sequential narrative. Adam's fall must be seen not as an action that had had an origin chronologically in time but as one that called for a different view of time altogether and was to be understood as above or transcending it: an enduring allegory of what the relationship between humanity and the divine must for ever be.

From the beginning Coleridge sees Christian truth as more than a code of ethics; despite its simplicity, it exists at a remove from everyday love, and may indeed require the shock of fear to help establish it—which can be an important use of superstition.[1]

> And what if some rebellious, o'er dark realms
> Arrogate power? yet these train up to God,
> And on the rude eye, unconfirmed for day,
> Flash meteor-lights better than total gloom . . .
> Fancy is the power
> That first unsensualizes the dark mind,
> Giving it new delights; and bids it swell
> With wild activity; and peopling air,
> By obscure fears of Beings invisible,
> Emancipates it from the grosser thrall
> Of the present impulse, teaching Self-control,
> Till Superstition with unconscious hand
> Seat Reason on her throne. Wherefore not vain,
> Nor yet without permitted power impressed,
> I deem those legends terrible, with which
> The polar ancient thrills his uncouth throng:

Many years later he produces another version of this, using the image of the shadow on a cloud that can project a normal-sized human figure as a fearful giant form.[2]

> O! Superstition is the Giant Shadow
> Which the Solicitude of weak Mortality
> Its Back toward Religion's rising Sun,
> Casts on the thin mist of the uncertain Future.

In 1794 he is intent to stress the essential benevolence of the Creator, using an organic image for the proper human response.[3]

Your remark of the Physical Evil in the long Infancy of men would indeed puzzle a Pangloss—puzzle him to account for the wish of a benevolent heart like your's to discover malignancy in it's Creator. Surely every Eye but an Eye jaundiced by habit of peevish Scepticism must have seen, that the Mother's cares are repaid even to rapture by the Mother's endearments—and that the long helplessness of the Babe is the *means* of our superiority in the filial & maternal Affection & Duties to the same feelings in the Brute Creation—it is likewise among other causes the *means* of Society—that thing which makes Man a little lower than the Angels . . .

All necessary knowlege in the Branch of Ethics is comprised in the Word Justice—that the Good of the whole is the Good of each Individual. Of course it is each Individual's *duty* to be Just, *because* it is his *Interest*. To perceive this and to assent to it as an abstract proposition— is easy—but it requires the most wakeful attentions of the most reflective minds in all moments to bring it into practice—It is not enough, that we have once swallowed it—The *Heart* should have *fed* upon the *truth*, as Insects on a Leaf—till it be tinged with the colour, and shew it's food in every the minutest fibre.

Meanwhile, the growth of his optimism concerning the possibility of improving human moral nature by exposure to natural beauty is checked by other experiences of nature, including the pains and dangers of pregnancy.[4]

I think the subject of Pregnancy the most obscure of all God's dispensations—it seems coercive against Immaterialism—it starts uneasy doubts respecting Immortality, & the pangs which the Woman suffers, seem inexplicable in the system of optimism—Other pains are only friendly admonitions that we are not acting as Nature requires—but here are pains most horrible in consequence of having obeyed Nature. Quere—How is it that Dr Priestley is not an atheist?—He asserts in three different Places, that God not only *does*, but *is*, every thing.—But if God *be* every Thing, every Thing is God—: which is all, the Atheists assert—. An eating, drinking, lustful *God*—with no *unity* of *Consciousness*——these appear to me the unavoidable Inferences from his philosophy—Has not Dr Priestly forgotten that *Incomprehensibility* is as necessary an attribute of the First Cause, as Love, or Power, or Intelligence?——

The problem of guilt is the most intractable.[5]

Of GUILT I say nothing; but I believe most stedfastly in original Sin; that from our mother's wombs our understandings are darkened; and even where our understandings are in the Light, that our organization is depraved, & our volitions imperfect; and we sometimes see the good without *wishing* to attain it, and oftener *wish* it without the energy that wills & performs—And for this inherent depravity, I believe, that the *Spirit* of the Gospel is the sole cure—but permit me to add, that I look for the *spirit* of the Gospel 'neither in the mountain, nor at Jerusalem'—.

As the grip of his opium addiction begins to tighten a few years later, he does not blame exclusively his moral failings, since there is an intimate connection between the drug and the pain that he seeks to relieve by his recourse to it, both affecting his failure of will – as he tries to show when describing the illness that has deprived him even of the power to open his letters. This, he argues, has not penetrated to the sense of his own Being.[6]

. . . not that my inner Being was disturbed—on the contrary, it seemed more than usually serene and self-sufficing—but the exceeding Pain, of which I suffered every now and then, and the fearful Distresses of my sleep, had taken away from me the connecting Link of voluntary power, which continually combines that Part of us by which we know ourselves to be, with that outward Picture or Hieroglyphic, by which we hold communion with our Like—between the Vital and the Organic— or what Berkley, I suppose, would call—Mind and it's sensuous Language.

In the autumn of 1803, discussions with Wordsworth and Hazlitt about the Wisdom of the Creator have led him on to consider the origin of evil.[7]

I made out the whole business of the Origin of Evil satisfactorily to my own mind, & forced H. to confess, that the metaphysical argument ~~to~~ reduced itself to this: Why did not infinite Power *always* & exclusively produce such Beings as in each moment of their Duration were infinite/ why, in short, did not the Almighty create an absolutely infinite number of Almighties?—The Hollowness & Impiety of the Argument will be felt by considering, that suppose a universal Happiness & Perfection of the moral as well as natural world, still the whole objection applies, just as forcibly as at this moment. The malignity of the Deity (I shudder even at the assumption of this affrightful & satanic Language) is manifested in the creation of Archangels & Cherubs & the whole Company of pure Intelligences burning in their unquenchable Felicity equally as in the creation of ~~the~~ Neros, & Tiberiuses, of Stone & Leprosy— Suppose yourself perfectly happy, yet according to this argument you *ought* to charge God with Malignity for having created you—Your own Life & all its Comforts are in the Indictment against the Creator—for surely even a child would be ashamed to answer—No! *I* should still exist; only in that case instead of being a Man I should be an infinite Being—as if the word *I* here had even the remotest Semblance of a meaning—Infinitely more absurd, than if I should write ⟨the Fraction⟩ "$\frac{1}{1000}$"on a slate, then rub it out with my spunge, & write in the same place ⟨the integral number⟩, "555,666,879"—and then observe, that the former figure was greatly *improved* by the measure—That *it* was grown a far finer figure?—Conceiting a *change*, where there had been positive Substitution.—

Thus then it appears, that the sole Justification of those who offended by the Vice & misery of the created world, as far as we know it, impeach the power or goodness of the Almighty, making the proper cause of such vice & misery to have been a defect either of power or goodness,— it appears, that their sole Justification rests on an argument; which has nothing to do with vice or misery, as vice & misery—on an argument, which would hold equally good in Heaven, as in Hell—on an argument, which, it might be demonstrated, no human Being in a state of Happiness could ever have conceived—an argument which a Millenium would annihilate, & which yet would hold equally good ~~in~~ then as now?—But even in point of metaphysic the whole rests ~~on~~ at last on the Conceivable. Now I appeal to every man's internal consciousness, if he will but sincerely & in brotherly simplicity silence the bustle of argument in his mind & the ungenial Feelings that mingle with & fill up the mob—& then ask his own Intellect, whether supposing he could conceive the creation of positively Infinite & coequal Beings, & whether, supposing this not only possible but real, this has exhausted his notion of *Creatability*? Whether the Intellect by an inborn, and original Law of its Essence, does not demand of infinite Power more than merely infinity of Number—infinity of *Sorts* & orders?—Let him have created this infinity of Infinites—Still there is space in the Imagination for the Creation of Finites—but instead of these let him again create Infinites— Yet still the same Space is left—it is no way filled up. I feel too, that the whole rests on a miserable Sophism of applying to an Almighty Being such words as *All*. Why were not *all*—Gods? But there is no *all*, in creation—It is composed of Infinites—& the Imagination bewildered by heaping Infinites on Infinites, & wearying of demanding increase of number to a number which it conceives already infin., deserted by Images, and mocked by words, whose sole Substance is the inward sense of Difficulty that accompanies all our notions of infinity applied to number, turns with delight to distinct Images, & clear Ideas—contemplates *a World*, an harmonious System where an infinity of Kinds subsist each in a multitude of Individuals apportionate to its Kind in conformity to Laws existing in the divine Nature—& therefore in the nature of Things. We cannot indeed *prove* this in any other way than by finding it as impossible to deny omniform, as eternal, agency to God—by finding it impossible to conceive that an omniscient Being should not have a distinct Idea of finite Beings, or that distinct Ideas in the mind of God should be without the perfection of real Existence—i.e. imperfect—But this is a proof, subtle indeed, yet not more so than the difficulty. The intellect that can stand the one can understand the other, if his vices do not prevent him. Admit for a moment, that "to conceive" is = with creation in the divine nature, synonimous with "to beget," (a feeling of which has given to Marriage a mysterious sanctity & sacramental significance in the mind of many great & good men). Admit this, and all difficulty ceases—all Tumult is hushed—all is clear & beautiful—/We sit in the Dark, but each by the side of his little Fire in his own group, & lo! the summit of the distant mountain is smitten with Light—all night long it has dwelt there—& we look at it, & know that the Sun is not extinguished/yea, that he is elsewhere bright & vivifying—that he is coming to us, to make our fires needless—yet even now that our Cold & Darkness are so called only in comparison with the Heat & Light of the Coming Day/never wholly deserted of the Rays.—Ask it as a Duty to choose Good rather than evil—even tho' there were a choice.—

A further attempt next day to solve the problem.[8]

To return to the Question of Evil—woe to the man, to whom it is an uninteresting Question—tho' many a mind, overwearied by it, may shun it with Dread/and here, N.B. scourge with deserved & lofty Scorn those Critics who laugh at the discussion of old Questions—God, Right & Wrong, Necessity & Arbitrement—Evil, &c—No! forsooth!—the Question must be new, *new spicy hot* Gingerbread, a French Constitution, a Balloon, change of Ministry, or which had the best of it in the Parliamentary Duel, Wyndham or Sheridan, or at the best, a chemical Theory, whether the new celestial Bodies shall be called Planets or Asteroids—&c—Something new, something *out* of themselves—for whatever is *in* them, is deep within them, must be *old as* elementary Nature. To find no contradiction in the union of old & novel—to contemplate the Ancient of Days with Feelings new as if they then sprang forth at his own Fiat—this marks the mind that feels the Riddle of the World, & may help to unravel it. But to return to the Question—the whole rests on the Sophism of imagining Change in a case of positive Substitution.—This, I fully believe, *settles* the Question/—The assertion that there is in the essence of the divine nature a necessity of omniform harmonious action, and that Order, & System/not number—in itself base & disorderly & irrational—/define the creative Energy, determine & employ it—& that number is subservient to order, regulated, organized, made beautiful and rational, an object both of Imag. & Intellect, by Order—this is no mere assertion/it is strictly in harmony with the Fact, for the world appears so—& it is proved by whatever proves the Being of God—. Indeed, it is involved in the Idea of God.—

Further hard cases of innocent suffering prompt recourse again to assurance of benevolent purpose.[9]

Poor Miss Dane!—born with a wrong Conformation that prophesied the early Death, it occasioned—Such are generally gentle & innocent Beings—God himself seems to stamp on their Forehead the Seal of Death, in sign of Appropriation/no evil dares approach—the sacred Hieroglyphic on this Seal of Redemption we on earth interpret early Death; but the heavenly Spirits, that minister around us, read in it "Abiding Innocence."—

Something to me delicious in the Thought that one who dies a Baby presents to its glorified Saviour & Redeemer that same sweet Face of Infancy which he blessed when on earth, & sanctified with a kiss—& solemnly pronounced to be the Type, & Sacrament of Regeneration.

Another attempt to solve the problem brings in his thinking about the nature of subconscious thinking.[10]

I will at least make the attempt to explain to myself the Origin of moral Evil from the *streamy* Nature of Association, which Thinking = Reason, curbs & rudders/how this comes to be so difficult/Do not the bad Passions in Dreams throw light & shew of proof upon this Hypothesis?—Explain those bad Passions: & I shall gain Light, I am sure—A Clue! A Clue!—an Hecatomb a la Pythagoras, if it unlabyrinths me.—Dec. 28, 1803—Beautiful luminous Shadow of my pencil point following it from the Candle—rather going before it & illuminating the word, I am writing. 11°clock/—But take in the blessedness of Innocent Children, the blessedness of sweet Sleep, &c &c &c: are these or are they not contradictions to the evil from *streamy* association?—I hope not: all is to be thought *over* and *into*—but what is the height, & ideal of mere association?—Delirium.—But how far is this state produced by Pain & Denaturalization? And what are these?—In short, as far as I can see any thing in this Total Mist, Vice is imperfect yet existing Volition, giving diseased Currents of association, because it yields on all sides & *yet* is— So think of Madness.

The death of John Wordsworth at sea prompts a recourse to the morally chaotic world of the oriental tales and so to a renewed respect for John's unflinching regard for Duty – a quality to become a prime value during the next few years for both himself and William Wordsworth.[11]

8 Apr. 1805. Monday.—The favorite Object of all oriental Tales, & that which inspiring their Authors in the East inspires still their Readers every where, is the impossibility of baffling Destiny, & that what we considered as the means of one thing becomes in a strange manner the direct means of the Reverse. O dear John Wordsworth! what Joy at Grasmere that you were made Captn of the Abergavenny/so young too! now it was next to certain that you would in a few years settle in your natives Hills, and be verily one of *the Concern.*—Then came your Share in the brilliant action with Linois—I was at Grasmere in spirit only. but in spirit I was one of the Rejoicers—As Joyful as any, & perhaps more Joyous!—This doubtless not only enabled you to lay in ~~more~~ a larger and more advantageous Cargo, but procured you a voyage to India instead of China/& in this a next to certainty of Independence/—and all these were Decoys of Death!—Well!—but a nobler feeling than these vain regrets would become the Friend of the man whose last words were—"I have done my Duty! let her go!"—Let us do our *Duty*: all else is a Dream, Life and Death alike a Dream/this short sentence would comprize, I believe, the sum of all profound Philosophy, of ethics and metaphysics conjointly, from Plato to Fichte.—S.T.C.—

Writing to J.P. Estlin in April 1814 about the latter's book on Universal Restitution he agrees concerning the incompatibility of vindictive justice with the infinite love of God, but argues from his own point of view, that the vindictiveness must be found in the mind of the sinner, where it can only be vanquished by a miraculous divine operation.[12]

I believe, that punishment is essentially *vindictive*, i.e. expressive of abhorrence of Sin for it's own exceeding sinfulness: from all experience as well as a priori from the constitution of the human Soul I gather that without a miraculous Intervention of Omnipotence the Punishment must continue as long as the Soul—which I believe imperishable.—God has promised no such miracle—he has covenanted no such mercy—I have no right therefore to believe or rely on it—It *may* be so; but wo to me! if I presume on it.—There is a great difference, my dear Sir! between the assertion—'It ɪs so!' & 'I have no right to assert the contrary!'

As to eternal punishment, he writes to Cottle:[13]

The literal meaning of *'aionios'* is, 'through ages;' that is, indefinite; beyond the power of imagination to bound. But as to the effects of such a doctrine, I say, First,—that it would be more pious to assert nothing concerning it, one way or the other. . . . Second,—that however the doctrine is now broached, and publicly preached by a large and increasing sect, it is no longer possible to conceal it from such persons as would be likely to read and understand the Religious Musings.

All such assertions relate back to his conviction that human beings are fallen creatures – which grows, if anything, with the years. As he puts it in 1830.[14]

A *Fall* of some sort or other—the creation, as it were, of the Non-Absolute—is the fundamental *Postulate* of the Moral History of Man. Without this hypothesis Man is unintelligible; with it, every phenomenon is explicable. The Mystery itself is too profound for human insight.

Coleridge enunciates his own solution to the problem by excluding various unacceptable alternatives and concluding that the remaining position, however mysterious, must be the correct one.[15]

Omnia exeunt in mysterium, says a Schoolman: i.e. *There is nothing, the absolute ground of which is not a Mystery.* The contrary were indeed a contradiction in terms: for how can that, which is to explain all things, be susceptible of an explanation? It would be to suppose the same thing first and second at the same time.

If I rested here, I should merely have placed my Creed in direct opposition to that of the Necessitarians, who assume (for observe *both* Parties begin in an *Assumption*, and cannot do otherwise) that motives act on the Will, as bodies act on bodies; and that whether mind and matter are essentially the same or essentially different, they are both alike under one and the same law of compulsory Causation. But this is far from exhausting my intention. I mean at the same time to oppose the Disciples of SHAFTESBURY and those who, substituting one Faith for another, have been well called the pious Deists of the last Century, in order to distinguish them from the Infidels of the present age, who *persuade* themselves, (for the thing itself is not possible) that they reject all Faith. I declare my dissent from these too, because they imposed upon themselves an *Idea* for a Reality: a most sublime Idea indeed, and so necessary to human Nature, that without it no Virtue is conceivable; but still an Idea! In contradiction to their splendid but delusory Tenets, I profess a deep conviction that Man was and is *a fallen* Creature, not by accidents of bodily constitution, or any other cause, which *human* Wisdom in a course of ages might be supposed capable of removing; but diseased in his *Will*, in that Will which is the true and only strict synonime of the word, I, or the intelligent Self. Thus at each of these two opposite Roads (the Philosophy of Hobbes and that of Shaftesbury), I have placed a directing Post, informing my Fellow-travellers, that on neither of these Roads can they see the Truths to which I would direct their attention.

But the place of starting was at the meeting of *four* Roads, and one only was the right road. I proceed, therefore, to preclude the opinion of those likewise, who indeed agree with me as to the moral Responsibility of Man in opposition to Hobbes and the Anti-Moralists, and that He was a fallen Creature, essentially diseased, in opposition to Shaftesbury and the Misinterpreters of Plato; but who differ from me in exaggerating the diseased *weakness* of the Will into an absolute privation of all Freedom, thereby making moral responsibility, not a mystery *above* comprehension, but a direct contradiction, of which we do distinctly comprehend the absurdity. Among the consequences of this Doctrine, is that direful one of swallowing up all the attributes of the supreme Being in the one Attribute of infinite Power, and thence deducing that Things are good and wise because they were created, and not created through Wisdom and Goodness. Thence too the awful Attribute of *Justice* is explained away into a mere right of absolute *Property*; the sacred distinction between Things and Persons is erased; and the selection of Persons for Virtue and Vice in this Life, and for eternal Happiness or Misery in the next, is represented as the result of a mere *Will*, acting in the blindness and solitude of its own Infinity. The Title of a Work written by the great and pious Boyle is "Of the Awe, which the human Mind owes to the supreme Reason." This, in the language of these gloomy Doctors, must be translated into—"the horror, which a Being capable of eternal Pleasure or Pain is compelled to feel at the idea of an infinite Power, about to inflict the latter on an immense majority of human Souls, without any power on their part either to prevent it or the actions which are (not indeed its causes but) its assigned *signals*, and preceding links of the same iron chain!"

Against these Tenets I maintain, that a Will conceived separately from Intelligence is a Non-entity, and a mere Phantasm of Abstraction; and that a Will, the state of which does in *no sense* originate in its own act, is an absolute contradiction. It might be an Instinct, an Impulse, a plastic Power, and, if accompanied with consciousness, a Desire; but a Will it *could* not be! And this *every* Human Being *knows* with equal *clearness*, though different minds may *reflect* on it with different degrees of *distinctness*; for who would not smile at the notion of a Rose *willing* to put forth its Buds and expand them into Flowers? That such a phrase would be deemed a *poetic* Licence proves the difference in the things: for all metaphors are grounded on an apparent likeness of things essentially different. I utterly disclaim the idea, that any *human* Intelligence, with whatever power it might manifest itself, is *alone* adequate to the office of restoring health to the Will: but at the same time I deem it impious and absurd to hold, that the Creator would have *given* us the faculty of Reason, or that the Redeemer would in so many varied forms of Argument and Persuasion have *appealed* to it, if it had been either totally useless or wholly impotent. Lastly, I find all these several Truths reconciled and united in the belief, that the imperfect human understanding can be effectually exerted only in *subordination* to, and in a dependent *alliance* with, the means and aidances supplied by the all-perfect and supreme Reason; but that under these conditions it is not only an admissible, but a necessary, instrument of ameliorating both ourselves and others.

The question of free will remains thorny.[16]

Dr Davison has threshed over again the bruised, and chopped Straw of the ? respecting the compossibility of Prescience with Free Will; but setting aside the passage borrowed from (at least, pre-existing in) Phil[ip] Skelton, without beating out a single additional Grain—a mournful proof of the incommunion with IDEAS in the ablest men of the present Age.—Yet methinks, even without the Idea an acute Thinker might have seen that the difficulty lies in the antithesis ⟨(= opposition)⟩ Knowlege [opposed to] Will, which is rendered a catathesis (= contrareity) by the predicates Præ [contrary to] Post—i.e. by supposing Will posterior to Knowlege. Now if *Pre*science is a predicable of God, this objection must hold equally good of the Divine *Will*—but if Prescience with respect to *this* would argue an imperfection in Deity, why not in the case of the *human* Will.—Can the imperfection of the Object ⟨known⟩ affect the perfection of the Subject knowing? But if omniscience, the necessary perfection of the Eternal, remain omniscience under the form of Eternity whatever the Object may be—is it not evident, that the whole difficulty resolves itself into the impossibility of *expressing* the Idea, Eternity, (i.e. presenting it in the forms of the Understanding or Discursive Faculty) except by two contra-dictory Conceptions?—Now this is only saying, that Eternity is an IDEA, not a Conception—for it is the common characteristic of all Ideas.—But the truth lies deeper. The real contrariety consists in Will = Object, i.e. in making *Will* an Object at all. A Deed, a Thought, *are* possible objects of a knowlege relatively anterior—and from the Deed, the Thought, the Will may be certainly known. The mistake lies in supposing Contingency to be the necessary character of Will or *Free* Agency/for if so, God could not be *free*. Are or are not, all things simultaneously present to God—Is, or is not, his knowlege always equally certain? If so, and if God knows his own Will & yet that remains free, why should his certain knowlege of *our* Will be incompatible with its freedom? Its *presentness* to God is not affected by its finiteness or evil Nature—.—There is an Equivoque in the term, or rather a confusion in Man's Notions of Necessity—God's Will is necessarily free by virtue of its own absoluteness—the Devilish Will necessarily bound by force of its own predestinating self-determination. Properly speaking, Freedom of Will is one and the same with co-incidence with the Will of God—as far as it is one with this, it is known with all its products in the same Light in which God knows his own Will and Works—as far as it is not, it is a necessitated Will, the necessary tendencies of which are known to the Omniscient in the absolute Will of itself/but the direction is given by the Machinery in which & by which it is permitted to manifest ⟨itself⟩—but this is of God alone—. Consequently, its products are equally capable of being pre-calculated as the movements of the Planets. In either case therefore God's knowlege

& (relatively to our conceptions of ourselves relatively to God) his *Fore-knowlege* is certain—in the one case, the Will is known as the *Subject*, in the other ⟨fore-known⟩ as an *object.*—The question—but how is it fore-known that Herod or Judas should be the Individuals whose Will was evil—is senseless.—The evil Will constituted itself Judas here and Herod there.—Finally, the Disputant will complain that I have not enabled him to *understand* the matter better than he did before—And that is very true. I cannot enable him to smell Music or hear a color. Eternity and Eternal Things are not Objects of Conception—but pass all understanding.

It is a belief in the necessity of a redeemer that makes the Unitarian position untenable.[17]

There is an immense difference between negative & positive Socinianism—I doubt not, that the idiotæ of Tertullian were *negative* Socinians—they did not believe *explicitly* because they did not think about the nature of the union of the Godhead with Christ—yet *implicitly* they believed it inasmuch as they believed redemption *by* Christ, not merely *thro'* him—because they did not only believe Christ, but believed *in* him—which are contradictions in thought with the notion of a mere Prophet, or passive vehicle—

Belief in the Devil speaks to a similar subconscious assumption.[18]

That our religious faith & the instincts which lead us to metaphysical investigation, are founded on a practical necessity not a mere intellectual craving after knowlege, & systematic computings, is evinced by the interest which all men take in the question of future Existence, and the Being of God/while even among those, who are speculative by profession, a few Phantasts only have troubled themselves with the questions of pre-existence, or with attempts to demonstrate the posse and esse of a Devil. But in the latter case more is involved—concerning Pre-existence men in general have neither care or belief; but a Devil is taken for granted, and if we might trust words, with the same faith as a Deity—"He neither believes God or Devil"—and yet while we are delighted in hearing proofs of the one, we never think of asking a single question concerning the other/This too originates in a practical source—The Deity is not a mere solution of difficulties concerning origination; but a truth which spreads Light, and Joy, & Hope, & Certitude thro' all things—while a Devil *is* a mere solution of an Enigma—an assumption to silence our uneasiness—That end answered (and most easily are such ends answered) we have no further concern with it—

In the same way, Unitarians speak of the sufferings of Christ in a manner which shows that they cannot believe them to be no more than a simple martyrdom.[19]

The instances are so numerous of men who have endured Sufferings far more dreadful, and Deaths of studied Torture in a good cause, to rescue their Country from civil and religious Tyranny or to introduce the knowlege of the Truth among nations in darkness—who have from the beginning steadfastly looked forward to it, as the probable, nay almost certain final result of their labors of Love, and without that supernatural Assurance of an immediate Assumption into Bliss and Glory, which even the Unitarians attribute to Jesus—and without betraying any other Enthusiasm, than accompanies all great Thoughts & Actions grounded on strong convictions—. Nay, I confess that when I began to suspect that tho' the Faith of the Church might be false, Unitarianism could not be true; that if the one was absurd, the other was trifling—that if the one was an Enthusiasm soaring beyond Reason, the other was a Superstition darting its forked tongue at her Heel, at enmity with the interests of Science, and with the conditions of ⟨all⟩ genuine and statutable Experience—in short, that there was no medium between Deism and Orthodoxy (i.e. the Belief common to all the established Churches, Greek & Latin, Catholic & Protestant) or rather between the philosophy of Spinoza and the Creed of the Council of Nice—I confess, I say, that one of the disturbing Difficulties was how in the scheme of the Psilanthropists to reconcile the mental agonies of Jesus with heroic fortitude & greatness of mind on the one hand, or with his superhuman Certainty of the unspeakable Glory & Beatitude after a few hours of bodily Sufferings. It is true indeed, that Persistency of Purpose under such a weight of Terror & Reluctancy is exemplary; but when we reflect how few would persist under such emotions, the so extraordinary Dread of Death can scarcely be considered as such ⟨. . . and sure I was, that the same doubt would have perplexed the minds of the old Fathers who placed the agony and bloody sweat of our Lord among the chief mysteries of the Gospel—⟩ Now I ask whether the emotions connected with the latter half of this sentence, and the horror with which a ⟨even an ignorant⟩ Christian whose religious information is perhaps comprized in the Apostles' Creed, recoils from the *thought* of the former, could have been felt by a Roman in the reign of Honorius for Quintus Curtius;

or by a Greek, who owed his knowledge of a pure system of Morality &
his confidence in a future state to the records of the Life and Death of
Socrates, for the deified Socrates; or by a Scottish Protestant for the
Martyr Wishart. I cannot believe it—I cannot understand how it is
possible—& when I hear a Unitarian talk the language of Christians in
general respecting the sufferings & death of Christ, I attribute his feeling
to the insensible influence of the Creed of his Country, & his unconscious
sympathy with those among whom he lives/ so that he cannot bring
down his feelings to a level with his Opinions—A unitarian will speak
of the Martyrdom of Stephen, or Peter, or Polycarp, &c—but there is
a something that checks him from saying, the Martyr Jesus—or calling
his Crucifixion a Martyrdom, as he would call Peter's or Paul's Death on
the Cross I say, I cannot understand it—I cannot refer the feeling, the
peculiar impression, even of the Unitarians, to a Unitarian Belief—

*The true 'atonement' is regarded in 1804 as a matter of intellectual harmon-
ization.*[20]

Each man having a spark (to use the old metaphor) of the Divinity, yet
a whole fire-grate of Humanity (each therefore will legislate for the
whole, spite of the De gustibus non est disputandum [there is no
accounting for tastes], even in trifles, till corrected by experiences—and
at least in this endless struggle of presumption, really occasioned by the
ever-working Spark of the Universal, and the disappointments & baffled
attempts of each, all are disposed to the jus extrinsecum fortioris [the
external law of stronger force] ⟨(Spinoza)⟩, & recognize that reason as
the highest, which may not be understood as the best, but of which the
Concrete Possession is felt to be the strongest—Then comes Society,
Habit, Education, Sleepiness, misery, intrigue, oppression—Then *Revolution*/& the circle begins anew/:—Each man will universalize his notions,
& yet each is variously finite. To *reconcile* therefore is truly the work of
the Inspired! This is the true *Atonement*—/i.e. to reconcile the struggles
of the infinitely various Finite with the *Permanent*.

*The idea of sacrificial atonement certainly calls, in his view, for extreme
mental strenuousness, rather than compliance with current complacency.*[21]

In the plausible passage in Paley's Sermons respecting Sacrifi[ci]al
Atonement—&c—We may hope to learn what it means in a *future* state!

We *may* then PERHAPS see how true it is—tho' at present it is, it must be confessed, sad nonsense!!—This will, however, be popular—1,0001 of good sober pious Christians will echo the words & adopt them as their Makers faith. Why? it is feeble—& who ever is feeble favors mental indolence. It is feeble: and feebleness in the disguise of confessing and condescending Strength is always popular. It flatters the Reader by removing the apprehended distance between him & the superior Author—& it flatters him still more by enabling him to transfer to himself and appropriate this superiority, and to make his very weakness a mark & proof of his strength. Aye—or a ⟨sighing self-soothing⟩ sound between Aye and Ah.! I think with the great Dr Paley &c.

His own position demands both a recognition of the incommunicable reality of sin and an equally mysterious working of the Logos through the human mentality.[22]

Some unknown Person, soon after the publication of the Aids to Reflection, sent me Relly's Treasury of Faith (See Southey's Life of Wesley, Vol. II. p. 315) whether imagining a resemblance in my tenets with his, I know not. If so, the Sender must have been a very careless reader—⟨the actuality of Sin—⟩ "the exceeding sinfulness of Sin"—and its essential incommunicability—being my foundation stones/and the conversion of Sin into Disease or Calamity the error of errors, against which I cry out. No less expressly have I declared the nature (τό *quid et quale* [the what and of what quality]) of the Redemptive Act, and the subsumption of the Humanity by the co-eternal Son of God, an incomprehensible Mystery/to the belief of which we can *intellectually* supply one indirect argument, viz. an exposure of the Absurdity of every comprehensible Substitute, that has been imagined.

Nevertheless, there are certain Appertinents, for which we have the authority of Redemption—for instance, that the fallen Nature, which Christ was born into, was capable of acting on his Will—and that this is a concerning truth is evident from its being recorded in each of the three Gospels.—And there are, I believe, certain Positions, in such apparent harmony with Scripture Declarations, & which, if admitted, would intelligibly connect all the various declarations of the Scripture into a Whole, that they may be innocently and profitably set forth—provided that it be done modestly, as an aid to individual conviction respecting the doctrines of Faith, not as an addition. Such I hold the two following—that a finite Will can become personal, an I am, only under the condition of the Eternal Logos enlightening it, or that we call Reason is the Light or Manifestation of the Divine Intelligence; and that the finite "I" can exist really (or actually [as opposed to] potentially) only as it has a ground or Base of existence in a Life or Nature; and that this Life or Nature is not individual & imparticipable in the sense in which the "I" itself is; but *generic*—or a Common Nature, so that each man speaks of his Nature, as a somewhat with which he is united but not identified, as mine not I, as *mine* & yet *our*; it being the incommunicable Perfection of God to contain in himself the Ground of his own existence.

7
'Science, Freedom and the Truth...'

From the time of the early poem in which he asserted his allegiance to 'Science, Freedom and the Truth in Christ', Coleridge displayed an acute interest in the new discoveries that were being made in his time and in the wide conspectus of scientific knowledge that was by now available. He catalogued the range of scientific subjects he would feel it necessary to master if he were to embark on the writing of an epic poem for the new age and engaged himself with the various theories of life that were being bandied about. In the 1790s his chief contemporary hero was Joseph Priestley, well known in scientific circles for his work on oxygen, whose liberal political attitudes were accompanied by Unitarianism. As has already been mentioned, he was disturbed by some of his religious doctrines, which seemed to open the gates to pantheist beliefs; yet he could not find unattractive a man who struggled so valiantly for freedom in every sphere. A few years later he was even more drawn to Humphry Davy, whom he encountered at the end of the decade and who brought a poetic intellect to the work he was pursuing, initially in Bristol and then at the Royal Institution in London. For a time he even envisaged an alliance between Wordsworth, Davy and Godwin and himself in the hope of renovating English intellectual life.

Coleridge followed Davy's career with close interest and under his influence engaged in chemical and scientific experimentation himself for a time, even though his friend's scientific path took a different turn. He increasingly came to believe that the way forward for science should be to develop what he thought of as a 'dynamic' method, whereas he saw Davy falling into the British mainstream of empiricism. From now on, nevertheless, he would maintain a close interest in what was happening scientifically abroad as well as at home, relating what he learned, wherever possible, to his own metaphysical and psychological concerns.

After his return from Italy and Malta in 1806 the latter took a new turn. His hopes of finding an exemplary Platonic love with Words-worth's sister-in-law Sara Hutchinson seemed to have moved no further towards fulfilment, while his plan to establish new religious attitudes by way of his psychological investigations and speculations needed, it seemed, to be deferred as a distant project. Davy, too, must be left to pursue his work on a long timescale in the hope that his ideas might achieve some convergence with the dynamic ideal.

His friendship with Wordsworth remained meanwhile the chief stay and source of hope. Both men still nursed an aspiration to be of service to younger men who had found their political idealism dashed by the failure of the French Revolution and yet wished to guide their society into a better way of life. While unsure of the status of the autobiograph-ical poem (later to be published as *The Prelude*) that he had completed during Coleridge's absence in Malta and dedicated to him, Wordsworth hoped to fulfil his larger project by writing a longer poem, tentatively called 'The Recluse'. Coleridge, meanwhile, while urging him on in his poetic endeavours, agreed with him also as to the need for better ideals in political and social life, and set out to promulgate some of his ideas—initially by founding a journal, *The Friend*. In this he tried to move towards the establishment of fixed principles, while also arguing, in accordance with his retreat from Unitarianism, that acceptance of Christianity purely as a system of ethics was inadequate to the true underlying needs of human beings. This reverberated in his thinking about the physical sciences by fostering, across the whole intellectual scale, attention to the concept of law.

In the context of this renewed interest the question of miracles, involving events in which the laws of nature seem temporarily ignored, continued to be important. This contradiction of the normal order of things, presenting a challenge that bordered on an offence to common eighteenth-century thinking and therefore the subject of much contro-versy, was an issue to which he returned several times, insisting that attempts to base religious belief on miracles were mistaken, even when, as was often the case, he had no wish to deny their existence. In his view miracles must always follow on Faith, and not (as seemed to be the common contemporary assumption) vice versa.

His scientific thinking took a new turn as renewed relations between Britain and Continental Europe at the end of the Napoleonic wars opened up channels of information about recent developments of thought in the universities there, including intimations of a renewed interest in ideas that had captivated him in the 1790s. In particular, news reached him that Blumenbach had now become a convert to belief in the existence of hypnotic powers: as a result of which he for some years engrossed himself in recent treatises on the subject, many of them emanating from Germany. This was not all, however, for there was now in Germany a flourishing school of *Naturphilosophen* who were devoting themselves to the elaboration of systems from which all the phenomena of nature could be deduced. Coleridge found this method appealing and spent some time in letters and discussions with friends in which he tried to work out schematic explanations of his own. Although there is no room to include all these in the present collection, their existence is another testimony to his desire to find an interpretation of nature that could be more readily reconciled with a divine purpose.[1]

On one matter of current scientific theory he was particularly firm. Since the appearance of Edward Tyson's *Orang-Outang* in 1699 and Lord Monboddo's chapter on the subject in *Of the Origin and Progress of Language* (1774–92), followed by Erasmus Darwin's theories concerning the progress of life in *Zoonomia*, it had been not uncommon to discuss the possibility that human beings were descended from the apes. Coleridge was firm in his denial, believing that the appearance of human beings on the scene had been a supernaturally ordained event, an embodying of human and intellectual qualities from which they had henceforward deteriorated. At the same time he was also sure that a full survey of the animated beings in nature revealed a progressive development towards the emergence of humanity; he simply rejected the notion that there had been a continuous evolution in time, including that humanity as part of the process: his religious beliefs involved an affirmation of the intellectual and moral stature of his fellows that would not easily survive such a diminution of their status. In spite of that he would, nevertheless, continue to insist equally on the fact of their degeneracy from an original ideal state, and seek to establish the reasons for such a falling away.

In his early years Coleridge projects the kind of scientific knowledge he would need in order to prepare himself for the writing of a great epic poem.[1]

I would be a tolerable Mathematician, I would thoroughly know Mechanics, Hydrostatics, Optics, and Astronomy, Botany, Metallurgy, Fossilism, Chemistry, Geology, Anatomy, Medicine—then the *mind of man*—then the *minds of men*—in all Travels, Voyages and Histories. So I would spend ten years—the next five to the composition of the poem—and the five last to the correction of it.

At the same time he is fascinated by the different theories of life and their implications for knowledge of oneself.[2]

. . . true or false, Heaven is a less gloomy idea than Annihilation!—Dr Beddoes, & Dr Darwin think that *Life* is utterly inexplicable, writing as Materialists—You, I understand, have adopted the idea that it is the result of organized matter acted on by external Stimuli.—As likely as any other system; but you *assume* the thing to be proved—the '*capability* of being stimulated into sensation' *as* a *property* of organized matter—now 'the Capab.' &c is *my* definition of *animal Life*——Monro believes in a plastic immaterial Nature—all-pervading—

> And what if all of animated Nature
> Be but organic harps diversely fram'd
> That tremble into *thought* as o'er them sweeps
> Plastic & vast &c—

(by the bye—that is my favorite of *my* poems—do *you* like it?) Hunter that the *Blood* is the Life—which is saying nothing at all—for if the blood were *Life*, it could never be otherwise than Life—and to say, it is *alive*, is saying nothing—& Ferrir believes in a *Soul*, like an orthodox Churchman—So much for Physicians & Surgeons—Now as to the Metaphysicians, Plato says, it is *Harmony*—he might as well have said, a fiddle stick's end—but I love Plato—his dear *gorgeous* Nonsense! And *I, tho' last not least,* I do not know what to think about it—on the whole, I have rather made up my mind that I am a mere *apparition*—a naked Spirit!—And that Life is I myself I! which is a mighty clear account of it.

By 1801 his intercourse with Humphry Davy has convinced him of the importance of chemistry in understanding the natural world.[3]

—As far as *words* go, I have become a formidable chemist—having got by heart a prodigious quantity of terms &c to which I attach *some* ideas—very scanty in number, I assure you, & right meagre in their individual persons. That which most discourages me in it is that I find all *power* & vital attributes to depend on modes of *arrangement*—and that Chemistry throws not even a distant rush-light glimmer upon this subject. The *reasoning* likewise is always unsatisfactory to me—I am perpetually saying—probably, there are many agents hitherto undiscovered. This cannot be *reasoning;* for in all conclusive reasoning we must have a deep conviction that all the *terms* have been exhausted.

This is saying no more than that (with Dr Beddoes's leave) chemistry can never possess the same kind of certainty with mathematics—in truth, it is saying nothing. I grow however exceedingly interested in the subject.—

Biology seems even more important, when he considers the apparently endless divisibility of life and its implications.[4]

Wonderful, perplexing divisibility of Life/it is related by D. Unzer, an authority wholly to be relied on, that an Ohrwurm (Earwig?) cut in half eat its own hinder half!—Will it be the reverse with G. Britain & America? The Head of the rattle-snake severed from the body bit at, & squirted out its poison/Related by Beverley in his Hist. of Virginia. Lyonnet/ in his Insect-Theol./tore a wasp in half, & 3 days after the fore-half bit whatever was presented to it of its former food, & the hind-half darted out its sting on being touched. Boyle mentions a female butterfly that when beheaded not only admitted the male but lay eggs in consequence of the impregnation. But a Turtle has lived six months with his Head off—& wandered about/yea, six hours after its heart & bowels (all but the Lungs) were taken out—How shall we think of this compatible with the *monad* Soul? If I say what has Spirit to do with space—what odd dreams it would suggest? Or is every animal a republic in se? Or is there one Breeze of Life—at once the soul of each & God of all?

Discussions with Humphry Davy led to the adumbration of a unified theory of matter. As always, however, the ultimate task is to reconcile natural science with moral science.[5]

Davy supposes that there is only one power in the world of the senses; which in particles acts as chemical attractions, in specific masses as electricity, & on matter in general, as planetary Gravitation. Jupiter est, quodcumque vides [Jupiter is whatever you see]; when this has been proved, it will then only remain to resolve this into some Law of vital Intellect—and all human Knowlege will be Science and Metaphysics the only Science. Yet after all, unless all this be identified with Virtue, as the ultimate and supreme Cause and Agent, all will be a worthless Dream. For all the Tenses and all the Compounds of *Scire* will do little for us, if they do not draw us closer to the Esse and Agere [Being and Acting].—

Writing to Estlin a year later and having temporized a little concerning his withdrawal from Unitarianism—while trying to explain it—he turns to his new venture, The Friend.[6]

As to 'THE FRIEND', I make no request to you. You will do me all the good, you can, compatible with the approbation of your own mind. I have received promises of Support from men of very high name in the literary world—and as to my own Efforts, I consider the work as the main Pipe of my intellectual Reservoir.—The first Essay will be—On the nature and importance of *Principles*.

A few days later he elaborates on this statement, explaining that his "principles" are first and foremost those of Reason, though a Reason that must take account of all that is involved in Religion.[7]

My first Essay will be on the Nature and the Importance of *Principles*— i.e. of the pure REASON, which dictates unconditionally, in distinction from the prudential understanding, which employing it's mole Eyes in an impossible calculation of Consequences perverts and mutilates its own Being, untenanting the function which it is incapable of occupy-ing. This is Infidelity, essential Infidelity, however goodly it's Garb, however seemly it's name—and this I have long deemed the Disease, nay, let me speak out—the *Guilt* of the Age—therefore, and not *chiefly* because it has produced a spirit of enquiry into the external evidences of instituted Religion, it is an Infidel age. Will the Truth of the Tale exculpate me from the crime of personal calumny, if I illustrate—(thus, and to you alone, and in a confidential Letter)—my general Charge by a particular instance? If I tell you, that I know a Bishop, an English Bishop, who professing Socinianism (not indeed all the heresies of Drs Priestley & Co, but absolutely all the distinguishing tenets of Socinus) affirms the innocence & the duty of offering Adoration and *ultimate* Prayer to Christ, whom he yet Zealously contends to have been & to be not only a finite Creature, but a mere MAN! adding—*I can see* no harm, in this practice—it leaves untouched all the motives of future reward and punishment, which is the *essence* of Religion. Merciful Heaven! *this* the Essence of that Religion, which permits the degraded man to com-mence with terror only as the means of enabling him finally to arrive at itself, which is perfect Love shutting out Fear. Shall I hesitate to deem such a man an infidel, who rejects the fundamental *principle* of all Reli-gion, propounded amid the Thunders of Mount Sinai, and revealed even to Heathen Philosophers by 'the still small voice' of Conscience, simply because in counting the Consequences, that people the tiny field of his dim Vision, he had seen *no Harm* from it!

The writing of The Friend *thus gives him various opportunities to expound his view of 'Reason' in its supersensuous form—an idea which he expounds with particular vigour to Davy in a letter of 1807.*[8]

. . . tho I did not see, as clearly as I could wish, the pertinence of the religious declaration quoted from you and am not quite at ease (especially when I think of Darwin) when I find Theosophy mingled with Science; and tho' I wished to have been with you to have expressed my doubts concerning the accuracy of your comparison between the great Discoverers of Science, and the Miltons, Spinozas, & Rafaels; yet the intervening History—it is only that I am writing to you that I stopped & hesitate in using the word—overwhelmed me—and I dare avow, furnished to my Understanding & Conscience proofs more convincing, than the dim Analogies of natural organization to human Mechanism, both of the Supreme Reason as superessential to the World of the Senses; of an analogous Mind in Man not resulting from it's perishable Machine, nor even from the general Spirit of Life, it's inclosed steam or perfluent water-force; and of the moral connection between the finite and the infinite Reason, and the aweful majesty of the former as both the Revelation and the exponent Voice of the Latter, immortal Time-piece [of] an eternal Sun.

He hopes that the labours of the physiologists, in particular, assisted by psychological insight, will lead to the formation of laws of organic nature.[9]

. . . and hence proceeds the striving after unity of principle through all the diversity of forms, with a feeling resembling that which accompanies our endeavors to recollect a forgotten name; when we seem at once to have and not to have it; which the memory feels but cannot find. Thus, as "the lunatic, the lover, and the poet," suggest each other to Shakspeare's Theseus, as soon as his thoughts present him the ONE FORM, of which they are but varieties; so water and flame, the diamond, the charcoal, and the mantling champagne, with its ebullient sparkles, are convoked and fraternized by the theory of the chemist. This is, in truth, the first charm of chemistry, and the secret of the almost universal interest excited by its discoveries. The serious complacency which is afforded by the sense of truth, utility, permanence, and pro-gression, blends with and ennobles the exhilarating surprise and the pleasurable sting of curiosity, which accompany the propounding and the solving of an Enigma. It is the sense of a principle of connection given by the mind, and sanctioned by the correspondency of nature. Hence the strong hold which in all ages chemistry has had on the imagination. If in SHAKSPEARE we find nature idealized into poetry, through the creative power of a profound yet observant meditation, so through the meditative observation of a DAVY, a WOOLLASTON, or a HATCHETT;

> By some connatural force,
> Powerful at greatest distance to unite
> With secret amity things of like kind,

we find poetry, as it were, substantiated and realized in nature: yea, nature itself disclosed to us, GEMINAM *istam naturam, quæ fit et facit, et creat et creatur* [that dual nature, which becomes and makes, creates and is created] as at once the poet and the poem!

His turn to a more orthodox Christianity has meanwhile caused him to look again at the defences which are mounted in its favour, writing in Malta:[10]

The Grotian Paleian Defences of X how injurious to X develope/—never would the number of Infidels have been so great, if to each attack it had been answered/Well, Brother! but granting these miracles to have been false, or the growth of delusion at the time, and of exaggeration after-ward from Reporter to Reporter, yet still all the doctrines remain bind-ing on thee? Still must thou repent, & be regenerated, and be crucified to the flesh, & this not by thy own mere being, but by a mysterious action of the Moral world on thee, of the ordo ordinans [ordering order]. Still will the Trinity, the Redemption, the assumption of Humanity by the Godhead remain Truth/& still will the Faith in these Truths be the living fountain of all true virtue, the seed like a mustard Seed, all the leaves, sprays, flowers, & trunks of true good being only the develope-ment of *that* form, & its combination with the real world, it the vital form, that its materiale? Believe all these so as thy Faith be not merely *real* but *actual*/Then shalt thou know from God whether or no Christ be of God—It is the importance and *essentiality* attributed to miracles that has tempted men to deny them!—They are extra-essential, tho' not use-less or superfluous.—

In reply to a query from a friend in 1807 he outlines his view of miracles.[11]

My whole & sincere opinion is this: that Miracles are a condition & necessary accompaniment of the Christian Religion; but not it's specific & characteristic Proof. They were not so even to the first eye-witnesses; they cannot be so to us. I believe the Miracles, because many other evidences have made me believe in Christ; & thus, no doubt, the faith in miracles does then react on it's cause, & fills up & confirms my faith in Christ.—

After the final issues of The Friend *he turns back to the question in more detail, remarking in notebook entries how important it seems to the position of Paley, Priestley and like-minded Christian apologists.*[12]

Quere. Have we any more right to expect that the Miracles worked by Christ on his Contemporaries should act on our minds with the same degree of evidence, than that our diseases should be cured by them/? Did the cure of the paralytic patient imply by antecedent proxy the cure of Palsy in perpetuum?—Can a wise man alter the essences of things? Must not ocular evidence with all its accompanying opportunities of examination, all its security from omissions & additions, be transferred to & identified with historical Testimony?—The instances of Pompey, or William the Conqueror are not cases in point/no one, who saw them, saw any thing strange/and what we do not wonder at when we see, we can find no reason to doubt when we hear—

The question exercises him again, probably as he prepares to meet the opinions of an unsophisticated listener for the Philosophical Lectures of 1819.[13]

You seem to me first to ask & crave for an impossible result, videlicet, that a conviction of the understanding should have the unfelt compulsion, the necessity combined with complacency, of an impression on the senses made under the conditions of experience—i.e. under such circumstances as permit no doubt of its Objectivity.—And secondly, I cannot but think, that you deceive yourself in supposing that the actual Beholding of any thing irreconcileable with all your former experience, such for instance, as a Butt of Water being changed by force of a few words uttered by a Man ten yards off into Port or Sherry Wine, would produce the same complacency & inward acquiescence in your

Thought & Feelings, that the change of Brandy, Rum, Lemon Juice, Sugar and Hot Water into Punch would do—A If we are to learn the definition of the term, Miracle, from the Bible—and not from Logic-choppers—we find no other than what the word itself means—namely, an act exciting wonder in those who saw & in those who recorded it—& for the life of me I cannot conceive more than two rational deductions from such an act, taken *singly*—tho' from a series of such wonder-exciting Acts, and Events there may arise a powerful argument from their harmony of the Series, & the confirmation that one might give to the others—as if, for instance, Isaiah had prophesied that 760 years after his time a Man should multiply a few Loaves & Fishes into food sufficient for 4000 Persons./ The argument from the harmony, however, does not apply to the Incidents, *as* Miracles, peculiarly—not the Links, but their making a *Chain*, is the Proof. But taking a single miracle, I say, I can see but two consequences—one, the exciting *attention* to the purpose for which the Miracle was worked, to the Person's Teachings & Declarations—and supposing these were found to merit the attention, then to justify an especial attention to that Person's assertions respecting the source & way by which he had acquired this power of producing effects beyond the power of other men . . .

In 1817 Coleridge registers a query concerning the refusal by certain contemporaries even to examine the growing evidence in favour of Animal Magnetism, and in the spring and summer of 1819 writes a note reinforcing his own recent, less sceptical views.[14]

Whence the contemptuous rejection of Animal Magnetism, before and without examination? How am I to account for this extraordinary Antipathy?—Had it been a discovery, of the same kind with that of the simple magnet, of electricity, above all, of the almost miraculous powers of transferring substances at indefinite distances belonging to Galvanism, then its apparent contradiction to all the Laws hitherto known, as those of Cohesion, Gravitation &c, might have justified it.—Or had it been like the discovery of Copernicus, then its broad blank contradiction to the apparent evidence of the Senses would make it at once intelligible to me, that men should refuse even to attend to the Question—and place it (as even so late as the Restoration of Ch. 2. Sir T. Brown did) among the proofs, that no absurdity can be so wild, but that some Philosopher or Sect of Philosophy will assert it:—A collection of the a priori verdicts passed by men of highest character, and pre-eminent in their generation, from the reign of Elizabeth to that of James the Second, against the Copernican—(and in France, Spain, and Italy to a much later period)—would be not merely entertaining but highly instructive. For who were those who ⟨built Cenotaphs⟩ and passed into a reverence of the prophets (as of Jeremiah &c) far too near Idolatry—the prophets, whom their Fore-Fathers had abused, ridiculed, and murdered? "WE" would not have done it! No!—but yet these very "WE" were the persons who bellowed out "crucify him! Crucify him! And loose unto us Barabbas" "Now Barabbas was a Murderer"!—But in the case of Animal Magnetism there is no question concerning a Theory—the whole and sole demand is, to examine with common honesty and inward veracity a series of Facts—and these again not as the evidence of the circumstances that accompanied the first promulgation of Christianity, mere *historical Facts*, the irrecoverable property and (as it were) the *fixtures* of the Past; but the reproducible Facts, facts as strictly analogous to those of Galvanism as the difference of the subjects ⟨and the continual changes of organic Life⟩ make possible. The only position asserted by Magnetists as Magnetists (and independent of all particular theory, or explanation) as is most evident from its being held in common without the least shade of variation in their facts & in those statements, of which their facts are mere generalization, (even as Gravitation in the first and purest sense of the word as solicitously determined by Sir I Newton, expressed as a general Term the aggregate of effects—namely, that all Bodies tend to their centers in the direct proportion of their relative masses) the only position, I say, asserted by all Magnetists as Magnetists is, that the will or (if you prefer it as even less theoric) the vis vitæ [vital power] of Man is not confined in its operations to the Organic Body, in which it appears to be seated; but under certain previously defined Conditions of distance and position, and above all of the relation to the Patient to the Agent, and of the Agent to the Patient, is capable of acting and producing certain pre-defined Effects on the human living Bodies external to it.—Thus the Gymnotus Electricus, and the two other Fishes, possess a power of acting on bodies at a distance. In them, it is true, the power is given to them merely for self-defence—and likewise an organic apparatus has been discovered—but these differences are no more than what might have been certainly and securely anticipated from universal analogy.—Every power which man has in common with the Insects, the Bees for instance, is subjected to his Will, and capable of voluntary application—the very faculty of continuing his Species in projective reproduction is in his instance only entrusted in great measure to his *Will*.—Again no man has yet discovered any organic apparatus for Thought, Passion, Volition—we have discovered the Instrument set in action by them but not the specific organs—but simply this, that in some way or other the whole nervous system is the organ.—What then is asked of any man? To believe? No! but merely to review the mass of evidence supplied by every variety of witness, from almost every part of Europe—and to show if you can some instances in the past experience of Mankind, of Evidence so concurrent from so many quarters under such very marked and even hostile differences of the attesters themselves, in respect of Country, Religion, Philosophic Sect, Rank, Talent, and even of personal Antipathies, in any thing afterwards proved to be false.—But even on this Ground no faith is demanded—nothing more than the admission that a position as analogous to many known facts of Animal Electricity and Galvanism as two series of facts can be, and so attested, should be put to the test of impartial examination. There is but one demand made—Viz. Try it yourself.—There are but three essential Conditions—the first, that the patient should labor under some disturbance of Health. Secondly, that the Agent should sincerely and humanely wish to relieve him, if it be in his power to do so—and lastly that he should to the utmost of his power fix his attention and devote his will to this one object.—The external manipulations (the necessity of which is not yet demonstrated; but the expedience of which as a means of facilitating the act of *attending* is undeniable; were it only on the same principle that men play with their buttons, watch-chain, or take snuff when they are desirous of attending earnestly to any one object) the external manipulation is far less complex than what is required in the ordinary medical administration of Electricity—.To place yourself face to face with the patient—to lay your left hand on his right shoulder, and your right hand on his left shoulder, to move your hands down his Arms to the tips of his fingers, then to hold his thumbs for a few moments, his right thumb between the thumb and forefinger or little finger of your left hand, and his left thumb in the same manner with your right Hand—And having repeated this process half a dozen times, then to draw your hand and Arm in a sweep from his head downwards—and if he complain of any local pain, to touch the part repeatedly—and at all events, to draw your hand either with the flat palm, or with the fingers' ends; from the Neck to the Abdomen, either by direct touch, or at a distance of one or two inches.—Doubtless, the manipulations vary with the case; and every magnetist is led by his own experience, one to prefer one plan, and one another, or to unite all at different times, such as alternating the sweep from the Head downwards by laying one hand on the person's brow and another on his navel—or breathing on the part affected, as in the Eye, in cases of Amaurosis, in the cure of which Animal Magnetism has been found particularly successful—or *flipping*, as it were, the flat of the thumbs with the forefinger at the part—or the placing the one hand on the correspondent region of the back, while the other is employed on the gastric or abdominal region. And during all this no other state of mind is required ~~that~~ than what you would think it your duty to produce in yourself, if you were trying over again an experiment (chemical) concerning which you entertained some doubts—as for instance, when Sir H. Davy repeated the experiments of Berzelius with regard to the metal of Barytes, or Mr. Brand Professor Clark's experiments on the fusions of stones, ⟨earth, and⟩ metals by Newman's Blow-pipe with the condensed Gasses—.

If it be said, that Mesmer was a Character who wanted to make his fortune by his Secret and that he did so—first of all, he fairly revealed his whole secret to those who bought it, and of the hundred Gentlemen, who paid him a hundred louis each, not *one* complained of having been deceived. Secondly do you not give Dr. James's powders? Was it the case with Vaccination in the first year of its Introduction—in Germany, and Italy? or are there none who *get money* by Medical Electricity and Galvanism? Besides, Mesmer and Mystery are now gone by forever—So far from any secret being made, the cases are published at present in all the respectable foreign Journals, medical and philosophical, as any other cases in medicine and physics.—Even the sturdy Leader of the *matter-of-fact* Experimentalists, Gilbert, has at length admitted the subject into his annals, and he himself *most reluctantly* has been obliged to concede the *facts*. Nearly two years have passed since the Prussian and Austrian Governments have demanded a report on the subject from the Physicians and Eminent Naturalists of Berlin and Vienna, and the report of the French Committee under Dr. Franklin has been subjected to a careful revision, and declared partial. And yet has there arisen one man, among all, who has detected falsehood or delusion! Not one—The Theory of Magnetic Fluids, the Vortices of Mesmer and the crude Materialists, have been attacked by the *Dynamic* Philosophers— the transcendent Visions of the Mystics & Spiritualists have been ridiculed by the Materialists—the followers of Puységur (the Marquis, who at his own expence has founded Magnetic Hospitals out of his princely fortune) declare against all Theory as premature, and press for a multiplication of experiments—and yet not one solitary instance of a denial of the *Facts*. Whence then comes this Incredulity? The English World are against it— . . .

If additional proof respecting the facts or real phænomena of Animal Magnetism were necessary, it might be found in the contrast between the Reports of the German Magnetisers and those of the French. Suppose the facts real and grounded *quovis modo* [in whatever way] in some general Law, but not yet brought into clear connection with our former experience, and the Attesters would feel, act and express themselves, just as the German Naturalists & Physicians do and have done.

Suppose them *subjective* accidents, & illusions, or intentional tricks, observed without caution and recorded without accuracy, and you have the natural Product in the Bibliothéque magnetisme animale, or Magazine by the Société du Magnetisme at Paris—first published I July 1814.—Yet the German Credulity and its honorable derivation from their own scrupulous Veracity (to which, however, we must add their rage for Theory and Prepossession in favor of whatever strange phænomena they think, that they have found out how to account for) are amusingly exemplified in Kieser's reflections on this Contrast. An English Physiologist with the same facts before him (ex. gr. that the most powerful Magnetizers in Germany out of a hundred sick Patients all females do not produce or expect more than one or two Somnambulists often after a month's manipulation, while according to the French Account a First Beginner makes 5 out of 6 healthy Persons of both sexes Somnambulists in the first attempt!!) would exclaim—What a nation of LIARS the French are! Only where immediate Detection is foreseen (as in Mathematics & Chemistry) can you rely on a word, they say!—Not so honest Kieser's *"most believing mind."* He takes both statements for granted: & gravely sets about a solution of the difference. . . .—If there were any ground for Kieser's speculation on the dependence of the *sorts and comparative excitability* of the magnetic State on national character, so that France being = 10, Germany is but = 1, I fear that old England will be −1 = + 0: i.e. not mere absence of sufficing evidence with its consequent Unbelief, but positive *Dis*belief.—

As to my own creed, I am more and more inclined to revert to my first notion, that the French Report under Dr Franklin was a glimpse of the truth, but such as might be expected from French Eyes filmed and gummy with French Sensualism/. Relying on the German Statements exclusively, and the special circumstance that it is always *der* Magnetiseur, and *die* Magnetesirte, I infer that the sexual relation excited by and thro' the Skin contains the *main* solution, if we do not forget to take in the properties of the Skin (among which I for the last 20 years have reckoned *Voli*tion) and the actions of the Nerves, as well as the re-actions of the whole & of all the parts, some parts more remarkably

& with a sort of specific Sympathy, as must needs be the case when so very important an organ as the Skin is aff- and inf-ected (contagium quasi in*generatio* [contagion that is almost in*generation*])—but then I hold that the very contrary of the French Reporter's Theory is the Fact— namely, that the Act of Magnetism is to *transmute* the infra-abdominal Appetite into pectoral Sentimental Fruition or Sensation. Opium will, in a less degree, produce the same effect on men of feminine Constitu- tion—Hence its temporary cures in women's hysterics—it dissolves the *uterifaction* or rather the tumultuous struggle of the whole nervous system to resist the despoinism of the Uterus—and diffusing calms it as by an equation./S. T. C. 16 April, 1819.

Whether Mesmer were the Discoverer of a New Power, standing in a similar ratio to Galvanism as Galvanism to common Electricity, or only on the surprizing both psychological and medical effects of cutaneous excite- ment or sedation, in either case the phænomena remain the same, and the cures unquestionable. Our Memory suffers no revolution: tho' our Hopes of the Future may be narrowed. On either supposition, therefore, Mesmer deserves that we should proceed to the examination both of his claims as a Physiologist and of his character and conduct, as a Man, without *pre- judice*—nay, I do not hesitate to add, with a prepossession in his favor.

Soon he is ready to consider the phenomenon in relation to the early records of the Church.[15]

And first, let it be understood that the solution of the Phænomena, and their true character, are not the points in question. Let them be effects or results of the Imagination—tho' here it may fairly be asked, what then <u>is</u> this Imagination capable of producing such effects, and in many instances without any consciousness of the operation ab extra on the part of the individual so acted on?—or let them be only indirect con- sequences of the outward Agency & the accidental Results of disorder in the functions of the Nervous System, of a metastasis, for instance, of it's <u>poles</u> or foci; or let them depend on a magnetic, electric or galvanic Fluid or Action modified and potenziated by Life and the living Organismus/ as the later Disciples of Mesmer suppose; or let them be referred to the immediate influence of an intense Volition extending the sphere of the Will beyond the outline of the Operator's own Body; or lastly, combin- ing the two latter, let us assume that the Will by a concentration of it's energies is capable of exciting, accumulating and directing some physical <u>Materia</u> or equivalent Activity of Matter, the possibility of which is proved by the Torpedo, Gymnotus Electricus, &c—these, I say, are not the ground of the Inquiry nor would the answer to these questions in any way concern or affect the argument. The only Questions are—Are the Phænomena and the accompanying Circumstances described and the Cases related in instance & illustration of the same, by Gmelin, Weinholt, Marquis Puységur, Kluge, Wolfart, Keyser, and many others; Italian, French, German, Swedish, Danish, Dutch and Swiss Physicians, and Naturalists—<u>Facts</u>? Are the numerous Historians of Zoo-magnetism, <u>all</u> of whom profess to relate as certain, such phænomena only as they have themselves seen and in the majority of instances, have themselves repeatedly produced,—are these, I say, together with the Committees appointed by the Austrian, Prussian, Hanoverian, and Saxon and Danish Governments the Reports of which are subscribed by the most splendid Names of Continental Europe—veracious Historians? or have they all, in so many different countries, & languages and religions, combined in giving publicity to a complex Lie—not only without, but against every conceivable motive?— —Now, I do not hesitate to affirm, that the denial or doubt of the actual truth of these Relations, viz. that such Phænomena have actually presented themselves under such Circumstances, is little less than <u>impossible</u>, by any honest and sober-minded Man, except from ignorance of the evidence. Even the French Commissioners, appointed by Louis the XVI in the first <u>Blaze & Blair</u> of Animal Magnetism, exposed to suspicion as it was by the Quackery and mysterious Jargon of Mesmer, notoriously unfair as their proceedings were, and violently prejudiced as the Inspectors—and tho' it was their avowed Object to explode the pretended Science and to heap contempt and Opprobrium on ~~the~~ supposed Discover,—did not, and could not, deny the <u>Facts</u>; but only endeavored to explain them on the principles of the then received physiological System.—Indeed the evidence is such and so overwhelming from the number, independence, and high character of the Attesters, (differing from that of common Electrical Chemistry only by the impossibility of commanding or ascertaining the requisite conditions in a living subject with the same regularity as when the Agent has inorganic substances to operate on) that the man who being perfect Master of the facts and documents should bring into comparison therewith the similar external and testimonial evidence of the extraordinary Cures and Phænomena of the First Century would be either deranged, or did not mean honestly by Religion. Even respecting the far more aweful and important Facts of the Gospel, the Miracles of our Lord himself, what more can a Believer be required to prove, than that the evidence is as great as it <u>ought to be</u>, and as great as it <u>can be</u>

without destroying or counteracting the very objects and purposes of
the Religion which the Miracles were worked to confirm?— —The next
Question is—What is the degree of resemblance between the facts of
Animal Magnetism, and the miraculous power exercised ~~by~~ in the
Apostolic Age, and confidently pretended to during the two first
Centuries of the Church/— —. If after due allowance made for the characteristic exaggeration of the early Fathers of the Church, and the want
of precision in all unscientific statements, the resemblance shall be
found such as in any other case would warrant a presumption of identity in kind—how is this to be explained?— —And if no satisfactory
explanation can be given, none, I mean, which at once accounts for the
Appearance, and disproves the reality, of their both being <u>ejusdem
generis</u> [of the same kind], in what manner & to what extent will the
evidence, the true, proper, and efficient Evidence, of the Truth in
Christ, as contained in the Gospel of John and the Epistles of Paul, or in
the Confessions of the Lutheran, and the Reformed Churches, be
endangered thereby?—Nay, <u>supposing</u> that such an Inquisition should
lead us to the discovery and establishment of a difference <u>in kind</u>
between the Miracles of Christ, and the extraordinary Gifts and Perform-
ances of the Primitive Church—would not the Cause of Christianity be
benefited rather than injured thereby?—Believing that this might be
shewn without detriment ~~even~~ to the character of the Primitive Christians, and so as to confirm rather than invalidate the report of their
Sanctity & singleness of heart, I have little hesitation in answering this
question in the Affirmative.—

Later, however, after nine years' study, he has to confess himself still baffled.[16]

Were I asked, what *I* think—my answer would be—that the evidence
enforces Scepticism and a Non liquet. Too strong & consentaneous for
a candid mind to be satisfied of its falsehood, or its solvibility in the
supposition of Imposture or casual Co-incidence;—too fugacious and
unfixible to support any Theory that supposes the always potential &
under certain conditions & circumstances occasionally actual existence of a correspondent faculty in the human Soul. And nothing less
than such an hypothesis would be adequate to the *satisfactory*
explanation of the Facts—tho' that of a metastasis of specific functions of the nervous energy taken in conjunction with extreme nervous excitement, +some delusion, +some illusion, +some imposition,
+(plus) some chance & accidental coincidence, might determine the

direction, in which the Scepticism vibrated. Nine years has the subject of Zoo-magnetism been before me—I have traced it historically— collected a Mass of documents in French, German, Italian, & the Latinists of the 16th century—have never neglected an opportunity of questioning Eye witnesses, (ex. Gr. Tieck, Treviranus, De Prati, Meyer, and others of literary or medical celebrity) and I remain where I was, & where the first perusal of Klug's work had left me, without having advanced an inch backward or forward. Treviranus the famous Botan-ist's reply to me, when he was in London, is worth recording. . . . I have seen what I am certain I would not have believed on *your* telling; and in all reason therefore I can neither expect nor wish that you should believe on mine.

Writing to Lord Liverpool in 1817, meanwhile, he has argued against a mech-anical view of the universe.[17]

What indeed but the wages of Death can be expected from a Doctrine which degrades the Deity into a blank Hypothesis, and that the Hypo-thesis of a clock-work-maker—say rather, the Hypopoiesis or suffection, fairly open to Darwin's sarcasm—the 15th part of the atmosphere per-ishes we know not how—therefore, there is a Green Dragon at the north-pole—a Godless Nature and a Natureless abstract God, now an extramundane homo magus, from whom the world *had* its being, the Allah of Mahometan Mono-idolism, and now the Sunday, or red-letter name of Gravitation, wherever the Pater-omnipotens Æther is not employ'd instead. One good thing, however, we owe to this Æther—it detects the hollowness of the usual excuse of the Doctors of the corpus-cular system that their attraction & repulsion are but fictions in a Memoria Technica, meant to connect, not explain, the phaenomena of which they are the generic exponents. With the truly great Kepler's Centripetal and Centrifugal agencies this is really the case—the terms simply generalize the facts—But the very terms substituted and chosen instead imply causative agency: and I will hazard an assertion, that there is not a single chapter in the works of any modern Theorist, a dis-ciple of Locke, Hartley, & Condillac, that will not be found to contain positions utterly subversive of this pretence. If any thing could have recalled the Physics & Physiology of the age to the Dynamic Theory of the eldest Philosophy, it must have been the late successful researches of the Chemists, which almost force on the very senses the facts of mutual penetration & intus-susception which have supplied a series of experimental proofs, that in all pure phaenomena we behold only the copula, the balance or indifference of opposite energies. The recent relapse therefore of the Chemists to the atomistic scheme, and the almost unanimous acceptance of Dalton's Theory in England, & Le Sage's in France, determine the intellectual character of the age with the force of an experimentum crucis [a crucial experiment].

I reverence the sublime & prosperous application of the higher Geometry to the investigation of the world, as far as the nature of Masses is revealed by Quantity, and thus, as it were, self-submitted to the processes of scientific calculus. But let it not be forgotten, that this is a scyon, the one healthy & prosperous graft from the Platonic tree! I appreciate at their full value the useful inventions and brilliant discoveries of modern chemistry, from Stahl to Davy; but I dare not overlook that they were made during the *suspension* of the mechanic Philosophy relatively to chemical Theory, and I know, that since the year 1798 every experiment of importance had been distinctly pre-announced by the founders or restorers of the constructive or dynamic philosophy, in the only country where a man can exercise his understanding in the light of his *reason*, without being supposed to be *out of his senses*. And I persist in the belief . . . that a few brilliant discoveries have been dearly purchased at the loss of all communion with life and the spirit of Nature.

Most significantly, my Lord, did the ancients name the object of Physiology the Genesis, the φύσις, the natura rerum—i.e. the birth of things. They searched after, and recorded the *acts* of the world: and the self-subsistence, yet interdependence, the difference yet Identity of the forms they express'd by the symbol of begetting. With the Moderns, on the contrary, nothing grows; all is made—

Aware of contemporary theories that human beings descended from the apes he wrote to Wordsworth in his 1815 letter concerning The Excursion *that he had hoped to find among its achievements a spirited attack on the idea (as fostered by Charles Darwin's grandfather Erasmus).*[18]

Next, I understood that you would take the Human Race in the concrete, have exploded the absurd notion of Pope's Essay on Man, Darwin and all the countless Believers—even (strange to say) among Christians of Man's having progressed from an Orang Outang state—so contrary to all History, to all Religion, nay, to all Possibility . . .

In his Philosophical Lectures he comments again on the opinion that the human race 'gradually from a monkey came up through various states to be man'.[19]

Which reminds one of the French lady who hearing a story that a dead man had walked a league with his head under his arm, somebody exclaimed, "What! A league!" with surprise. "Aye!", said the lady, "the first step was the thing". If, however, man began to exist in the infancy of his race, he must like every other animal have been protected by an instinct; but as he was protected by an instinct, so surely, must it have been a human and intellectual instinct, and that this might have existed in imperfect degrees and will go on even to its last decay appears to me, I confess, not at all extravagant.

He takes up the point again in 1821, defending the biblical version of events.[20]

And here, once for all, I beg leave to remark that I attach neither belief nor respect to the Theory, which supposes the human race to have been gradually perfecting itself from the darkest Savagery, or still more boldly tracing us back to the bestial as to our Larva, contemplates the Man as the last metamorphosis, the gay *Imago* of some lucky species of Ape or Baboon. . . . The History, I find in my ~~Being~~ible, is in perfect coincidence with the opinion, which I should form on grounds of Experience and Common Sense—. But our belief, that Man first appeared with all his faculties perfect & in full growth, by virtue of the anticipation exercised in the supernatural Act of Creation, in no wise contravenes or weakens the assertion, that these faculties, maturely considered, presupposed and in each successive Individual born according to nature must be preceded by a process of growth, and consequently a state of involution or latency correspondent to each successive Moment of Development . . .

In spite of rejecting the idea that human beings actually evolved from animal ancestors, however, he is equally anxious to argue for the development towards human characteristics in the lower orders of nature. He attempts, for example, to portray the natural development of the caterpillar to the butterfly as an analogue of the human advance from the discursive powers of the mind to the illuminated Reason.[21]

In the Aurelian Metamorphosis the Head of the canker (caterpillar) becomes the Tail of the Butterfly/—The discursive Intellect in man sub-ordinated to the Intuitive/—

In a corresponding longer note, he attempts to show the process in history by which the human race has moved towards the present establishing of the infinite by developing a deeper internal psychology.[22]

To shew the best means of leading the mind to Science, that is, to its true Object there are two ways—the one strictly scientific, and therefore requiring a degree of attention not to be expected in a numerous Audience, and a frequent recurrence to precedent proofs, in aid of the memory, which is not possible except in private/this is, the proof from an analysis of the human mind in itself, in its component forms and faculties—. the other, not less efficacious, and more suited to the pres-ent occasion, is from History. What *has been* ~~the~~ Ladder, what have been the various Rounds by which what may be called the continuously successive portions of the Human Race, have ascended to the present Height. From this we may abstract perhaps, and certainly in this we may exemplify, the principles, by which we may arrive at our desired end—namely, that of preparing the mind of the Individual for the acquirement of Truth, and in that of course, for the Progress of Know-ledge in general, as effected by the efforts of Individuals.—If, I thought, I can point out how it pleased Providence to educate the earliest period of the Human Race, then its Youth, and lastly if not its Manhood yet the preparation for its Manhood, I shall derive a lesson applicable to particular states and even to Individuals—for as the Instincts, by which Providence works, so are the correspondent Objects and Results—The Butterfly is not led in vain for a purpose unknown to itself & un-connected with any existing desire or want, to lay its eggs on the par-ticular Sort of Leaf that is fitted to sustain the Caterpillar—and is it in Man, the sole magnificent Temple in the world of visible Existence, and is it in the Holy of Holies of this Temple, that is, in the moral & rational part of Humanity, that Nature tells her first and only Lie?—Impossible.

Therefore I attempted to represent the periods of the human Race hitherto, as a Line with two opposite Poles—the patriarchal Period, best represented and longest preserved in the Hebrew nation as the primary or mid point from which both were produced, the Greeks as the Ideal Pole, and the Romans as the Real—and I observed that the synthesis or Union of Both was in Christendom.—From this point therefore I now take up the Disquisition—It is but a simile, and no Simile is expected to be compleat in all points—Else it would not be a Simile, but an Instance—I have said, that the Greeks succeeded just so far & no further, than as they acted upon the stores which the mind found within itself, awakened indeed by excitement from external objects, but not afforded by them/and instanced it, in Poetry, the other Fine Others, pure Mathematics, and Universal Logic—and that the Romans, adding nothing to these, yet were the instruments of realizing, of fixing them, and of preparing a soil properly cleared and fenced for their after growth & ramification by War, Empire, and Law—I have now to add, that the first influences that followed this period, were to neutralize.— The World during the existence of the Roman Empire presents at large (not in Individuals: for as is always the case in periods of preparation, these were many & most illustrious—but in the World at large) a state in which Christianity was still held in check, & incapable of shewing itself in its full influences upon Society by Paganism, and Paganism reduced to a Caput Mortuum by Christianity. This I should characterize as our fourth point—that of Indifference/At length, in the destruction of the Roman Empire the intermedium was furnished, in the stern and austere habits, and more indefinite and imaginative Superstitions of the Gothic Nations—and the fifth Point, or Period, that of the Union of the Ideal and Real by combination, in which each power acts but in harmony with the other, began—and in an advanced part of this period we ourselves are now living—

Thus we have accompanied the Race first through its boyhood, then thro' its Youth, and lastly in the preparation of making the practical use of its acquirements/—Palestine, Greece, and Rome (*observe* here as to smallness of the 2 former & of 3 orig.) But as between our quitting the universities, and final Establishment there intervenes a period of Travel and Excursions, or what is called the Grand Tour; even so with the Human Race—Travels almost guideless into the world within us, and into the external World—A Great Revolution had taken place—consisting chiefly in this—that in the elder world the Infinite was hidden in the Finite— Every Stream had its Naiad—the Earth its Cybele, the Ocean its Neptune/ the upper Air was Jupiter, the lower Juno—Fire was Vesta, as the fixive, preservative Power—and the artificial technical Fire Neptune—all was reduced to the Finite—The Ages, we call the Dark, were the counterpart—

Lord Bacon—his true Principles—he had to attack Schoolmen—and Alchemists—but as the former were the most to be feared against those he chiefly directed his attacks—hence aided by Commerce his Philosophy has been perhaps injurious by being but half understood/

Questions of Identity.[23]

If it were asked of me to justify the interest, which many good minds—what if I speak out, and say what I believe to be the truth—which the majority of the best and noblest minds feel in the great questions—Where am I? What and for what am I? What are the duties, which arise out of the relations of my Being to itself as heir of futurity, and to the World which is its present sphere of action and impression?—I would compare the human Soul to a Ship's Crew cast on an unknown Island (a fair Simile: for these questions could not suggest themselves unless the mind had previously felt convictions, that the present World was not its whole destiny and abiding Country)—What would be their first business? Surely, to enquire what the Island was? in what Latitude? what ships visited that Island? when? and whither they went?—and what chance that they should take off first one, & then another?—and after this—to think, how they should maintain & employ themselves during their stay— & how best stock themselves for the expected voyage, & procure the means of inducing the Captain to take them to the Harbour, which they wished to go to?—

The moment, when the Soul begins to be sufficiently self-conscious, to ask concerning itself, & its relations, is the first moment of its *intellectual* arrival into the World—Its *Being*—enigmatic as it must seem—is posterior to its *Existence*—. Suppose the shipwrecked man stunned, & for many weeks in a state of Ideotcy or utter loss of Thought & Memory—& then gradually awakened/

The uniqueness of man by comparison with the animal kingdom.[24]

Instinct = continuous Impressions producing *memory* on the organs made susceptible thereof by the vital Principle—Man has a *portion* of this, perhaps, equal to that of any other animal; but he has likewise evidently another Substratum or Repository of Impressions, the mind—& this so overdazzles the other, that we call it by impropriation the Memory—An argument hence for the immortality of Man versus beast. For that seems ever to me the main point—not to prove the imperishability of Life, which is a mathematical *Idea*, but of man's individuality—arguments that apply to man & man only. The procession of animal Life is a grand and cheerful Theory; but furnishes no moral bond.

Later, to Tulk he expounds this philosophy further, dwelling on the necessarily intuitive element involved:[25]

. . . the inclosed Scrawl contains a very, *very* rude and fragmentary delineation of the *Objective* Pole, or the Science of the Construction of *Nature*.—I first assume God, not as Ὁ Θεός sensu eminenti [God in an eminent sense] but as the τὸ Θεῖον [God] or the Absolute, as the Identity or *Pro*thesis of Unity and Omnëity. This is the Plenum, the Position, the *Est* of Nature: abstracted from which all forms are either mere *logical Entities*, or mere Umbrae apparentiae [shadows of appearance], i.e. either mere νούμενα ['noumena'] or mere φαινόμενα ['phaenomena']. Without *this* (the Ens ideale, et idcirco realissimum, and the Ens realissimum, et idcirco ideale [ideal Being, and what is most real around it, and the most real Being, and what is ideal around it], the identity of the Self-affirmant and the Self-affirmed) we launch into a vain metaphysical Vacuum; but with this, as a perpetual *Subintelligitur*, we may profitably avail ourselves of the Relations or polarities, as so many organs of thought, as so many intellectual *Senses*. But it is the Intuition, the direct Beholding, the immediate Knowlege, which is the *substance* and true *significance* of all—But to *give* or to *convey* to another the *Immediate* is a contradiction in terms—all that a Teacher can do is, 1. to demonstrate the hollowness and falsehood of the Corpuscular Theory and of every other scheme of Philosophy which commences with matter as a jam datum [given], or under any disguise substitutes the Lockian, and Newtonian—From God we *had* our Being—for the Pauline—*In* whom we move and live and *have* our Being. The moderns take the Ὁ θεός [god], as an hypothetical Watchmaker, and degrade the τὸ θεῖον [divine] into a piece of Clock-Work— they live without God in the world. The ancients are (at least some of them) chargeable with the contrary extreme—they take [the τὸ θεῖον to the omission of the ὁ Θεός [God], and make the world the] total God. True Philosophy begins with the τὸ θεῖον in order to end in the Ὁ Θεός; takes it's root in Science in order to blossom into Religion. All false Systems may be reduced into these two genera—instead of the κόσμος ἐν Θεῷ [cosmos in God] the former assumes a θεὸς ἔξω τοῦ κόσμου [god outside the cosmos] the latter a θεὸς ἐν κόσμῳ [god in cosmos]. In the one the World *limits* God, in the other it *comprehends* him. Now the *falsehood* of both may be *taught*, both directly by subversion of the premises, and indirectly by the absurdity, and immoral *un*human nature, of the inevitable consequences. But the *Truth* of the Contrary must be *seen*—we must *be* it in order to *know* it.—2. to excite the mind to the effort, and to encourage it by sympathy—. Suppose a world of blind men with a few scattered exceptions. How gladly would each of these meet another, as a confirmation that he did indeed *see*—a confirmation to the feelings at least. . . . For it is not of a dead machine that I speak; but I am endeavoring to trace the Genesis, the φύσις [nature], the *Natura* rerum, the *Birth* of Things: and this under the disadvantage of beginning (as far as the mere *science* is concerned) with the lowest, per ascensum: whereas the only true point of view is that of Religion, namely, per descensum.—Observe too, that the two great poles of manifestation are Continuity (Lex Continui [Law of the Continuous]) and Individuation—the latter being the final cause of nature, or her object, from the Coral which is almost confounded with Nature to the Man of Genius and *genial* Goodness, the maximum of Individuation in the present Life; yet so as that the whole process is cyclical tho' progressive, and the Man separates from Nature only that Nature may be found again in a higher dignity in the Man. For as the Ideal is realized in Nature, so is the Real idealized in man.

He moves on to consider the role of God in the Creation and how His nature means that He does not initiate it in time.[26]

All that exists has a beginning—and God, whose essence is the *ground* of all things, is by his Will, thro' the *utterance* of his Will (= the Word, Λόγος) the Beginner of their *existence*; i.e. God *createth* all things. He not only *formeth* them, i.e. establisheth their relativity and correspondent relations, but he likewise *groundeth* them—*in* him they have their *Being*, *from* him they receive their *existence*. God is not merely the Cause of the Universe, for that would be atheism, in which the Mens or Noῦς would be a part of the Universe, viz. the first Link of the Chain. Thus instead of a *Cosmo*gony we should have a *Theo*gony, and the philosophic, or rather philopseudic, Monster of a Θεὸς ἐσόμενος [future God] ('there is none yet, but when the World is compleatly organized, there *will be* a God') would cease to be absolutely *absurd*. . . . —The Text cannot refer to any particular Time any more than to any particular Space: for it speaks of the Act which gave birth to Time and Space.

He concludes a long account of the resultant philosophy by claiming that his adoption of it preceded the work of Germans such as Schelling—whom he welcomes as an ally. Such a thinker may, as in his early allegory, be thought of as the only sane person in a world of madmen.[27]

Accept this very rude sketch of the very rudiments of *'Heraclitus redi-vivus'* [Heraclitus renewed]—One little presumption of their truth is, that as Wordsworth, Southey, and indeed all my intelligent Friends well know & attest, I had formed it during the study of Plato, and the Scholars of Ammonius, and in later times of Scotus (Joan. Erigena), Giordano Bruno, Behmen, and the much calumniated Spinoza (whose System is to mine just what a Skeleton is to a Body, fearful because it is only the *Skeleton*) long before Schelling had published his first and imperfect view—. If I had met a friend & a Brother in the Desart of Arabia, I could scarcely have been more delighted than I was in finding a fellow-laborer and in the only Country in which a man dare exercise his *reason* with-out being thought to have lost his Wits, & be out *of his Senses*.

8
Original Sin and the True Reason

The spiritual crisis which resulted in Coleridge's turning back resolutely to Anglicanism after his alienation from Wordsworth has already been mentioned more than once. His new attitude was recorded with pleasure by Hannah More, who wrote to Wilberforce in April 1814 about a visit she had just received from him, displaying 'great reverence for Evangelical religion and considerable acquaintance with it'. He had also shown her a letter from Dr Estlin, forbidding him his house on account of his remarks concerning Socinianism during his Bristol lecture; she had further learned from him of the reform of Alfred Elwyn, who had lent him the work of Archbishop Leighton, his favourite author.[1]

This loan, which had, she said, led to his sitting up to four in the morning reading it, was also recorded in his marginal notes to the volume, where he 'blessed the Hour' that had introduced him to Leighton's works and expressed admiration for the quality of mind and spirituality they displayed—together with remorse for the tyranny of the opium habit over him, coupled with cries for mercy and a rueful identification of his initials as those of a 'Sinful, Tormented Culprit'.[2] Later readings and annotations of Leighton contributed to his religious thinking as he thought about the immediate problems of the age. During this time he was moving towards the construction of a great work to justify all his reading and speculation of the previous period, which would, he knew, call for presentation on a grand scale; but in view of the pressing problems of the time he also felt that some immediate and timely commentary was called for while the larger work was in gestation.

His first impulse was to call on the work that had been of such service to him during his own period of crisis. The writing of Leighton, as we have seen, had spoken to him with an extraordinary directness, reminding him of truths he felt he had been in danger of forgetting. He had

154

enjoyed a refreshment like that which T.S. Eliot, over a century later, was to receive from the writings of Lancelot Andrews—the experience, that is, of a simple writing that seemed to convey, in a manner not available from the sinuous and contorted logic of other Renaissance writers, a direct sense of the beauty of holiness.

The work he originally planned would have been called, adapting a contemporary literary fashion to religious uses, 'The Beauties of Leighton'; his first hope was evidently that his contemporary readers, if properly guided, would need only to be exposed to specimens of Leighton's work to have an experience of enlightenment similar to his own. As he began work on the project, however, his own habits of analysis and organization came to the fore, and he began to consider how to deal with the separate divisions he had projected. Once he came to the 'Spiritual' section the need for commentary of his own took over—indeed, he made two separate starts on it, his comments becoming longer and longer until they became a near substitute for the 'Assertion of Religion' he was planning as a part at least of his 'Opus Maximum'. In the passages extracted for the present section he gave considered versions of two of his favorite themes: the need for redemption, with his own interpretation of the term 'original sin', and a distinguishing of the difference between Reason and Understanding.

The existence of sin and the need for a redeemer he took to be incontestable facts—though at the same time he found orthodox accounts and explanations deficient in important respects. These included a central discussion by Jeremy Taylor which he thought suggested a lack of common justice on the part of the punishing divinity. In attempting an adequate account of his own he was forced to fall back on the conception of human evil as mysterious, a problem to be resolved only by way of another mystery, that of faith, which in turn rested on yet another, that of Reason, the God-given endowment of human beings. This was to be distinguished from the Understanding, a power which humans shared with the animal and even the vegetable creation. It was this Reason alone that could respond intuitively to the divine Grace and Truth—which in turn were marks of the divine redemption.

Coleridge now brings all his learning together in an attempt to show how Reason, properly invoked, may solve the problem of Original Sin.[1]

The most *momentous* question a man can ask is, Have I a Saviour? And yet as far as the individual Querist is concerned, it is premature and to no purpose, except another question has been previously put and answered, (alas! too generally put after the wounded Conscience has already given the answer!) *viz.*, Have I any need of a Saviour? For him who *needs* none, (O bitter irony of the evil Spirit, whose whispers the proud Soul takes for its own thoughts, and knows not how the Tempter is scoffing the while!) there *is* none, as long as he feels no need. On the other hand, it is scarce possible to have answered this question in the affirmative, and not ask—first, *in what* the necessity consists? secondly, *whence* it proceeded? and, thirdly, how far the answer to this second question is or is not contained in the answer to the first? I intreat the intelligent Reader, who has taken me as his temporary guide on the straight, but yet, from the number of cross roads, difficult way of religious Inquiry, to halt a moment, and consider the main points, that in this last division of our work have been already offered for his reflection. I have attempted then to fix the proper meaning of the words, Nature and Spirit, the one being the *antithesis* to the other: so that the most general and *negative* definition of Nature is, Whatever is not Spirit; and *vice versâ* of Spirit, That which is not comprehended in Nature: or in the language of our elder Divines, that which transcends Nature. But Nature is the term in which we comprehend all things that are representable in the forms of Time and Space, and subjected to the Relations of Cause and Effect: and the cause of the existence of which, therefore, is to be sought for perpetually in something Antecedent. The word itself expresses this in the strongest manner possible: Natura, that which is *about to be* born, that which is always *becoming*. It follows, therefore, that whatever originates its own acts, or in any sense contains in itself the cause of its own state, must be *spiritual*, and consequently *supernatural*: yet not on that account necessarily *miraculous*. And such must the responsible WILL in us be, if it be at all.

A prior step had been to remove all misconceptions from the subject; to show the reasonableness of a belief in the reality and real influence of a universal and divine Spirit; the compatibility and possible communion of such a Spirit with the Spiritual in Principle; and the analogy offered by the most undeniable truths of Natural Philosophy.*

These Views of the Spirit, and of the Will as Spiritual, form the groundwork of our Scheme. Both Reason and Experience have convinced me,

---

* It has in its consequences proved no trifling evil to the Christian World, that Aristotle's Definitions of Nature are all grounded on the petty and rather rhetorical than philosophical Antithesis of Nature to Art—a conception inadequate to the demands even of *his* Philosophy. Hence in the progress of his reasoning, he

that in the greater number of our ALOGI, who feed on the husks of Christianity, the disbelief of the Trinity, the Divinity of Christ included, has its origin and support in the assumed self-evidence of Natural Theology, and in their ignorance of the insurmountable difficulties which (on the same mode of reasoning) press upon the fundamental articles of their own Remnant of a Creed. But arguments, which would prove the falsehood of a known truth, must themselves be false, and can prove the falsehood of no other position in eodem genere [that kind].

This *hint* I have thrown out as a *Spark* that may perhaps fall where it will kindle.... And worthily might the wisest of men make inquisition into the three momentous points here spoken of, for the purposes of speculative Insight, and for the formation of enlarged and systematic views of the destination of Man, and the dispensation of God. But the *practical* Inquirer (I speak not of those who inquire for the gratification of Curiosity, and still less of those who labor as students only to shine as disputants; but of one, who seeks the truth, because he feels the want of it,) the practical Inquirer, I say, hath already placed his foot on the rock, if he have satisfied himself that whoever needs not a Redeemer is more than human. Remove for him the difficulties and objections, that oppose or perplex his belief of a crucified Saviour; convince him of the reality of Sin, which is impossible without a knowledge of its true nature and inevitable Consequences; and then satisfy him as to the *fact* historically, and as to the truth spiritually, of a redemption therefrom by Christ; do this for him, and there is little fear that he will permit either logical quirks or metaphysical puzzles to contravene the plain dictate of his Common Sense, that the Sinless One that redeemed Mankind from Sin, must have been more than Man; and that He who brought Light and Immortality into the World, could not in his own nature have been an inheritor of Death and Darkness. It is morally impossible, that a man with these convictions should suffer the Objection of Incomprehensibility (and this on a subject of *Faith*) to overbalance the manifest absurdity and contradiction

---

confounds the Natura *Naturata* (that is, the sum total of the Facts and Phaenomena of the Senses) with an hypothetical Natura *Naturans*, a *Goddess* Nature, that has no better claim to a place in any sober system of Natural Philosophy than the Goddess *Multitudo*; yet to which Aristotle not rarely gives the name and attributes of the Supreme Being. The result was, that the Idea of God thus identified with this hypothetical *Nature* becomes itself but an *Hypothesis*, or at best but a precarious inference from incommensurate premisses and on disputable Principles: while in other passages, God is confounded with (and every where, in Aristotle's *genuine* works, *included in*) the Universe: which most grievous error it is the great and characteristic Merit of Plato to have avoided and denounced.

in the notion of a Mediator between God and the Human Race, at the same infinite distance from God as the Race for whom he mediates.

The Origin of Evil, meanwhile, is a question interesting only to the Metaphysician, and in a *system* of moral and religious Philosophy. The Man of sober mind, who seeks for truths that possess a moral and practical interest, is content to be *certain*, first, that Evil must have had a beginning, since otherwise it must either be God, or a co-eternal and co-equal Rival of God; both impious notions, and the latter foolish to boot. 2dly, That it could not originate in God; for if so, it would be at once Evil and not Evil, or God would be at once God (that is, infinite Goodness) and not God—both alike impossible positions. Instead therefore of troubling himself with this barren controversy, he more profitably turns his inquiries to *that* Evil which most concerns himself, and of which he *may* find the origin.

The entire Scheme of *necessary* Faith may be reduced to two heads, 1. the Object and Occasion, and 2. the Fact and Effect, of our redemption by Christ: and to this view does the order of the following Comments correspond. I have begun with ORIGINAL SIN, and proceeded in the following Aphorism to the doctrine of Redemption. The Comments on the remaining Aphorisms are all subsidiary to these, or written in the hope of making the minor tenets of general belief be believed in a spirit worthy of these. They are, in short, intended to supply a febrifuge against aguish Scruples and Horrors, the hectic of the Soul! and "for servile and thrall-like fear to substitute that adoptive and chearful boldness, which our new alliance with God requires of us as Christians." (*Milton*). NOT the Origin of Evil, NOT the *Chronology* of Sin, or the chronicles of the original Sinner; but Sin originant, underived from without, and no passive link in the adamantine chain of Effects, each of which is in its turn an *instrument* of Causation, but no one of them a Cause! NOT with Sin *inflicted*, which would be a Calamity! NOT with Sin (*i.e.* an evil tendency) *implanted*, for which let the Planter be responsible! But I begin with *Original* Sin. And for this purpose I have selected the Aphorism from the ablest and most formidable Antagonist of this Doctrine, Bishop JEREMY TAYLOR, and from the most eloquent work of this most eloquent of Divines. Had I said, of Men, Cicero would forgive me, and Demosthenes nod assent!

ON ORIGINAL SIN[2]

Is there any such Thing? That is not the question. For it is a fact acknowledged on all hands almost: and even those who will not confess it in words, confess it in their complaints. For my part I cannot but confess that *to be*, which I feel and groan under, and by which all the world is miserable.

Adam turned his back on the Sun, and dwelt in the Dark and the Shadow. He sinned, and brought evil into his *Supernatural* endowments, and lost the Sacrament and instrument of Immortality, the Tree of Life in the centre of the Garden. He then fell under the evils of a sickly Body, and a passionate and ignorant Soul. His Sin made him sickly, his Sickness made him peevish: his Sin left him ignorant, his Ignorance made him foolish and unreasonable. His sin left him to his *Nature*: and by Nature, whoever was to be born at all, was to be born a child, and to do before he could understand, and to be bred under laws to which he was always bound, but which could not always be exacted; and he was to choose when he could not reason, and had passions most strong when he had his understanding most weak; and the more need he had of a curb, the less strength he had to use it! And this being the case of all the world, what was *every* man's evil became *all* men's greater evil; and though alone it was very bad, yet when they came together it was made much worse. Like ships in a storm, every one alone hath enough to do to outride it; but when they meet, besides the evils of the Storm, they find the intolerable calamity of their mutual concussion; and every Ship that is ready to be oppressed with the tempest, is a worse Tempest to every Vessel against which it is violently dashed. So it is in Mankind. Every man hath evil enough of his own, and it is hard for a man to live up to the rule of his own Reason and Conscience. But when he hath Parents and Children, Friends and Enemies, Buyers and Sellers, Lawyers and Clients, a Family and a Neighbourhood—then it is that every man dashes against another, and one relation requires what another denies; and when one speaks another will contradict him; and that which is well spoken is sometimes innocently mistaken; and that upon a good cause produces an evil effect; and by these, and ten thousand other concurrent causes, man is made more than most miserable.

COMMENT

The first question we should put to ourselves, when we have to read a passage that perplexes us in a work of authority, is; What does the Writer *mean* by all this? And the second question should be, What does he intend by all this? In the passage before us, Taylor's *meaning* is not quite clear. A Sin is an Evil which has its ground or origin in the Agent, and not in the compulsion of Circumstances. Circumstances are compulsory from the absence of a power to resist or control them: and if this absence likewise be the effect of Circumstance (*i.e.* if it have been neither directly nor indirectly caused by the Agent himself) the Evil *derives* from the Circumstances; and therefore (in the Apostle's sense of the word, Sin, when he speaks of the exceeding sinfulness of Sin) such *evil* is not *sin*; and the person who suffers it, or who is the compelled instrument of its infliction on others, may feel *regret*, but cannot feel *remorse*. So likewise of the word origin, original, or originant. The reader cannot too early be warned that it is not applicable, and, without abuse of language, can never be applied, to a mere *link* in a chain of effects, where each, indeed, stands in the relation of a *cause* to those that follow, but is at the same time the *effect* of all that precede. For in these cases a cause amounts to little more than an antecedent. At the utmost it means only a *conductor* of the causative influence: and the old axiom, Causa causae causa causati [The cause of a cause is the cause of what is caused], applies, with a never-ending regress to each several link, up the whole chain of nature. But this (as I have elsewhere shown at large) *is* Nature: and no *Natural* thing or act can be called originant, or be truly said to have an *origin* in any other. The moment we assume an Origin in Nature, a true *Beginning*, an actual First—that moment we rise *above* Nature, and are compelled to assume a *supernatural* Power. (Gen. i. 1.)

It will be an equal convenience to myself and to my Readers, to let it be agreed between us, that we will generalize the word Circumstance so as to understand by it, as often as it occurs in this Comment, all and every thing not connected with the Will, past or present, of a Free Agent. Even though it were the blood in the chambers of his Heart, or his own inmost Sensations, we will regard them as *circumstantial*, *extrinsic*, or *from without*.

In this sense of the word Original, and in the sense before given of Sin, it is evident that the phrase, Original Sin, is a Pleonasm, the epithet not adding to the thought, but only enforcing it. For if it be Sin, it must be *original*: and a State or Act, that has not its origin in the will, may be calamity, deformity, disease, or mischief; but a *Sin* it cannot be. It is not enough that the Act appears voluntary, or that it is intentional; or that it has the most hateful passions or debasing appetite for its proximate cause and accompaniment. All these may be found in a Mad-house, where neither Law nor Humanity permit us to condemn the Actor of Sin. The Reason of Law declares the Maniac not a Free-Agent; and the Verdict follows of course—Not guilty. Now Mania, as distinguished from Idiocy, Frenzy, Delirium, Hypochondria, and Derangement (the last term used specifically to express a suspension or disordered state of the Understanding or Adaptive Power) is the Occultation or Eclipse of Reason, as the Power of ultimate ends. The Maniac, it is well known, is often found clever and inventive in the selection and adaptation of means to *his* ends; but his *ends* are madness. He has lost his Reason. For though Reason, in finite Beings, is not the Will—or how could the Will be opposed to the Reason?—yet it is the *condition*, the *sine qua non* of a *Free*-will.

We will now return to the Extract from Jeremy Taylor on a theme of deep interest in itself, and trebly important from its *bearings*. For without just and distinct views respecting the Article of Original Sin, it is impossible to understand aright any one of the peculiar doctrines of Christianity. Now my first complaint is, that the eloquent Bishop, while he admits the *fact* as established beyond controversy by universal experience, yet leaves us wholly in the dark as to the main point, supplies us with no answer to the principal question—why he names it Original Sin? It cannot be said, We know what the Bishop *means*, and what matters the name? for the *nature* of the fact, and in what light it should be regarded by us, depends on the nature of our answer to the question, whether Original Sin is or is not the right and proper designation. I can imagine the same quantum of *Sufferings*, and yet if I had reason to regard them as symptoms of a commencing Change, as pains of growth, the temporary deformity and misproportions of immaturity, or (as in the final sloughing of the Caterpillar) as throes and struggles of the waxing or evolving Psyche, I should think it no stoical flight to doubt, how far I was authorised to declare the Circumstance an *Evil* at all. Most assuredly I would not express or describe the fact as an evil having an origin in the Sufferers themselves, or as Sin.

Let us, however, wa[i]ve this objection. Let it be supposed that the Bishop uses the word in a different and more comprehensive Sense, and that by Sin he understands Evil of all kind connected with or resulting from *Actions*—though I do not see how we can represent the properties even of inanimate Bodies (of poisonous substances for instance) except as *Acts* resulting from the constitution of such bodies! Or if this sense, though not unknown to the Mystic Divines, should be *too* comprehensive and remote, we will suppose the Bishop to comprise under the term Sin, the Evil accompanying or consequent on *human* Actions and Purposes:—though here too, I have a right to be informed, for what reason and on what grounds Sin is thus limited to *human* Agency? And truly, I should be at no loss to assign the reason. But then this reason would instantly bring me back to my first definition; and any other reason, than that the human Agent is endowed with Reason, and with a Will which can place itself either in subjection or in opposition to his Reason—in other words, that Man is alone of all known Animals a responsible Creature—I neither know or can imagine.

Thus, then, the Sense which Taylor—and with him the Antagonists generally of this Article as propounded by the first Reformers—attaches to the words, Original Sin, needs only be carried on into its next consequence, and it will be found to *imply* the sense which I have given— namely, that Sin is Evil having an *Origin*. But inasmuch as it is *evil*, in God it cannot originate: and yet in some *Spirit* (*i.e.* in some *supernatural* power) it *must*. For in *Nature* there is no origin. Sin therefore is spiritual Evil: but the spiritual in Man is the Will. Now when we do not refer to any particular Sins, but to that state and constitution of the Will, which is the ground, condition, and common Cause of all Sins; and when we would further express the truth, that this corrupt *Nature* of the Will must in some sense or other be considered as its own act, that the corruption must have been self-originated;—in this case and for this purpose we may, with no less propriety than force, entitle this dire spiritual evil and source of all evil, that is absolutely such, Original Sin. (I have said, "the corrupt *Nature* of the Will." I might add, that the admission of a *Nature* into a spiritual essence by its own act *is* a corruption.)

Such, I repeat, would be the inevitable conclusion, *if* Taylor's Sense of the term were carried on into its immediate consequences. But the whole of his most eloquent Treatise makes it certain that Taylor did not carry it on: and consequently Original Sin, according to his conception, is a Calamity which being common to all men must be supposed to result from their common Nature: in other words, the universal Calamity of Human *Nature*!

Can we wonder, then, that a mind, a heart like Taylor's should reject, that he should strain his faculties to explain away, the belief that this Calamity, so dire in itself, should appear to the All-merciful God a rightful cause and motive for inflicting on the wretched Sufferers a Calamity infinitely more tremendous? nay, that it should be incompatible with Divine Justice *not* to punish it by everlasting torment? Or need we be surprised if he found nothing, that could reconcile his mind to such a belief, in the circumstance that the acts now *consequent* on this Calamity and either directly or indirectly *effects* on the same were, five or six thousand years ago in the instance of a certain Individual and his Accomplice, *anterior* to the Calamity, and the *Cause* or *Occasion* of the same? that what in all other men is *Disease*, in these two Persons was *Guilt*? that what in *us* is *hereditary*, and consequently *Nature*, in *them* was *original*, and consequently *Sin*? Lastly, might it not be presumed, that so enlightened, and at the same time so affectionate, a Divine, would even fervently disclaim and reject the pretended justifications of God grounded on flimsy analogies drawn from the imperfections of human ordinances and human justice-courts—some of very doubtful character even as human Institutes, and all of them just only as far as they are necessary, and rendered necessary chiefly by the weakness and wickedness, the limited powers and corrupt passions, of mankind? The more confidently might this be presumed of so acute and practised a Logician, as Jeremy Taylor, in addition to his other extraordinary Gifts, is known to have been, when it is demonstrable that the most current of these justifications rests on the palpable equivocation: viz. the gross misuse of the word Right. An instance will explain my meaning. In as far as, from the known frequency of dishonest or mischievous persons, it may have been found *necessary*, in so far is the Law *justifiable* in giving Landowners the Right of proceeding against a neighbour or fellow-citizen for even a slight trespass on that which the Law has made their Property:—nay, of proceeding in sundry instances criminally and even capitally. (Where at least from the known property of the Trespasser it is fore-known that the consequences will be penal. Thus: three poor men were fined Twenty Pounds each, the one for knocking down a Hare, the other for picking it up, and the third for carrying it off: and not possessing as many Pence, were sent to Jail.) But surely, either there is no religion in the world, and nothing obligatory in the precepts of the Gospel, or there are occasions in which it would be very *wrong* in the Proprietor to exercise the *Right*, which yet it may be highly *expedient* that he should possess. On this ground it is, that Religion is the sustaining Opposite of Law.

That Jeremy Taylor, therefore, should have striven fervently against the Article so interpreted and so vindicated, is, (for me, at least,) a subject neither of Surprise nor of Complaint. It is the doctrine which he *sub-stitutes*, it is the weakness and inconsistency betrayed in the defence of this substitute, it is the unfairness with which he blackens the established Article—for to give it, as it had been caricatured by a few Ultra-Calvinists during the fever of the (so called) *quinquarticular* Controversy, was in effect to blacken it—and then imposes another scheme, to which the same objections apply with even increased force, a scheme which seems to differ from the former only by adding fraud and mockery to injustice: these are the things that excite my wonder, it is of these that I complain! For what does the Bishop's scheme amount to? God, he tells us, required of Adam a perfect obedience, and made it possible by endowing him "with perfect rectitudes and super-natural heights of grace" proportionate to the obedience which he required. As a *consequence* of his disobedience, Adam lost this rectitude, this perfect sanity and proportionateness of his intellectual, moral and corporeal state, powers and impulses; and as the *penalty* of his crime, he was deprived of all super-natural aids and graces. The Death, with whatever is comprised in the scriptural sense of the word, Death, began from that moment to work in him, and this *consequence* he conveyed to his offspring, and through them to all his posterity, *i.e.* to all mankind. They were *born* diseased in mind, body and will. For what less than disease can we call a necessity of error and a predisposition to sin and sickness? Taylor, indeed, *asserts*, that though perfect Obedience became incomparably more difficult, it was not, however, absolutely *impossible*. Yet he himself admits that the contrary was *universal*; that of the countless millions of Adam's Posterity, not a single Individual ever realized, or approached to the realization of, this possibility; and (if my memory does not deceive me) Taylor himself has elsewhere exposed—and if he has not, yet Common Sense will do it for him—the sophistry in asserting of a whole what may be true of the whole, but—is in fact true only, of each of its component parts. Any one may snap a horse-hair: therefore, any one may perform the same feat with the horse's tail. On a level floor (on the hardened sand, for instance, of a sea-beach) I chalk two parallel strait lines, with a width of eight inches. It is *possible* for a man, with a bandage over his eyes, to keep within the path for two or three paces: therefore, it is *possible* for him to walk blindfold for two or three leagues without a single deviation! And this *possibility* would suffice to acquit me of *injustice*, though I had placed man-traps within an inch of one line, and knew that there were pit-falls and deep wells beside the other!

This *assertion*, therefore, without adverting to its discordance with, if not direct contradiction to, the tenth and thirteenth Articles of our Church, I shall not, I trust, be thought to rate below its true value, if I treat it as an *infinitesimal* possibility that may be safely dropped in the calculation: and so proceed with the argument. The consequence then of Adam's Crime was, by a natural necessity, inherited by Persons who could not (the Bishop affirms) in any sense have been accomplices in the crime or partakers in the guilt: and yet consistently with the divine Holiness, it was not possible that the same perfect Obedience should not be required of them. Now what would the Idea of Equity, what would the Law inscribed by the Creator in the heart of Man, seem to dictate in this case? Surely, that the supplementary Aids, the super-natural Graces correspondent to a Law above Nature, should be increased in proportion to the diminished strength of the Agents, and the increased resistance to be overcome by them! But no! not only the consequence of Adam's act, but the penalty due to his crime, was perpetuated. His descendants were despoiled or left destitute of these Aids and Graces, while the obligation to perfect obedience was continued; an obligation too, the non-fulfilment of which brought with it Death and the unutterable Woe that cleaves to an immortal Soul for ever alienated from its Creator.

Observe, Reader! all these *results* of Adam's Fall enter into Bishop Taylor's scheme of Original Sin equally as into that of the first Reformers. In this respect the Bishop's doctrine is the same with that laid down in the Articles and Homilies of the Established Church. The only difference that has hitherto appeared, consists in the aforesaid *mathematical* possibility of fulfilling the whole Law, which in the Bishop's scheme is affirmed to remain still in human Nature, or (as it is elsewhere expressed) in the Nature of the human Will. But though it were possible to grant this existence of a power in all men, which in no one man was ever exemplified, and where the *non*-actualization of such power is, a priori, so certain, that the belief or imagination of the contrary in any Individual is expressly given us by the Holy Spirit as a test, whereby it may be known that the truth is not in him! as an infallible sign of imposture or self-delusion! Though it were possible to grant this, which, consistently with Scripture and the principles of reasoning which we apply in all other cases, it is not possible to grant; and though it were possible likewise to overlook the glaring sophistry of concluding in relation to a series of indeterminate length, that whoever can do any one, can therefore do all; a conclusion, the futility of which must force itself on the commonsense of every man who understands the proposition;—still the question will arise—Why, and on what principle of equity, were the unoffending sentenced to be born with so fearful a disproportion of their powers to their duties? Why were they subjected to a Law, the fulfilment of which was all but impossible, yet the penalty on the failure tremendous? Admit that for those who had never enjoyed a happier lot, it was no punishment to be made to inhabit a ground which the Creator had cursed, and to have been born with a body prone to sickness, and a Soul surrounded with temptation, and having the worst temptation within itself in its own *temptibility*! To have the duties of a Spirit with the wants and appetites of an Animal! Yet on such imperfect Creatures, with means so scanty and impediments so numerous, to impose the same task-work that had been required of a Creature with a pure and entire nature, and provided with super-natural Aids—if this be not to inflict a penalty!—Yet to be placed under a Law, the difficulty of obeying which is infinite, and to have momently to struggle with this difficulty, and to live in momently hazard of these consequences—if this be no punishment!—words have no correspondence with thoughts, and thoughts are but shadows of each other, shadows that own no substance for their anti-type!

Of such an outrage on common-sense, Taylor was incapable. He himself, calls it a penalty; he admits that in effect it is a punishment: nor does he seek to suppress the question that so naturally arises out of this admission—On what principle of Equity were the innocent offspring of Adam *punished* at all? He meets it, and puts-in an answer. He states the problem, and gives his solution—namely, that "God on Adam's Account *was so exasperated with Mankind, that being angry* he would still continue the punishment!" The case (says the Bishop) is this: "Jonathan and Michal were Saul's Children. It came to pass, that seven of Saul's Issue were to be hanged: all equally innocent, EQUALLY CULPABLE." [*Before I quote further, I feel myself called on to remind the Reader, that these two last words were added by Jeremy Taylor without the least ground of Scripture, according to which*, (2 Samuel, lxxi.) *no crime was laid to their charge, no blame imputed to them. Without any pretence of culpable conduct on their part, they were arraigned as Children of Saul, and sacrificed to a point of state-expedience. In recommencing the quotation, therefore, the Reader ought to let the sentence conclude with the words*—] "all equally innocent. David took the five Sons of Michal, for she had left him unhandsomely. Jonathan was his friend: and therefore he spared *his* Son, Mephibosheth. Now here it was indifferent as to the guilt of the persons (*Bear in mind, Reader! that no guilt was attached to either of them!*) whether David should take the Sons of Michal or Jonathan's; but it is likely that as upon the kindness that David had to Jonathan, he spared his son; so upon the just provocation of Michal, he made that evil fall upon them, which, it may be, they should not have suffered, if their mother had been kind. ADAM WAS TO GOD, AS MICHAL TO DAVID." (Taylor's Polem. Tracts, p. 711.)

This Answer, this Solution, proceeding too from a Divine so preeminently gifted, and occurring (with other passages not less startling) in a vehement refutation of the received doctrine on the express ground of its opposition to the clearest conceptions and best feelings of mankind—this it is, that surprises me! It is of this that I complain! The Almighty Father *exasperated* with those, whom the Bishop has himself in the same treatise described as "innocent and most unfortunate"—the two things best fitted to conciliate love and pity! Or though they did not remain innocent, yet those whose abandonment to a mere nature, while they were left amenable to a law above nature, he affirms to be the irresistable cause, that they one and all *did* sin! And this decree illustrated and justified by its analogy to one of the worst actions of an imperfect Mortal! Let such of my Readers as possess the Volume of Polemical Discourses, or the opportunity of consulting it, give a thoughtful perusal to the pages from 869 to 893, (*Third Edition enlarged*, 1674). I dare anticipate their concurrence with the judgment which I here transcribe from the blank space at the end of the Deus Justificatus in my own Copy; and which, though twenty years have elapsed since it was written, I have never seen reason to recant or modify. "This most eloquent Treatise may be compared to a Statue of Janus, with the one face, which we must suppose fronting the Calvinistic Tenet, entire and fresh, as from the Master's hand: beaming with life and force, witty scorn on the Lip, and a Brow at once bright and weighty with satisfying reason! the other, looking toward the '*something to be put in its place*,' maimed, featureless, and weather-bitten into an almost visionary confusion and indistinctness."

With these expositions I hasten to contrast the *scriptural* article respecting Original Sin, or the corrupt and sinful Nature of the Human Will, and the belief which alone is required of us, as Christians. And here the first thing to be considered, and which will at once remove a world of error, is; that this is no Tenet first introduced or imposed by Christianity, and which, should a man see reason to disclaim the authority of the Gospel, would no longer have any claim on his attention. It is no perplexity that a man may get rid of by ceasing to be a Christian, and which has no existence for a philosophic Deist. It is a FACT, affirmed, indeed, in the Christian Scriptures alone with the force and frequency proportioned to its consummate importance; but a fact acknowledged in *every* Religion that retains the least glimmering of the patriarchal faith in a God infinite, yet *personal*! A Fact assumed or implied as the basis of every Religion, of which any relics remain of earlier date than the last and total Apostacy of the Pagan World, when the faith in the great I AM, the *Creator*, was extinguished in the sensual polytheism, which is inevitably the final result of Pantheism or the Worship of Nature; and the only form under which the Pantheistic Scheme—that, according to which the World is God, and the material universe itself the one only *absolute* Being—can exist for a People, or become the popular Creed. Thus in the most ancient Books of the Brahmins, the deep sense of this Fact, and the doctrines grounded on obscure traditions of the promised remedy, are seen struggling, and now gleaming, now flashing, through the Mist of Pantheism, and producing the incongruities and gross contradictions of the Brahmin Mythology: while in the rival Sect—in that most strange Phaenomenon, the religious Atheism of the Buddhists! with whom God is only universal Matter considered abstractedly from all particular forms—the Fact is placed among the delusions natural to man, which, together with other super-stitions grounded on a supposed *essential* difference between Right and Wrong, *the Sage* is to decompose and precipitate from the menstruum of *his* more refined apprehensions! Thus in denying the Fact, they virtually acknowledge it.

From the remote East turn to the mythology of Minor Asia, to the Descendants of Javan *who dwelt in the tents of Shem, and possessed the Isles*. Here again, and in the usual form of an historic Solution we find the same *Fact*, and as characteristic of the Human *Race*, stated in that earliest and most venerable Mythus (or symbolic Parable) of Prometheus—that truly wonderful Fable, in which the characters of the rebellious Spirit and of the Divine Friend of Mankind (Θεὸς φιλάνθρωπος [philanthropic God]) are united in the same Person: and thus in the most striking manner noting the forced amalgamation of the Patriarchal Tradition with the incongruous Scheme of Pantheism. This and the connected tale of Io, which is but the sequel of the Prometheus, stand alone in the Greek Mythology, in which elsewhere both Gods and Men are mere Powers and Products of Nature. And most noticeable it is, that soon after the promulgation and spread of the Gospel had awakened the moral sense, and had opened the eyes even of its wiser Enemies to the necessity of providing some solution of this great problem of the Moral World, the beautiful Parable of Cupid and Psyche was brought forward as a *rival* FALL OF MAN: and the fact of a moral corruption con-natural with the human race was again recognized. In the assertion of ORIGINAL SIN the Greek Mythology rose and set.

Coleridge now turns to the relationship between Evil and the human will.[3]

A moral Evil is an Evil that has its origin in a Will. An Evil common to all must have a ground common to all. But the actual existence of moral evil we are bound in conscience to admit; and that there is an Evil common to all is a Fact; and this Evil must therefore have a common ground. Now this evil ground cannot originate in the Divine Will: it must therefore be referred to the Will of Man. And this evil Ground we call Original Sin. It is a *Mystery*, that is, a Fact, which we see, but cannot explain; and the doctrine a truth which we apprehend, but can neither comprehend nor communicate. And such by the quality of the subject (*viz.* a responsible *Will*) it must be, if it be truth at all.

From the mystery of Evil his readers are drawn to the mysteries of Faith, as the proper context for any consideration of morality.[4]

In whatever age and country, it is the prevailing mind and character of the nation to regard the present life as subordinate to a Life to come, and to mark the present state, *the World of their Senses*, by signs, instruments, and mementos of its connexion with a future state and a spiritual World; where the Mysteries of Faith are brought within the *hold* of the people at large, not by being explained away in the vain hope of accommodating them to the average of their Understanding, but by being made the objects of Love by their combination with events and epochs of History, with national traditions, with the monuments and dedications of Ancestral faith and zeal, with memorial and symbolical observances, with the realizing influences of social devotion, and above all, by early and habitual association with Acts of the Will; *there* Religion is. *There*, however obscured by the hay and straw of human Will-work, the foundation is safe! In *that* country, and under the predominance of such Maxims, the national church is no mere State-*Institute*. It is the State itself in its intensest federal union; yet at the same moment the Guardian and Representative of all personal Individuality. For the Church is the Shrine of Morality: and in Morality alone the Citizen asserts and reclaims his personal independence, his *integrity*. Our outward Acts are efficient, and most often possible, only by coalition. As an efficient power, the Agent, is but *a fraction* of Unity: he becomes an *integer* only in the recognition and performance of the Moral Law. Nevertheless it is most true (and a truth which cannot with safety be overlooked) that Morality *as* Morality, has no existence for *a People*. It is either absorbed and lost in the quicksands of Prudential Calculus, or it is taken up and transfigured into the duties and mysteries of Religion. And no wonder: since Morality (including the *personal* being, the I AM, as its subject) is itself a Mystery, and the ground and *suppositum* of all other Mysteries, relatively to Man.

This leads to his central distinction between Reason and Understanding, Reason being the power at the heart of Mystery—as he believes he can demonstrate by analogy with the natural world.[5]

. . . Reason is the Power of universal and necessary Convictions, the Source and Substance of Truths above Sense, and having their evidence in themselves. Its presence is always marked by the *necessity* of the position affirmed: this necessity being *conditional*, when a truth of Reason is applied to Facts of Experience, or to the rules and maxims of the Understanding, but *absolute*, when the subject matter is itself the growth or offspring of the Reason. Hence arises a distinction in the Reason itself, derived from the different mode of applying it, and from the objects to which it is directed: accordingly as we consider one and the same gift, now as the ground of formal principles, and now as the origin of *Ideas*. Contemplated distinctively in reference to *formal* (or abstract) truth, it is the *speculative* Reason; but in reference to *actual* (or moral) truth, as the fountain of Ideas and the *Light* of the Conscience, we name it the *practical* Reason. Whenever by self-subjection to this universal Light, the Will of the Individual, the *particular* Will, has become a Will of Reason, the man is regenerate: and Reason is then the *Spirit* of the regenerated man, whereby the Person is capable of a quickening intercommunion with the Divine Spirit. And herein consists the mystery of Redemption, that this has been rendered possible for us. "And so it is written: the first man Adam was made a living soul, the last Adam a quickening Spirit." (1 Cor. xv. 45.) We need only compare the passages in the writings of the Apostles Paul and John, concerning the *Spirit* and Spiritual Gifts, with those in the Proverbs and in the Wisdom of Solomon respecting *Reason*, to be convinced that the terms are synonymous. In this at once most comprehensive and most appropriate acceptation of the word, Reason is pre-eminently spiritual, and a Spirit, even *our* Spirit, through an effluence of the same grace by which we are privileged to say Our Father!

On the other hand, the Judgments of the Understanding are binding only in relation to the objects of our Senses, which we *reflect* under the forms of the Understanding. It is, as Leighton rightly defines it, "the Faculty judging according to Sense." Hence we add the epithet *human*, without tautology: and speak of the *human* Understanding, in disjunction from that of Beings higher or lower than man. But there is, in this sense, no *human* Reason. There neither is nor can be but one Reason, one and the same: even the Light that lighteth every man's individual Understanding (*Discursus*), and thus maketh it a reasonable Understanding, *Discourse of Reason*—"one only, yet manifold; it goeth through all understanding, and remaining in itself regenerateth all other powers." (Wisdom of Solomon, c. viii.) The same writer calls it likewise "an influence from the *Glory of the Almighty*," this being one of the names of the

Messiah, as the Logos, or co-eternal Filial Word. And most noticeable for its coincidence is a fragment of Heraclitus, as I have indeed already noticed elsewhere. "To discourse rationally it behoves us to derive strength from that which is common to all men: for all human Understandings are nourished by the one DIVINE WORD."

Beasts, we have said, partake of Understanding. If any man deny this, there is a ready way of settling the question. Let him give a careful perusal to Hüber's two small volumes, on Bees and Ants (especially the latter), and to Kirby and Spence's Introduction to Entomology: and one or other of two things must follow. He will either change his opinion as irreconcilable with the facts: or he must deny the facts, which yet I cannot suppose, inasmuch as the denial would be tantamount to the no less extravagant than uncharitable assertion, that Hüber, and the several eminent Naturalists, French and English, Swiss, German, and Italian, by whom Hüber's observations and experiments have been repeated and confirmed, had all conspired to impose a series of falsehoods and fairy-tales on the world. I see no way at least, by which he can get out of this dilemma, but by over-leaping the admitted Rules and Fences of all legitimate Discussion, and either transferring to the word, Understanding, the definition already appropriated to Reason, or defining Understanding *in genere* by the *specific* and *accessional* perfections which the *human* Understanding derives from its co-existence with Reason and Free-will in the same individual person; in plainer words, from its being exercised by a self-conscious and responsible Creature. And, after all, the supporter of Harrington's position would have a right to ask him, by what other name he would designate the faculty in the instances referred to? If it be not Understanding, what is it?

In no former part of this volume has the Author felt the same anxiety to obtain a patient Attention. For he does not hesitate to avow, that on his success in establishing the validity and importance of the distinction between Reason and Understanding, he rests his hopes of carrying the Reader along with him through all that is to follow. Let the Student but clearly see and comprehend the diversity in the things themselves, the expediency of a correspondent distinction and appropriation of the *words* will follow of itself. Turn back for a moment to the Aphorism, and having re-perused the first paragraph of this Comment thereon, regard the two following narratives as the illustration. I do not say proof: for I take these from a multitude of facts equally striking for the one only purpose of placing my *meaning* out of all doubt.

I. Hüber put a dozen Humble-bees under a Bell-glass along with a comb of about ten silken cocoons so unequal in height as not to be

capable of standing steadily. To remedy this two or three of the Humble-
bees got upon the comb, stretched themselves over its edge, and with
their heads downwards fixed their forefeet on the table on which the
comb stood, and so with their hind feet kept the comb from falling.
When these were weary, others took their places. In this constrained
and painful posture, fresh bees relieving their comrades at intervals, and
each working in its turn, did these affectionate little insects support the
comb for nearly three days: at the end of which they had prepared sufficient wax to build pillars with. But these pillars having accidentally
got displaced, the bees had recourse again to the same manœuvre (or
rather *pedœuvre*), till Hüber, pitying their hard case, &c.

II. "I shall at present describe the operations of a single ant that I
observed sufficiently long to satisfy my curiosity.

"One rainy day, I observed a Laborer digging the ground near the
aperture which gave entrance to the ant-hill. It placed in a heap the
several fragments it had scraped up, and formed them into small
pellets, which it deposited here and there upon the nest. It returned
constantly to the same place, and appeared to have a marked design,
for it labored with ardor and perseverance. I remarked a slight furrow,
excavated in the ground in a straight line, representing the plan of a
path or gallery. The Laborer, the whole of whose movements fell
under my immediate observation, gave it greater depth and breadth,
and cleared out its borders: and I saw at length, in which I could not
be deceived, that it had the intention of establishing an avenue which
was to lead from one of the stories to the under-ground chambers.
This path, which was about two or three inches in length, and formed
by a single ant, was opened above and bordered on each side by a but-
tress of earth; its concavity *en forme de gouttiere* was of the most perfect
regularity, for the architect had not left an atom too much. The work
of this ant was so well followed and understood, that I could almost to
a certainty guess its next proceeding, and the very fragment it was
about to remove. At the side of the opening where this path terminated, was a second opening to which it was necessary to arrive by
some road. The same ant engaged in and executed alone this
undertaking. It furrowed out and opened another path, parallel to the
first, leaving between each a little wall of three or four lines in height.
Those ants who lay the foundation of a wall, chamber, or gallery, from
working separately occasion now and then a want of coincidence in
the parts of the same or different objects. Such examples are of no
unfrequent occurrence, but they by no means embarrass them. What
follows proves that the workman, on discovering his error, knew how

to rectify it. A wall had been erected with the view of sustaining a vaulted ceiling, still incomplete, that had been projected from the wall of the opposite chamber. The workman who began constructing it, had given it too little elevation to meet the opposite partition upon which it was to rest. Had it been continued on the original plan, it must infallibly have met the wall at about one half of its height, and this it was necessary to avoid. This state of things very forcibly claimed my attention, when one of the ants arriving at the place, and visiting the works, appeared to be struck by the difficulty which presented itself; but this it as soon obviated, by taking down the ceiling and raising the wall upon which it reposed. It then, in my presence, constructed a new ceiling with the fragments of the former one."— *Hüber's Natural Hist. of Ants*, pp. 38–41.

Now I assert, that the faculty manifested in the acts here narrated does not differ *in kind* from Understanding, and that it *does* so differ from Reason. What I conceive the former to be, physiologically considered, will be shown hereafter. In this place I take the understanding as it exists in *Men*, and in exclusive reference to its *intelligential* functions; and it is in this sense of the word that I am to prove the necessity of contra-distinguishing it from Reason.

Premising then, that two or more Subjects having the same essential characters are said to fall under the same General Definition, I lay it down, as a self-evident truth (it is, in fact, an identical proposition) that whatever subjects fall under one and the same General Definition are of one and the same kind: consequently, that which does *not* fall under this definition, must differ in kind from each and all of those that *do*. Difference in degree does indeed suppose sameness in kind: and difference in kind precludes distinction from difference of degree. *Heterogenea non comparari, ergo nec distingui*, possunt [Heterogeneous things cannot be compared, therefore cannot be distinguished]. The inattention to this rule gives rise to the numerous Sophisms comprised by Aristotle under the head of Μετάθεσις εἰς ἄλλο γένος, *i.e.* Transition into a new kind, or the falsely applying to X what had been truly asserted of A, and might have been true of X, had it differed from A in its degree only. The sophistry consists in the omission to notice what not being noticed will be supposed not to exist; and where the silence respecting the difference in kind is tantamount to an assertion that the difference is merely in degree. But the fraud is especially gross, where the heterogeneous subject, thus clandestinely *slipt in*, is in its own nature insusceptible of degree: such as, for instance, Certainty or Circularity, contrasted with Strength, or Magnitude.

To apply these remarks for our present purpose, we have only to describe Understanding and Reason, each by its characteristic qualities. The comparison will show the difference.

UNDERSTANDING	REASON
1. Understanding is discursive.	1. Reason is fixed.
2. The Understanding in all its judgments refers to some other Faculty as its ultimate Authority.	2. The Reason in all its decisions appeals to itself, as the ground and *substance* of their truth. (*Hebrews* VI. 13.)
3. Understanding is the Faculty of *Reflection*.	3. Reason of Contemplation. Reason indeed is much nearer to SENSE than to Understanding: for Reason (says our great HOOKER) is a dircct Aspect of Truth, an inward Beholding, having a similar relation to the Intelligible or Spiritual, as SENSE has to the Material or Phenomenal.

The Result is: that neither falls under the definition of the other. They differ *in kind*: and had my object been confined to the establishment of this fact, the preceding Columns would have superseded all further disquisition. But I have ever in view the especial interest of my youthful Readers, whose reflective *power* is to be cultivated, as well as their particular reflections to be called forth and guided. Now the main chance of their *reflecting* on religious subjects *aright*, and of their attaining to the *contemplation* of spiritual truths *at all*, rests on their insight into the *nature* of this disparity still more than on their conviction of its existence. I now, therefore, proceed to a brief analysis of the Understanding, in elucidation of the definitions already given.

The Understanding then (considered exclusively as an organ of human intelligence,) is the Faculty by which we reflect and generalize. Take, for instance, any objects consisting of many parts, a House, or a group of Houses: and if it be contemplated, as a Whole, *i.e.* (as many constituting a One,) it forms what in the technical language of Psychology, is called a *total impression*. Among the various component parts of this, we direct our attention especially to such as we recollect to have noticed in other total impressions. Then, by a voluntary Act, we withhold our attention from all the rest to reflect exclusively on these; and these we henceforward use as *common characters*, by virtue of which the several Objects are referred to one and the same sort. Thus, the whole Process may be reduced to three acts, all depending on and supposing a previous impression on the Senses: first, the appropriation of our Attention; 2. (and in order to the continuance of the first) Abstraction, or the voluntary withholding of the Attention; and 3. Generalization. And these are the proper Functions of the Understanding: and the power of so doing, is what we mean, when we say we possess Understanding, or are created with the Faculty of Understanding.

The dependence of the Understanding on the representations of the Senses, and its consequent posteriority thereto, as contrasted with the independence and antecedency of Reason, are strikingly exemplified in the Ptolemaic System (that truly wonderful product and highest boast of the Faculty, judging according to the Senses!) compared with the Newtonian, as the Offspring of a yet higher Power, arranging, correcting, and annulling the representations of the Senses according to its own inherent Laws and constitutive Ideas.

Even greater than Reason is Wonder.[6]

In Wonder all Philosophy began: in Wonder it ends: and Admiration fills up the interspace. But the first Wonder is the Offspring of Ignorance: the last is the Parent of Adoration. The First is the birth-throe of our knowledge: the Last is its euthanasy and apotheosis.

SEQUELAE: OR THOUGHTS SUGGESTED BY THE PRECEDING APHORISM

As in respect of the first Wonder we are all on the same Level, how comes it that the philosophic mind should, in all ages, be the privilege of a Few? The most obvious reason is this: The Wonder takes place before the period of Reflection, and (with the great Mass of Mankind) long before the individual is capable of directing his attention freely and consciously to the Feeling, or even to its exciting Causes. Surprise (the form and dress which the Wonder of Ignorance usually puts on) is worn away, if not precluded, by Custom and familiarity. So is it with the Objects of the Senses, and the ways and fashions of the World around us: even as with the beat of our own hearts, which we notice only in moments of Fear and Perturbation. But with regard to the concerns of our inward Being, there is yet another cause that acts in concert with the power in Custom to prevent a fair and equal exertion of reflective Thought. The great fundamental Truths and Doctrines of

Religion, the existence and attributes of God, and the Life after Death, are in Christian Countries taught so early, under such circumstances, and in such close and vital association with whatever makes or marks *reality* for our infant minds, that the words ever after represent sensations, feelings, vital assurances, sense of reality—rather than thoughts, or any distinct conception. Associated, *I had almost said identified*, with the parental Voice, Look, Touch, with the living warmth and pressure of the Mother, on whose lap the Child is first made to kneel, within whose palms its little hands are folded, and the motion of whose eyes *it's* eyes follow and imitate—(yea, what the blue sky is to the Mother, the Mother's upraised Eyes and Brow are to the Child, the Type and Symbol of an invisible Heaven!)—from within and without, these great First Truths, these good and gracious Tidings, these holy and humanizing Spells, in the preconformity to which our very humanity may be said to consist, are so infused, that it were but a tame and inadequate expression to say, we all take them for granted. At a later period, in Youth or early Manhood, most of us, indeed, (in the higher and middle classes at least) read or hear certain PROOFS of these truths—which we commonly listen to, when we listen at all, with much the same feelings as a popular Prince on his Coronation Day, in the centre of a fond and rejoicing Nation, may be supposed to hear the Champion's challenge to all the Non-existents, that deny or dispute his Rights and Royalty. In fact, the order of Proof is most often reversed or transposed. As far, at least as I dare judge from the goings on in my own mind, when with keen delight I first read the works of Derham, Niewentiet, and Lyonet, I should say, that the full and life-like conviction of a gracious Creator is the Proof (at all events, performs the office and answers all the purpose of a Proof) of the wisdom and benevolence in the construction of the Creature.

Commenting on Jeremy Taylor's assertion that God had done 'Two Great Things' for mankind: to send His Son to take on the nature of humanity and to instil in all human beings an awareness that they were immortal, if only through their conviction that some state of redress for all their ills and injustices must exist, Coleridge objects to the last argument while accepting that of the universal assurance of immortality.[7]

... though I agree with Taylor so far, as not to doubt that the mis-allotment of worldly goods and fortunes was one principal occasion, exciting well-disposed and spiritually awakened Natures by reflections and reasonings, such as I have here supposed, to mature the presentiment of immortality into full consciousness, into a principle of action and a well-spring of strength and consolation; I cannot concede to this circumstance any thing like the importance and *extent* of efficacy which he in this passage attributes to it. I am persuaded, that as the belief of all mankind, of all tribes, and nations, and languages, in all ages and in all states of social union, it must be referred to far deeper grounds, common to man as man: and that its fibres are to be traced to the *tap-root* of Humanity. I have long entertained, and do not hesitate to avow, the conviction, that the argument, from Universality of Belief, urged by Barrow and others in proof of the *first* Article of the Creed, is neither in point of *fact*—for two very different objects may be intended, and two (or more) diverse and even contradictory conceptions may be expressed, by the same *Name*—nor in legitimacy of conclusion as strong and unexceptionable, as the argument from the same ground for the continuance of our personal being after death. The Bull-calf *buts* with smooth and unarmed Brow. Throughout animated Nature, of each characteristic Organ and Faculty there exists a pre-assurance, an instinctive and practical Anticipation: and no Pre-assurance common to a whole species does in any instance prove delusive.* All other prophecies of Nature have their exact fulfilment—in every other "ingrafted word" of Promise Nature is found true to her Word, and is it in her noblest Creature, that she tells her first Lie?—(The Reader will, of course, understand, that I am here speaking in the assumed character of a mere Naturalist, to whom no light of revelation had been vouchsafed; one, who

> ——with gentle heart
> Had worshipp'd Nature in the Hill and Valley,
> Not knowing what he loved, but loved it all!)

Whether, however, the introductory part of the Bishop's argument is to be received with more or less qualification, the *Fact* itself, as stated in the concluding sentence of the Aphorism, remains unaffected, and is beyond exception true.

---

* See Baron Field's Letters from New South Wales. The poor Natives, the lowest in the Scale of Humanity, evince no symptom of any Religion, or the belief of any Superior Power as the Maker of the World; but yet have no doubt that the Spirits of their Ancestors survive in the form of Porpoises, and mindful of their descendants with imperishable affection, drive the Whales ashore, for them to feast on.

Finally he returns to his main point, the human need for redemption, and argues concerning the nature of that need.[8]

Christ "redeemed mankind from the curse of the Law" (*Galatians* iii. 11): and we all know, that it was not from temporal death, or the penalties and afflictions of the present life, that Believers have been redeemed. The Law, of which the inspired Sage of Tarsus is speaking, from which no man can plead excuse; the Law miraculously delivered in thunders from Mount Sinai, which was inscribed on tables of stone for the *Jews*, and written in the hearts of *all* men (*Rom.* xi. 15.)—the Law "holy and *spiritual!*" what was the great point, of which this Law, in its own name, offered no solution? the mystery, which it left behind the veil, or in the cloudy tabernacle of types and figurative sacrifices? Whether there was a Judgment to come, and Souls to suffer the dread sentence? Or was it not far rather—what are the Means of escape? Where may Grace be found, and redemption? St. Paul says, the latter. The Law brings condemnation: but the conscience-sentenced Transgressor's question, What shall I do to be saved? Who will intercede for me? she dismisses as beyond the jurisdiction of her Court, and takes no cognizance thereof, save in prophetic murmurs or mute out-shadowings of mystic ordin-ances and sacrificial types. Not, therefore, *that* there is a Life to come, and a future state; but *What* each individual Soul may hope for itself therein; and on what grounds; and that this state has been rendered an object of aspiration and fervent desire, and a source of thanksgiving and exceeding great joy; and by whom, and through whom, and for whom, and by what means and under what conditions—*these* are the *peculiar* and *distinguishing* fundamentals of the Christian Faith! These are the revealed Lights and obtained Privileges of the Christian Dispensation! Not alone the knowledge of the Boon, but the precious inestimable Boon itself, is the "Grace and Truth that came by Jesus Christ!" I believe Moses, I believe Paul; but I believe *in* Christ.

9
Doctrines and Illuminations

Coleridge's rapprochement with the orthodox Anglican Church entailed frequent re-examination and re-evaluation of its doctrines. Over and above individual points loomed a larger question: what statements of belief was it reasonable to ask of a Christian? He interested himself in the historical issues involved, by which such assertions had grown and been elaborated, burgeoning from simple sets of statements to the more elaborate Nicene formula and so to the elaborate Athanasian creed, which he roundly branded on one occasion 'blasphemous, tautological, deficient and nonsensical'.[1] To John Wheeler he described it two years later as 'having done great mischief'. It was not by that father [Athanasius], he thought, and had misled thousands.[2]

Not unexpectedly, he made several attempts to devise creeds of his own, particularly after the débâcle initiated by the loss of Sara Hutchinson's presence and the quarrel with Wordsworth. These formulations were of several kinds, returning several times to the need to preserve a mean between damaging extremes.[3] Following the publication of *Aids to Reflection* he also took stock in a letter[4] of the elements in Christianity that he had not yet dealt with. Of these he would approach the political status of the Anglican Church in *On the Constitution of the Church and State* (1829) and questions of biblical criticism in the manuscript later published as *Confessions of an Inquiring Spirit* (1840). The other four topics he mentioned – faith, the Eucharist, the philosophy of prayer and prophecy – are the subject of brief discussions reproduced below.

Prayer, in particular, was a topic to which he returned time and again; while in his poetic expressions it was ideally a form of self-composure before God his actual experience made it quite often an involuntary expression of anxiety and agony, accompanied by a cry for mercy and help. In 1815 T.A. Methuen heard him say, 'Sir, it is my fixed persuasion

179

that no man ever yet prayed in earnest, who never felt the misery of being unable to pray. For when the soul feels that she is sinking, as it were, from Him who is the author of all happiness, she beseeches Him to stretch out his hand and suffer her to sink no further.'[5]

Just as he was aware of the extremes between which prayer existed, so he was always conscious that prophecy, if involved in the growth of the natural organism, was a matter simply of development and growth, yet once brought into conjunction with history it necessarily involved the ambiguities of time that he had explored in other contexts. These were all part of the strange contradictions inherent in the Christian religion. Even the Nature to which he had been so devoted at times could also appear like a witch that would in the end vanquish the human mind that tried to subdue her. In several poems during the time of his tribulation, similarly, he tried the experiment of imagining a world without Christianity in what he regarded as its essentials, either envisioning a lifeless state in which all the elements of the landscape shadowed the Christian illumination beautifully, yet without possessing the reality, as in 'Limbo', or trying to imagine what the total opposite of the divine would be like, as in 'Ne plus Ultra'. Yet in the larger irony of his complete philosophy such envisionings were no more than negatives to indicate sublime positives, just as one could not achieve a proper conception of the Christian God without the devil as a necessary part of one's negative thinking. The paradoxical figure in 'Limbo', 'His eyeless face all Eye', who 'seems to gaze at that which seems to gaze at him', was a perfect figuration of the unredeemed spirit, devoid of the power that would give life to its illumination and so transform it. The supravention of this extra power was what Coleridge projected when he thought of 'Reason', a power which for human beings of continuous minds set the finite into alignment with the infinite. When he tried to do proper justice to this sublime illumination the poet had to come to the rescue of the thinker.

Coleridge reviews the history of the creeds as it has affected Christian believers.[1]

The History of Creeds is a two-edged Sword, cutting equally the Socinians & the Romists, whose church ought to be called the Roman Tridentine Church/Every creed till Pope Pius the IV[th's] was or purported to be no other & no more than a fuller explication of the former, called for by heresies—but by no means any addition thereto—For this indeed would destroy the very essence of a Creed, which is the summary not of the whole Christian Doctrine, but of all its fundamental and universally necessary articles of Faith—and this so strictly, that even the Sacraments are omitted (unless the Eucharist be included in the communion of Saints) because circumstances are possible, in which a Christian may be saved without the *formal* reception of the bodily Elements, because tho' they are the ordinary & most solemn Mode of partaking in the Body and Blood (i.e. the divine Humanity, homo idealis realizatus [ideal man realized) of Christ, they are not the only possible modes—Vide John VI.—

The Creed therefore which was to be the introduction to the Scriptures for the instructed, the temporary Supplement for tribes barbarous & ἀναλφαβήτοις [unalphabeted], and the bond of Charity to all Christians— (i.e. that dear and aweful Remembrancer to them all in all their difference, how incomparably more & more important were the articles of Faith in which they agreed than the articles of opinion in which they differed) this has been perverted by the Tridentian Conspiracy to the antichristian purpose of superseding the Scriptures & introducing a *new Gospel*—So much for the Romish Tridentine—for the Socinians, ask concerning the history & motives of the new paraphrase of the Apostles' Creed by the first Nicene Council/was there a great struggle in the Christian World between the old plain simple Primitive Christians, ψιλανθρωπists, & the new-fangled Platonizing Doctors?—O no! not a word—but between the high Arians, who would have trembled at Socinianism even more than their opponents/—Into these the whole Christian World was divided—nor can the Socinians shew a *single Church* that held Socinianism—No! every attempt was by individuals, founding a new heretical *Church*—/This is, I think, an argument of weight/Many old Churches, even apostolical, became for a while Arian— Arius & his Disciples had persuaded them—not to alter the words of any Creed, not to reject the words Trinity in Unity, born before all worlds, creator of the world, redeemer &c &c—but that the homoiousian Interpretation was the right one/—they could therefore hold the apostolic Tradition & Arianism together—but what an instance is there of Paulus Samosatensis, having persuaded any Apostolic Church that the mere humanity of Christ was the doctrine it had received from its fathers?—

And Paul Samosateno—did he dare at Antioch to declare that Jesus Christ was only the chief & most fully inspired of the Prophets, that the Objects of his Mission were merely to teach a pure morality and to give a proof of a future state by his Resurrection, that the Trinity was an absurdity, that the phrases, ⟨the⟩ Word, the Holy Ghost, &c were mere modes of speech, and synonimes of God, = as the Justice of God, the Mercy of God—or as in ornamented Language, the munificence of

Trajan, the Obstinacy & Pride of Coriolanus—Did he dare declare to the Church at Antioch that this was the Tradition received by Men from their Fathers as the Apostolic Doctrine?—O no! he dared not—for he was not a madman/No, retaining all these words he began his attacks on the mode in which the Divine Word was present with the man Jesus, & so that plain men hearing the same words, they had been accustomed to hear, supposed the same meaning, or that the difference could not be great—this however, even this, was sufficient to alarm all Christendom, & of course, must have therefore alarmed all the more instructed Christians of Antioch first, who had given warning—From all parts the great Congregations of Bishops met, each with the solemn Suffrage of his Church—Did they all agree to a bare-faced Lie? Did P. S. appeal to any witnesses, any old men, of his own or of any other of the Churches of Asia, that of Jerusalem for instance, who gave evidence that they had heard their Fathers or Grandfathers say, that such was what *they* had understood from the Apostolic men who had converted them?—No! mere arguments that such might be the sense of the *words* of the uniform Διαδοσις—no pretence to innovate the words themselves./

When the first Council of Nice met, they had only the Apostles' Creed to repeat; they did so, and after due deliberation declared in what sense they had always understood each article of this Creed—and this *declaration* formed the Nicene Creed—i.e. a paraphrase of the Apostles. When the Council of Trent met, they had only the Apostles & Nicene/ they repeated the latter/well! did they paraphrase, i.e. make a declaration of the sense in which they had received & understood each article of it?—No! Nothing like this!—They left it as they found—but impudently added 12 *new* articles (new as a part of the *Essential Conditions* of Salvation: for that is the meaning & the purport of a Creed)—by their own confession—and yet dared to call it *Catholic*—when not only half the European Churches, & all the Oriental, gave no assent; but they themselves had *created* it for *themselves*. Good heavens! if candid men can withstand such palpable evidence as this, what can be done! and to men without the love of Truth what is the use of offering arguments?

In 1817 he puts together his beliefs in so far as they relate to morality.[2]

S. T. Coleridge's Confession of Belief with respect to the true grounds of Christian morality

1. I sincerely profess the Christian Faith, and regard the New Testament as containing all its articles: and I interpret the words ⟨not only⟩ in their

obvious, but in the *literal* sense, unless where Common Reason and the authority of the Church of England join in commanding them to be understood FIGURATIVELY: as for instance, "Herod is a Fox."—

2. Next to the holy Scriptures I revere the Liturgy, Articles, and Homilies of the Established Church: and hold the doctrines therein expressly contained.

3. I reject as erroneous, and deprecate as *most* dangerous, the notion, that our *Feelings* are to be the ground and guide of our Actions. I believe the Feelings themselves to be among the things that are to be grounded, and guided. The Feelings are effects, not causes; a part of the *instruments* of Action, but never can without serious injury be perverted into the *principles* of Action. ⟨Under *Feelings* I include all that goes by the names of *Sentiment*, Sensibility, &c &c. These, however pleasing, may be made and often are made, the instruments of Vice & Guilt, tho' under proper discipline they are fitted to be both aids and ornaments of Virtue. They are to Virtue what Beauty is to Health.—⟩

4. All men, the good as well as the bad, and the bad as well as the good, act with motives. But what is a motive to one person, is no motive at all to another—The pomps and vanities of the world supply *mighty* motives to an ambitious man; but are so far from being a *motive* to a humble Christian, that he rather wonders, how they can be even a temptation to any man in his senses who believes himself to have an immortal soul. Therefore that a Title, or the power of gratifying sensual Luxury, is the motive with which A acts, and no motive at all to B. must *arise from* the different state of the moral Being in A and in B: Consequently, *motives* too, as well as *Feelings*, are *effects*; and they become causes only in a secondary or derivative sense.

5. Among the motives of a probationary Christian the practical conviction, that all his intentional acts have consequences in a future State; that as he sows here, he must reap hereafter; in plain words, that according as he does or does not avail himself of the Lights and Helps given by God thro' Christ he must go either to Heaven or Hell; is the *most* impressive—were it only from pity to his own soul, as an everlasting sentient Being.

6. But that this *is* a motive, and the most impressive of motives, to any given Person arises from, and supposes, a commencing state of Regeneration in that Person's mind and heart/ That, therefore, which *constitutes* a regenerate State, is the true PRINCIPLE, *on* which, or with a *view* to which, all our Actions, Feelings, and Motives ought to be grounded.

7. The different *operations* of this radical Principle, (which Principle is called in Scripture sometimes Faith, and in other places Love) I have

been accustomed to call good *Impulses*: because they are the powers, that *impel* us to do what we ought to do.—

8. The Impulses of a full-grown Christian are 1. Love of God—2. Love of our Neighbor for the Love of God. 3. An undefiled Conscience, which prizes above every comprehensible advantage that *Peace* of God, which passeth all understanding!

9. Every Consideration, whether of Hope or of Fear, which *is*, and which is *adopted* by *us*, poor imperfect Creatures! in our present state of Probation, as a MEANS of *producing* such Impulses in our Hearts, is so far a *right* and *desirable* Consideration. He, that is weak, must take the medicine which is suitable to his existing weakness; but then he ought to know that it is a *medicine*, the object of which is to remove the Disease, not to feed and perpetuate it.

10. Lastly, I hold that there are two grievous mistakes,—both of which as *Extremes* equally opposite to Truth and the Gospel I equally reject and deprecate—. The first is that of Stoic Pride, which would snatch away his Crutches from a curable Cripple before he can walk without them. The second is that of those worldly and temporizing Preachers who would disguise from such a Cripple the necessary truth that Crutches are not Legs; but only temporary Aids and Substitutes.—

A final attempt, in the last years of his life, to define the 'Articles of Faith necessary to Christians' leads him on to define, once again, his attitude to members of other churches.[3]

N° 1. There is a Living God a Holy One who *affirmeth* his ~~own~~ Being, and that He is himself the Ground of his own Being. I AM, in that I AM, & ⟨who⟩ hath revealed himself, a God who heareth Prayer.

N° 2. That of all Beings, not made manifest to our *Senses* (⟨of⟩ Sight, Touch &c)—⟨that of all invisible, supersensuous Powers⟩ He alone is the rightful, the only permitted, Object of religious Worship, direct or indirect. For (see No. 1.) He is a god, who heareth PRAYER. And Prayer, *not* offered to an Omnipresent Being, that is, to a Being whose presentce to us is necessary and not contingent, must necessarily be itself contingent, that is, dependent on circumstances of Place and Time. "And the People fell on their faces, and worshipped God and King David." David was *then* ⟨and *there*⟩ present to their Eyes, Ears, &c; And they blamelessly worshipped him, as their lawful King—but Jehovah, the Invisible, they worshipped as God. Had any one of the Congregated Multitude retired to his Chamber, or to a Solitude in the distant Wilderness, and *there* offered prayers of thanksgiving to David, as to One whom he supposed to be conscious there⟨o⟩f, beyond doubt he would have been guilty of moral Idolatry. Prayer, including Petition, and Thanksgiving, addressed to a Being as *necessarily* present, is alone *religious* Worship.

Corollary. To fancy a Being, whose presence, it is acknowleged, can only be *contingently*, or accidentally present, nevertheless *actually* so, without any evidence of the Senses, or rational inference from such evidence: and on this ground to pray to him, is *Superstition*. The Worshipper is *out* of his *Senses*, and not in his right *Reason*.

N$^{o.}$ 3. Man, as he now is, can only address himself to God thro' a Mediator. (It is the conviction of this which forms the first ground of a Christian *Faith*. The *grounds* for such a conviction, the facts and reasons that justify it, it is the place of the Instructor of Catechumens to establish. *Here* we only assert it, as a Dictum: or assume it as a Postulatum.) Now N$^{o.}$ 3. can only be reconciled with N$^{o.}$ 1 and 2, under this Condition— that the Mediator is both God and Man. Therefore He is the only Mediator: for Prayer offered to a Being at all times and in all places, and to a Being as *necessarily* present independent of time and place, implies the same omnipresence in the Being, *thro'* whom we offer it. In praying *thro'* an invisible Being we *virtually*, tho' (and perhaps for very sufficient reasons) not *formally*, [? pray] *to* him.—

4. Man needs a Redemption, which of his own power he is incapable of effecting: but it hath been offered to Man in, by and thro' the Mediator, together with all the means of finally effecting it to as many, as truly receive the offer.—

5. *All* the particulars, historic, declarative, or preceptive, ~~necessarily~~ to the rational acceptance of this Offer, and to our availing ourselves of the same, singly and collectively, that is, as Individuals or as a Church, with many things most important to the Help and Furtherance of our Redemption, are contained in that collection of Books, received as Canonical, by the Churches *universally*, which we call *the Bible*. (Certain Books, called by us the Apocrypha, have been received by a large number of Christians; but those alone, contained in our Bible, by *all*,)— And no point, not expressly or by self-evident implication, contained in some of these Books, and ⟨so interpreted as to be⟩ *consistent* with the doctrines undeniably taught in some or all of the Others, dare be imposed on a Christian or on a Christian Church, as an Article of Faith, or an essential condition of Redemption.

Now these 5 Articles are all, I conceive necessary, in order to a *comprehension* of the different denominations of Christian Believers, without *Confusion*. And on this ground I feel compelled to disown, as members of the same Church with myself, the Parthenolators and Hagiolators of the *Romish* Communion, by virtue of N° 2. 3. and (in less degree) the 5th—and the Socinians, especially the modern Unitarians, by power of N° III:d and IVth—To the Ministers of all other Churches, Lutheran or Calvinistic, Arminian or [? Zwinglian], Presbyterian or Independent I say—or were it in my power, would say, "You neither need nor can *all* of you be Ministers of the National Church of England, any more than *all* Country Gentlemen can or need be Justices of Peace; but I receive you all, as Members of the *Christian* Church in England—& with any of you, whom I hold competent, I would interchange in the Pulpit"—S. T. C.

In addition, he has distinguished between three classes of religious faith.[4]

1. The essentials of universal immutable Religion, that of Men & Angels—
2. Of fallen man anticipatively—& then *met* by and filled up by Revealed Religion—
3. The essentials added to all these by *historical* revealed religion (i.e. the means & vehicle adopted by God & inseparable from the contents, without devitalizing of the latter, as the veins & arteries from the blood—) These are fully enumerated by St Paul. 1 Epist. to Tim. III. 16— Without controversy great is the mystery of Godliness! God was manifested in the flesh—justified in the Spirit—seen of Angels—preached unto the Gentiles—believed on in the World—received up into Glory—

With the above Creed no man can be a Heretic/let his opinions be what they will on subordinate questions, as of the canonical Books, what & what not—the *origin* of the Gospels—the inspiration & what & whether—&c &c

Here too we see why the suffering on the Cross is not mentioned, because this as the symbol of Redemption by Atonement belongs to the second Class—.

God was manifested in the flesh (well! grant that *this* might be explained away by the Socinians into the mere inspiration of Christ, yet) was *"received up into Glory"*.

What? was God, the father *received up* into Glory?—and "seen by Angels"—Suppose Christ a mere Man, ψιλος ανθρωπος [mere man], what is the significance, the specific purport, of this Clause? What could the Angels *see* that men could not?—But if it were ο θε ανθρωπος [the divine man], God incarnate, then indeed Angels *might* SEE, i.e. have a direct and *intuitive* knowlege of what men could only infer discursively & know by faith.

Later, he will also draw a distinction between the state of mind in which God is to be adored yet addressed in humility and that in which He can be thought about with a kind of rationality.[5]

The sublime and abstruse doctrines of Christian Belief belong to the Church—but the Faith of the Individual, centered in his heart, is or may be collateral to them. Faith is subjective—"I throw myself in adoration before God, acknowledge myself his creature—sinful, weak, lost—and pray for help and pardon"—but when I rise from my knees, I discuss the doctrine of the Trinity as I would a problem in Geometry—in the same temper of mind I mean, not by the same process of reasoning, of course.

Item: Launcelot Wade coincides with me in the full conviction, that neither the ceremony of Baptism under any form or circumstances, nor any other *ceremony*, but such a Faith in Jesus Christ as produces conformity to his holy doctrines and commandments in *heart* and *life*, that *properly* makes us Christians: that in the strict sense of the term essential, this alone is the *essential* of Christianity, that the same spirit should be growing in us which was in the fullness of all perfection in Christ Jesus. Whatever else is called essential is such only because and only as far as it is essential *to* this as its means or instrumental, or *evidently* and practically implied in this.—

His rapprochement to Anglicanism causes him to consider afresh the question of Baptism, first as a critique of a particular position and later as an account that will appear, revised, as a supplementary part of 'Aids to Reflection'.[6]

Mant's tract I have begun to read, and, as far as I have read, I should find no other difficulty in answering him than what arises from one or two passages of our Liturgy. The framers of that Liturgy were eminently pious, learned, and wise men. But they were not *inspired* men. Nor does the Church of England pretend to supersede the study of the Scripture by the pretences of infallible interpretation. The question of Baptism had not then been so deeply studied as it afterwards was; and the dreadful crimes, the fanatical exorbitances, and the seditious and outrageous doctrines of the Anabaptists at *Leyden*, *Munster*, and elsewhere, had prejudiced all sober Christians against every opinion supported by them;

even as too many zealous Protestants were irreconcileable to the noblest parts of our Book of Common Prayer, because they had pre-existed in the Mass-book, carrying the 'noscitur ex socio' ['it is known by its friend'] to a blameworthy excess. But so it is; so it has been; and probably, while this imperfect state continues, so it ever will be. And here too, as every where, the folly of man is the wisdom of God. For in this we find an additional and irrefragable proof of the divinity of the Scriptures, which everywhere, and under the strongest human inducements to do otherwise, preserve the Heavenly medium between extremes. What had been said of Baptism during the times when few, if any, but adult, tried, and *built-up* Christians were baptized, was incautiously (*as appears to me*) applied in these one or two passages to the baptism of infants; which (if we will not contradict the most positive commands and determinations of the Gospel, 'Repent and believe,' and 'thou mayest be baptized,') we must regard as a sacrament of *conditional promise* and as a *means* of grace, but not as a sacrament of *effect*, and an immediate *conveyance* of grace.

But still, my dear Sir, even with respect to the Liturgy, those who hold the doctrine I have now avowed stand on higher grounds than our opponents. For the prayer evidently implies that the actual operation of the Spirit is future and conditional. The whole prayer is *prospective*— 'Grant that this child *may* receive the fulness of grace,' and therefore all that follows *may* rationally, and in my view *ought* to be, likewise understood as *prospective*. For what could be more absurd in baptizing an unconscious infant, than to *pray* that he *might* receive the fulness of grace, if the *outward act* of Baptism were a *command* of God, of universal application to all ages from the birth (or, according to the Romanists, from the first quickening) of the babe to the last flutter of departing old age; if its operation were irrelative to age and to the development of consciousness; and if the regenerative influences were totally, and at one and the same instant, united with the visible ceremony; even as the power of consciousness in our mortal state with the organization and organic motions of the brain. Assuredly to pray as for a thing that may or may not be given, where God has solemnly announced that it is given, and when no possible repugnance or unfitness can exist in the subject, a helpless, passive infant, (for what obstacle can a *sinful nature* present to *Omnipotence*, when the holy and gracious decree, and the permission and appointment of free agency, present none to the infinite *wisdom?*) assuredly to *pray*, instead of returning *thanks*, would introduce a strange confusion into the services offered to the God of order. We *pray* for a gift yet to be vouchsafed; but we give thanks for that which is being, or has been, bestowed.

Instead of one or two sentences in the Liturgy, which the "Εν καὶ πᾶν υδρισταί [one and all waterists] (or those who teach that the Spirit is given all and at once with the water) can adduce in favour of their opinions, I can produce twice ten times the number irreconcileable with the practical conclusions which they draw from those passages.

Launcelot Wade and myself are agreed as as to the following:

1. That we are opposed equally to all attempts to explain any thing *into* Scripture, and to all attempts to explain any thing *out* of Scripture/ —i.e. to explain *away* the positive assertions of Scripture under pretence that the literal sense is not agreeable to *reason*, i.e. their notions drawn from *Their* school of phi- or psilosophizing. Thus a Platonist would believe as ideally true certain doctrines independent of Scripture and therefore anticipate their Scriptural realization which an Epicurean will not receive on the most positive declarations of the divine Word.—

We both agree likewise, that as the Unitarians (and a large part of the Arminians who will not allow themselves to be Unitarians in the fashionable plusquam-socinian sense) err grievously in the latter point, so tho' less grossly the Pædo-baptists err in the former. We both appear to ourselves to see, that there is no end or determinable Limit to these inferences and probable deductions; but that the final decision in each particular dispute, pro tempore isto et quo ad disputantes ipsos [so far as that time and those disputants are concerned] will depend on the accident of superior logical skill and rhetorical address and fluency in the victor of the moment. The vast & more than Alexandrine Library of theological Controversies affords one continued comment on and exemplification of this fact.—

In our conviction all the Texts of Scripture, appealed to by the Pædo-baptists as positively commanding or even authorizing & permitting infant baptism,—all without any exception, are made to bear a sense in no wise contained in the Text or communicated to it by the context, and in direct contradiction to other positive declarations of Scripture and to the Spirit of the whole L̶i̶v̶ Gospel *History*—so that as far as the question is an historical question, we have not a shade of doubt in our minds, that the Baptism of Infants was neither the practice or the purpose of the Apostles or the *Apostolic* Age.

P.S. More than this we do not consider as necessary to our argument/ and are far from joining with Robinson (Hist. of Bapt.) in his assertions respecting the late origin of Pædo-baptism, as commencing under, & at once condemned as general doctrine & yet allowed on the grounds of particular Charity, & because Charity is greater than doctrinal Faith, by

Cyprian; but as not becoming a general or ordinary practice till after Augustine's controversial Heats with the Pelagians, and his diffusion of the Calvinistic Article of Original Sin & the Devildom of Infants dying *unchristened*. We reject this statement as rash & believe it to have been unanswerably confuted by diverse Pædo-baptist Divines. Without any pretence to determine, how, where, or at what time Pædo-baptism began, we content ourselves with the negative assertion, that it did *not* begin in the *Apostles* and that it was not the practice of the *Apostolic* Churches.

As Aids to Reflection *approaches publication he looks forward to supplementary works which he hopes will add up to a more complete system.*[7]

I have six Disquisitions ready for the Press—as a sort of Supplement to this—the second of which was to have followed the disquisition on Baptism, and Infant Baptism; but was obliged to be left out from the length of the Volume.

1. On Faith. 2. The Eucharist. 3. The philosophy of PRAYER: and the three kinds of Prayer, Public, Domestic, and Solitary. 4. On the prophetic character of the Old Testament: and on the Gift of Prophecy. 5. On the Church + Establishment, and Dissent—and the true character & danger of the Romish Church. 6. On the right and the superstitious use and estimation of the Sacred Scriptures: this last in a series of Letters.

In the 'Aids to Reflection' I have touched on the Mystery of the Trinity only in a *negative* way. That is, I have shewn the hollowness of the arguments by which it has been assailed—have demonstrated that the doctrine involves nothing contrary to Reason, and the nothingness & even absurdity of a Christianity without it. In short, I have contented myself with exposing the causes of it's rejection and in removing (what by experience I know to be) the ordinary obstacles to it's belief.—But the positive establishment of the Doctrine as involved in the Idea, God—together with the *Origin* of EVIL, as distinguished from Original Sin (on which I *have* treated at large) and the Creation of the visible World—THESE as absolutely requiring the habit of abstraction, and *severe Thinking*, I have reserved for my larger Work—of which I have finished the first Division, namely, the *Philosophy* of the Christian Creed, or Christianity true in *Idea*. The 2nd. Division will be—Xty true in *fact*—i.e. historically. The third & last will be—Xty true in *act*—i.e. morally & spiritually.—

But with exception of the Trinity (the *positive* proof of)—the Origin of Evil, metaphysically examined—and the Creation—I may venture to say, that the Aids to Reflection (the latter $\frac{2}{3}$rds, I mean) with the six supplementary Disquisitions contain a compleat *System* of internal evidences. At least, I can think of no essential Article of Faith omitted.— At all events, no one hereafter can with justice complain that I have disclosed my sentiments only in flashes and fragments—

Reading an unidentified work in the 1820s, Coleridge argues the need for a different terminology when considering the Eucharist.[8]

This contra-distinction of *corporeal* from *spiritual* is the leaven of error that pervades the whole controversy respecting the Eucharist, and is partaken of by Romanist, Calvinist and Lutheran.—If instead of *corporeal* they had substituted the word, phænomenal, or corpus *phænomenon*, in antithesis to Corpus *noumenon*, or *reale* [phenomenal body in antithesis to noumenal or real Body], how many sanguinary conflicts would have been prevented, and how different a judgement would Philosophers have passed on the mystery itself! The Corpus *noumenon* of the impersonated Logos is the Finite, reunited with the Infinite in the *Divine* HUMANITY of Christ—the flesh and blood of the Son of God in his character and property as Son of Man.

The profoundest of the Christian Fathers seem to have held three Epiphanies of the Logos. First, the Birth of the Finite in the Infinite, του "Ο ΩΝ" εν κολπω τοῦ πατρος ["The Being" in the bosom of the father], in which he was begotten before all time (or creation. πρωτοτοκος πασης κτισεως [the firstborn of every creature]). Second, the *Utterance* in the creation. (εν τη του χαου κοσμησεῖ [in the ordering of the chaos]), in which the substance or base was the one, the form was the universal (generalization).

Thirdly, the incarnation or assumption of the finite personal, the Humanity—in which Substance was the Universal under the Form of Individuality.—But in all these the Substance and Form are indivisibly one, yet inconfusibly distinct.

In the light of these Ideas the Eucharist is a sublimation (by faith i.e. subjectively) of the 2nd to the third—a subsumption of the General (Bread & Wine) under the Individual (Flesh & Blood).

Further reflections on the Eucharist in his later Table Talk.[9]

No doubt, Chrysostom and the other rhetorical Fathers contributed a good deal by their rash use of figurative language to advance the superstitious notion of the Eucharist; but the beginning had been much earlier. In Clement, indeed, the mystery is treated as it was treated by John and Paul, but in Hermas we see the seeds of the error, and far more in Irenæus, and so it went on till the Idea was changed into an Idol.

The errors of the Sacramentaries on the one hand and of the Romanists on the other are equally great; the former have volatilized the Eucharist into a Metaphor; the latter have condensed it into an Idol.

Jeremy Taylor contends in his zeal against Transubstantiation that the sixth chapter of John has no reference to the Eucharist; if so, St John wholly passes over this sacred Mystery. It *is* a mystery; it is the only mystery in our Religious Worship. When many left Jesus and complained that his sayings were hard—he does not attempt to detain them by any explanation, but only tells them that his words are Spirit. If he had really meant that the Eucharist should only be a memorial or a celebration of his death, would it have been even honest to let these disciples go away from him upon such a gross misunderstanding? Would he not have said "You need not make a difficulty; I only mean so and so after all?"

Arnauld and the other learned Catholics are irresistible against the Sacramentary doctrine.

The Sacrament of Baptism applies itself and has reference to the Faith or Conviction and is therefore only to be performed once; it is the *Light* of Man. The Sacrament of the Eucharist is a Symbol of all our *Religion*; it is the *Life* of Man. We want it always; it is commensurate with our Will.

A parenthesis in his 1794 verse prayer for the health of Mary Lamb is followed three years later by a firm recantation.[10]

I utterly recant the sentiment contained in the lines
> Of whose omniscient and all-spreading Love
> Aught to *implore* were impotence of mind

it being written in Scripture '*Ask*, and it shall be given you,' and my human reason being convinced moreover of the propriety of offering *petitions* as well as thanksgivings to Deity.

A view of prayer in an earlier notebook.[11]

> Prayer—

First Stage—the pressure of immediate calamities without earthy aidance makes us cry out to the Invisible—

Second Stage—the dreariness of visible things to a mind beginning to be contemplative—horrible Solitude.

Third Stage—Repentance & Regret—& self-inquietude.

4th stage—The celestial delectation that follows ardent prayer—

5th stage—self-annihilation—the Soul enters the Holy of Holies.—

An account of his normal practice in prayer.[12]

> Ere on my bed my limbs I lay,
> It hath not been my use to pray
> With moving lips or bended knees;
> But silently, by slow degrees,
> My spirit I to Love compose,
> In humble trust mine eye-lids close,
> With reverential resignation,
> No wish conceived, no thought exprest,
> Only a sense of supplication;
> A sense o'er all my soul imprest
> That I am weak, yet not unblest,
> Since in me, round me, every where
> Eternal Strength and Wisdom are.

A not dissimilar account of his feelings after having heard Wordsworth recite his full version of 'The Prelude'.[13]

> Scarce conscious and yet conscious of it's Close,
> I sate, my Being blended in one Thought,
> (Thought was it? or aspiration? or Resolve?)
> Absorb'd, yet hanging still upon the sound:
> And when I rose, I found myself in Prayer!

A few years later caught in the tentacles of opium and urged by Cottle to 'pray earnestly', he protests that (like the Ancient Mariner in his agony) he does 'pray inwardly to be able to pray' *but that this can happen only as the reward of Faith; it is not a simple expedient. Later he returns to the question:*[14]

Christians expect no outward or sensible Miracles from Prayer—it's effects and it's fruitions are spiritual, and accompanied (to use the words of that true *Divine*, Archbishop Leighton) 'not by Reasons and Arguments; but by an inexpressible Kind of Evidence, which they only know who have it.'—To this I would add that even those who (like me, I *fear*) have not attained it may yet *presume* it—1. because Reason itself, or rather mere human Nature in any dispassionate moment, feels the *necessity* of Religion; 2. but if this be not true, there is no Religion, no *Religation* or Binding over again, nothing added to Reason—& therefore Socinianism is not only not Christianity, it is not even *Religion*—it doth not *religate*, doth not bind anew—

The first outward and sensible Result of Prayer is a penitent Resolution, joined with a consciousness of weakness in effecting it (yea, even a dread too well grounded, lest by breaking & falsifying it the soul should add guilt to guilt by the very means, it has taken to escape from Guilt—so pitiable is the state of unregenerated man!). Now I have resolved to place myself in any situation, in which I can remain for a month or two as *a Child*, wholly in the Power of others—But alas! I have no money . . .

Prayer is a matter on which he finds the contemporary Anglican Church failing.[15]

There are three sorts of Prayer—Public—Domestic—Solitary. Each has its peculiar uses and character. The Church ought to publish and authorize a directory of forms for the two latter.

The decay of the Devotional Spirit in the English Clergy is amazing. Witness the contemptible compositions which proceed from time to time from Lambeth and the Bishops generally, whenever a new Prayer is to be offered. Instead of New Forms of Prayer—they were happily blundered by the hawker into New Former Prayers.

Coleridge finds the manner of prophesying adopted by Moses exemplary.[16]

The manner of the predictions of Moses is very remarkable. He is like a man standing upon an eminence and addressing people below him, and pointing to things which he can and they cannot see. He does not say You will act in such and such a manner and the consequences will be so and so; but—so and so will take place, because you will act in such a way.

He develops further his view that Prophecy is not simply a straightforward foretelling of the future in chronological time.[17]

Finally, my dear Friend! the word, prophesy, may be taken in three senses.—Organization is either simultaneous as in an individual animal, or successive—as in one of Handel's or Mozart's Overtures. Now in every scheme of Organization Successive (and the great Scheme of Revelation is eminently such) every integral part is of necessity both prophecy & history, save the last or consummating Fact, which will be only History, and the initial which can only be prophecy: but of all the intervening Components of the Scheme every part is both at once—i.e. Prophecy in relation to what follows and History in relation to that which had preceded.—Now in this sense of the word I believe the whole Bible to be prophetic.—Secondly, in every perfect scheme there is an Idea of the whole, and in every *real* (i.e. not merely *formal* or abstract) Science there are Laws—& this is equally true in moral as in physical Science. But where ever Laws are, *Prophecy* may be—the difference between moral & physical Laws in this respect being only this, that in the physical the *Prophecy* is absolute, in the moral is it more or less conditional—according to the character of the moral Subject in whom it is to be fulfilled. In certain cases it will be *virtually* absolute— (Ex. gr. *If* that inveterate Sot and Dram-drinker does not conquer his habit, and it is *next* to certainty he never will—he will die of a rotten Liver.—Now would any man hesitate to abbreviate this into—'That man will die of a rotten Liver'?—Yet it *is possible*, that the man might reform.) and there are several instances of *verbally* unconditional Prophecies in scripture, both of Promise and of Threat, that were not fulfilled: and yet 'the Scripture not broken'. Why? because the condition, which in all moral prophecies is *understood*, did not take place.—Now of Prophecies in this sense of the word there are many and glorious ones— and such as bear witness to the divinity of the inspiring Spirit, the Santa SOPHIA, proceeding ἐκ τοῦ Ἀγαθοῦ, καὶ ἐκ τοῦ Ἀληθοῦς [from the Good, and from the True]. III. Prophecy is used for *prognostication*, with the precise time, individual person, and name—and this two or 3 hundred years before either the person was in existence or the name known.— Now of Prophecies in *this* third sense I utterly deny that there is any one instance delivered by any one of the illustrious Diadoche whom the Jewish Church comprized in the name *Prophets*—and I shall regard *Cyrus* as an exception when I believe the 137th Psalm to have been composed by David only because the collection in which it stands has, Psalms of David, for it's general Title.—Nay, I will go further—and assert, that the contrary belief, or the hypothesis of Prognostication, is in direct and irreconcileable oppugnancy to our Lord's repeated declaration, that the *times* hath the Father reserved to himself—a declaration drawn from the very depth of the profoundest Theology and Philosophy, aye and Morality to boot!

Meanwhile, in less optimistic mood, he rises to a tour de force in which he pictures the mind and nature as rival forces, each trying to subdue the other— the ultimate victory being destined to lie with Nature.[18]

My dear Friend

It is a flat'ning Thought, that the more we have seen, the less we have to say. In Youth and early Manhood the Mind and Nature are, as it were, two rival Artists, both potent Magicians, and engaged, like the King's Daughter and the rebel Genie in the Arabian Nights' Enternts., in sharp conflict of Conjuration—each having for it's object to turn the other into Canvas to paint on, Clay to mould, or Cabinet to contain. For a while the Mind seems to have the better in the contest, and makes of Nature what it likes; takes her Lichens and Weather-stains for Types & Printer's Ink and prints Maps & Fac Similes of Arabic and Sanscrit Mss. on her rocks; composes Country-Dances on her moon-shiny Ripples, Fandangos on her Waves and Walzes on her Eddy-pools; transforms her Summer Gales into Harps and Harpers, Lovers' Sighs and sighing Lovers, and her Winter Blasts into Pindaric Odes, Christabels & Ancient Mariners set to music by Beethoven, and in the insolence of triumph conjures her Clouds into Whales and Walrusses with Palanquins on their Backs, and chaces the dodging Stars in a Sky-hunt!—But alas! alas! that Nature is a wary wily long-breathed old Witch, toughlived as a Turtle and divisible as the Polyp, repullulative in a thousand Snips and Cuttings, integra et in toto! She is sure to get the better of Lady MIND in the long run, and to take her revenge too—transforms our To Day into a Canvass dead-colored to receive the dull featureless Portrait of Yesterday; not alone turns the mimic Mind, the ci-devant Sculptress with all her kaleidoscopic freaks and symmetries! into clay, but *leaves* it such a *clay*, to cast dumps or bullets in; and lastly (to end with that which suggested the beginning—) she mocks the mind with it's own metaphors, metamorphosing the Memory into a lignum vitae Escrutoire to keep unpaid Bills & Dun's Letters in, with Outlines that had never been filled up, MSS that never went farther than the Titlepages, and Proof-Sheets & Foul Copies of Watchmen, Friends, Aids to

Reflection & other *Stationary* Wares that have kissed the Publisher's Shelf with gluey Lips with all the tender intimacy of inosculation!—

In poems written about 1811 Coleridge imagines three great negatives: a lifeless, beautiful Limbo; an utter opposite to the Divine; and human life, once imagined devoid of immortality.[19]

Limbo

'Tis a strange Place, this Limbo! not a Place,
Yet name it so—where Time & weary Space
Fetter'd from flight, with night-mair sense of Fleeing
Strive for their last crepuscular Half-being—
Lank Space, and scytheless Time with branny Hands
Barren and soundless as the measuring Sands,
Mark'd but by Flit of Shades—unmeaning they
As Moonlight on the Dial of the Day—
But that is lovely—looks like Human Time,
An old Man with a steady Look sublime
That stops his earthly Task to watch the Skies—
But he is blind—a statue hath such Eyes—
Yet having moon-ward turn'd his face by chance—
Gazes the orb with moon-like Countenance
With scant white hairs, with fore-top bald & high
He gazes still, his eyeless Face all Eye—
As twere an Organ full of silent Sight
His whole Face seemeth to rejoice in Light/
Lip touching Lip, all moveless, Bust and Limb,
He seems to gaze at that which seems to gaze on Him!

No such sweet Sights doth Limbo Den immure,
Wall'd round and made a Spirit-jail secure
By the mere Horror of blank Nought at all—
Whose circumambience doth these Ghosts enthrall.
A lurid Thought is growthless dull Privation,
But the Hag, Madness, scalds the Fiends of Hell
With frenzy-dreams, all incompassible
Of aye-unepithetable Negation

A lurid thought is growthless dull Privation
Yet that is but a Purgatory Curse

Hell knows a fear far worse,
A fear, a future fate. Tis *positive Negation*!

Ne Plus Ultra

Sole Positive of Night!
Antipathist of Light!
Fate's only Essence! Primal Scorpion Rod!
The one permitted Opposite of God!
Condensed Blackness, and Abysmal Storm
Compacted to one Sceptre
Arms the Grasp enorm,
The Intercepter!
The Substance, that still casts the Shadow, Death!
The Dragon foul and fell!
The unrevealable
And hidden one, whose Breath
Gives Wind and Fuel to the fires of Hell!
Ah sole Despair
Of both th' Eternities in Heaven!
Sole Interdict of all-bedewing Prayer,
The All-compassionate!
Save to the Lampads seven
Reveal'd to none of all th' Angelic State,
Save to the Lampads seven
That watch the Throne of Heaven!

Human Life

ON THE DENIAL OF IMMORTALITY

If dead, we cease to be; if total gloom
   Swallow up life's brief flash for aye, we fare
As summer-gusts, of sudden birth and doom,
   Whose sound and motion not alone declare,
But *are* their whole of being! If the breath
   Be Life itself, and not its task and tent,
If even a soul like Milton's can know death;
   O Man! thou vessel purposeless, unmeant,
Yet drone-hive strange of phantom purposes!
   Surplus of Nature's dread activity,
Which, as she gazed on some nigh-finished vase,

Retreating slow, with meditative pause,
    She formed with restless hands unconsciously.
Blank accident! nothing's anomaly!
    If rootless thus, thus substanceless thy state,
Go, weigh thy dreams, and be thy hopes, thy fears,
The counter-weights!—Thy laughter and thy tears
    Mean but themselves, each fittest to create
And to repay the other! Why rejoices
    Thy heart with hollow joy for hollow good?
    Why cowl thy face beneath the mourner's hood?
Why waste thy sighs, and thy lamenting voices,
    Image of Image, Ghost of Ghostly Elf,
That such a thing as thou feel'st warm or cold?
Yet what and whence thy gain, if thou withhold
    These costless shadows of thy shadowy self?
Be sad! be glad! be neither! seek, or shun!
Thou hast no reason why! Thou canst have none;
Thy being's being is contradiction.

He also examines wryly the state and even the necessity of the Devil in Christian thought.[20]

All gross and vulgar Spirits are inclined to Devil-worship equally with Savages. In G. Britain they cannot do it avowedly; but I have observed in all the late evangelical magazines, Christian Observer, the works of Wilberforce, Hannah More, Porteus, and the whole of the Fanatics, Canters, or Sticklers for obsolete High-Church Orthodoxy for the sake of obsolete High Church Power a zealous advocacy for the existence & Agency of the Devil/who in this System is a sort of obnoxious Premier or Vizir of Providence, whose acts have no effect but in virtue of the Royal Signature, and yet his name & person take off the odium from the King—whom it is constitutional to abuse, in cases where without him Abuse would be Treason. All this has its uses; but nevertheless it is but a mask/and he who prays to God against his Devil, like those who petition his Majesty against his Ministers for measures which could not have taken place without the concurrence & authority of the Crown involve the Royal Person in the Blame actually, tho' in the least offensive manner. These glowing Diabolists have at the bottom the same state of religious feeling as their Cousins, the Theodiabolists of India or Africa/A. throws a sop to a savage Dog, B. offers a Bribe to his surly owner to keep him chained/—closely connected with this and using this as its means watch the love of Power; the pretence of *clerical conscience* attempted to be set up against the Laws of the Lands, in the Coroner's Verdict &c &c—in short, read with care the Christian Observer, & Works resembling it, & note down every instance/but priorly examine Warburton's Alliance of Church & State which contains the Germs of this Conspiracy. All these are mere, nay the merest *Hints*: the theme is, the Zeal for the existence and attributes of the Devil, and its conjunctions connective God and Reason require only virtue & reason; but the Devil needs an exorcist . . .

The Remark, which escaped my memory, or rather my recollection while the importance of the same lay heavy upon my memory, was simply this—and is, I believe, a perfectly new observation/that the Devil and Devils among Christians form precisely the same System, with the same Feeling, of *one* and at the same time *many*, as among the Pagan Greeks and Romans the ο Θεoς, and οι θεoι [God, and the gods]/the more philosophic part used even the οι θεoι, as synonimous with Ο θεoς [the god]—but the Generality explained away this feeling as far as they could, by a Jupiter and his variously Subordinated Gods/—yet even with these an obscure feeling of unity remained/—and *God* or the divine Nature without particularizing an individual God was sufficiently common among them/—So with our Evil Spirit/—*the Devil*/—and this again into Satan and his Subordinates.

Yet this cannot negate his belief in the ultimate triumph of life and light, which transcend Nature.[21]

Life is inward Light, and Light outward Life—and Light again = <u>objective</u> Being, <u>Actual</u> Being, Being manifested—whence the Word, the Supreme Reason, the Supreme Being is the Sun that rose and riseth with Healing in its wings, i.e. became—commences, to will, his redemptorial Office as the Light that lighteth every man that cometh into the world—

But what is Light to the Lifeless? Or rather what is <u>Outward</u> Light abstracted from the inward, as its <u>Sub</u>stance?—Answer.—A <u>Surface</u>— a glorious Shadow!

The Spirit proceedeth from the Son—and it is the Son's <u>Spirit</u>—"In him is Life"—and <u>this</u>, this Life, <u>substantial</u> Light, is the Light of Man, of which the outward Sun with its apparent Rays or Glory is the necessary Condition, and <u>Actuator</u>—evoking the former from potential Being

(Hades) into <u>Actual</u> Being.—And he breathed into Man a <u>living Soul</u>—of which <u>Conscience</u> is the evidence, the Soul's testimony of its own reality.

Soul, = principle of Individuality/Individuality the only Form and evidence of the participation of True Being in the Non-absolute.—Nature has no Reflex. Nature has no Conscience. She is soul-less, word-less, & thus yearning after Soul & the Word.

These are ultimately reflected in God's Ideas, and so those of the Trinity, reflecting like the sun in the fountain.[22]

Ideas things—God's *ideas* of finite things, *the finite things*—which originate in him but acquire separate existence.—God's *infinite idea of Himself an infinite thing eternally conceived*—this infinite thing or person conceived infinite Love of God, and God of it—and from God & his eternally conceived Idea of himself coeternally proceeded *infinite Love*—i.e. the Holy Spirit.

The Logos—or coeternal idea—feeling himself infinitely representative of God & infinitely happy in contemplation of himself as the absolutely infinite & perfect likeness of God was impelled by *infinite Love* to multiply finite images of Deity each happy in contemplating itself & the images around it—as being representative of Deity—Snatch a gaze at the Sun, then turn & contemplate them in the fountain—Prayer & meditation—Angels in the beatific Vision, then turn to created things—

The resulting vision can be expressed either in rather prosaic poetry:[23]

> ['Finally, what is Reason? You have often asked me: and this is my answer':—]

> Whene'er the mist, that stands 'twixt God and thee,
> Defecates to a pure transparency,
> That intercepts no light and adds no stain—
> There Reason is, and then begins her reign!

Or in a highly poeticized prose:[24]

A bodiless Substance, an unborrow'd Self, God in God immanent, the eternal Word, That goes forth yet remains, Crescent and Full, and

Wanes. Yet ever entire and one/—At the same time it dawns & sets & crowns the Height of Heaven the dawning, setting Son, at the same time the Tenant of each Sign Thro' all the zodiac/While each in its own Hour Boasts & beholds exclusive Presence, a Peculiar Orb. Each the great Traveller's Inn/Yet still the unmoving Sun—Great genial agent on all finite Souls, And by that action puts on finiteness absolute Infinite whose dazzling robe Flows in rich folds & plays in shooting Hues of infinite Finiteness.

10
Other Faiths

Coleridge's liberal-mindedness was evident in his attitude to religious toleration. In general, he was anxious to support it, but also clear-minded enough to see the almost insuperable difficulties of a total toleration for those who believed in any absolutes. Political toleration was easy enough for those who, like himself, believed in the need for a Redeemer, but there were certain activities—including, of course, political interference on the part of religious authorities, at which toleration must stop. He always tried to preserve an open mind regarding those who held beliefs other than his own—all the more because he knew how much his own faith had changed over the years. In addition to the Unitarianism that he embraced for several years, his search for religious truth had led him in his youth to investigate other sects. His early delight in the Moravian shoemaker Jacob Boehme was probably the reason for his short-lived schoolboy attempt to become apprenticed to one—and later for his brother's comment that he was not a Jacobin but a 'hot-headed Moravian'; while he was to recall humorously how his enthusiastic fondness for Quakerism when at Cambridge had led to his attending one of their meetings—which cured him.[1] His subsequent remarks about Quakers were increasingly hostile: he believed them to be 'altogether degenerated from their ancestors of the seventeenth century', and deplored their strong streak of commercialism.[2] His vehemence may well have been exacerbated by an uneasy consciousness that their belief in the 'inner light' corresponded rather closely with aspects of his own doctrine. In the same way he shared many of the contemporary prejudices concerning Judaism, failing to recognize the degree to which the commercial interests of Jews were a direct result of the disabilities imposed upon them in Christian cultures. Accordingly, he found himself marvelling at the contrast between the sublime pronouncements of an

Isaiah ('Give ear, O earth,' etc.) and the common cry of 'Old clothes!' to be heard from his successors in London streets.[3]

Roman Catholicism, though less well known in England when he was a young man, was to be a further long-standing interest. He would have come across it during the year he spent in Germany from 1798 and renewed his contact a few years later when he travelled to Malta and, subsequently, Italy. At times it could then seem impossibly alien: 'I have several times seen the stiletto and the rosary come out of the same pocket,' he noted on one occasion;[4] he also remarked on 'the immense *noise* and jingle-jingle as if to frighten away the daemon common-sense' which seemed always associated with what he termed Roman Catholic 'mummery'.[5] He remained fascinated with memories of his Mediterranean visit, nevertheless, speaking on one occasion of his 'Rome-haunting' mind.

His chief attachment, by contrast, particularly in later years, was to Martin Luther, whom he saw as a figure second only to St Paul and described as 'a hero, one fettered indeed with prejudices; but with those very fetters he would knock out the Brains of a modern Fort Esprit'.[6] His comments and marginal notes often expressed delight in his sturdy faith and vigorous expressions.

Roman Catholicism became a renewed issue in the 1820s with the calls for emancipation—finally met by the Act of 1829. The effect of this issue was the rise of urgent discussions concerning their proper standing, accompanied by investigations into the ultimate authority on which the English Church rested. Coleridge, who had been urgent in his own inquiries—particularly in works such as *Aids to Reflection*—was no less probing in the face of this new challenge. His *On the Constitution of the Church and State, according to the Idea of Each,* summed up a position that supported the traditional Establishment by arguing for a fortification of Church and State by mutual vivification. In a striking use of imagery, he drew a parallel with the cultivation of the Mediterranean countryside: 'As the olive-tree is said in its growth to fertilize the surrounding soil; to invigorate the roots of the vines in its immediate neighbourhood, and to improve the strength and flavour of the wines—such is the relation of the Christian and the National Church.'[7]

His views were seen as a significant contribution to the debate; they also proved catalysts to the evolving ideas of High Church thinkers, including John Henry Newman, who could not accept the idea that a Christianity that was destined to survive as sublime symbolism rather than as fact. Newman himself turned to Roman Catholicism rather than accept such a compromise; Sara Coleridge, the poet's daughter, on the other hand, felt able to carry his beliefs forward into the Oxford Movement. *On the Constitution of the Church and State*, would in any case remain for many Anglican thinkers her father's chief religious legacy.

On a larger scale, his religious thinking was by no means confined to Anglican—or even Christian—thought. At the time when he was exploring the implications of his thought concerning the 'one Life' he had also been absorbed in the religious beliefs of other cultures; his play *Osorio* and his plan to produce a joint poem with Southey on 'Mahomet' had led him to consider the qualities of the Mohammedan faith,[8] while study of his young son Hartley's desire to have ant-heaps near the house led him to relish 'his *Brahman* love and awe of life'.[9] His interest in Indian mythology, most active at the time of his greatest poetic achievements,[10] was still an object of musing concern when he wrote his 'Opus Maximum' fragments and reflected on his earlier attraction.

When he turned to what might be of lasting value in other faiths, however, it was to the best in Christian tradition that he looked. His deep interest in the life and writings of St Teresa was an example of his hope to find truths on which all believers might agree: far from the cold 'head-work' of Unitarianism, wary of the warm 'heart-work' of Methodism at its more frenetic, yet still finding community in devotion to a living illumination—rather as he felt that there were women who could breathe the hemlock of a false faith and turn it to music.

Coleridge shows concern for toleration, but does not agree that it can ever be a right.[1]

A *Right* to Protection I can understand; but *a right* to Toleration, seems to me a contradiction in terms. However, this be—I do not fear to avow my conviction, that Toleration, tho' from motives of expedience it may be wisely practised, can never be logically proved either a right on the part of the Sect, or a Duty on the part of a Government, if under the term, Religion, we are compelled to admit whatever hideous doctrine & practice any man or number of Men assert to be their Religion, & an article of their faith. Ex. gr. the same Pope commanded the Romish Catholics to rebel against Elizabeth—and if he had of right the power of commanding them to disobey the laws of the Land by separating themselves from the National Church, which previous to his command was not dictated by their Conscience or by any known decision of Council, he must have had the former likewise.

He develops his view in 'Omniana'.[2]

I dare confess that Mr. Locke's treatise on Toleration appeared to me far from being a full and satisfactory answer to the subtle and oft-times plausible arguments of Bellarmin, and other Romanists. On the whole, I was more pleased with the celebrated W. Penn's tracts on the same subject. The following extract from his excellent letter to the King of Poland appeals to the heart rather than to the head, to the Christian rather than to the Philosopher; and besides, overlooks the ostensible object of religious penalties, which is not so much to convert the heretic, as to prevent the spread of heresy. The thoughts, however, are so just in themselves, and exprest with so much life and simplicity, that it well deserves a place in the *Omniana*.

"Now, O Prince! give a poor Christian leave to expostulate with thee. Did Christ Jesus or his holy followers, endeavour, by precept or example, to set up their religion with a carnal sword? Called he any troops of men or angels to defend him? Did he encourage Peter to dispute his right with the sword? But did he not say, *Put it up*? Or did he countenance his over-zealous disciples, when they would have had fire from heaven, to destroy those that were not of their mind? No! But did not Christ rebuke them, saying, Ye know not what spirit ye are of? And if it was neither Christ's spirit nor their own spirit that would have fire from heaven—Oh! what is that SPIRIT that would kindle *fire on earth*, to destroy such as peaceably dissent upon the account of conscience!

"O King! when did the true RELIGION persecute? When did the true church offer violence for religion? Were not her weapons prayers, tears, and patience? Did not Jesus conquer by these weapons, and vanquish cruelty by suffering? Can clubs, and staves, and swords, and prisons, and banishments, reach the soul, convert the heart, or convince the understanding of man! When did violence ever make a true convert, or bodily punishment a sincere Christian? This maketh void the end of Christ's coming. Yea, it robbeth God's spirit of its office, which is to convince the world. That is the sword by which the ancient Christians overcame."

The *Theory* of Persecution seems to rest on the following assumptions. I. A duty implies a right. We have a right to do whatever it is our duty to do. II. It is the duty, and consequently the right, of the supreme power in a state, to promote the greatest possible sum of well-being in that state. III. This is impossible without morality. IV. But morality can neither be produced or preserved in a people at large without true religion. V. Relative to the *duties* of the legislature or governors, that is the true religion which they conscientiously believe to be so. VI. As there can be but one true religion, at the same time, this one it is their duty and right to authorise and protect. VII. But the established religion cannot be protected and secured except by the imposition of restraints or the influence of penalties on those, who profess and propagate hostility to it. VIII. True religion, consisting of precepts, counsels, commandments, doctrines, and historical narratives, cannot be effectually proved or defended, but by a comprehensive view of the whole, as a system. Now this cannot be hoped for from the mass of mankind. But it may be attacked, and the faith of ignorant men subverted, by particular objections, by the statement of difficulties without any counter-statement of the greater difficulties which would result from the rejection of the former, and by all the other stratagems used in the desultory warfare of sectaries and infidels. This is, however, manifestly dishonest, and dangerous; and there must exist therefore a power in the state to prevent, suppress, and punish it. IX. The advocates of toleration have never been able to agree among themselves concerning the limits to their own claims; have never established any clear rules, what shall and what shall not be admitted under the name of religion and conscience. Treason and the grossest indecencies not only may be, but have been called, by these names: as among the earlier Anabaptists. X. And last, it is a *petitio principii*, or begging the question, to take for granted that a state has no power except in case of overt acts. It is its duty to prevent a present evil, as much at least as to punish the perpetrators of it. Besides, preaching and publishing are overt acts. Nor has it yet been proved, though often asserted, that a Christian sovereign has nothing to do with the external happiness or misery of the fellow creatures entrusted to his charge.

In the last year of his life he addresses the question in greater detail.[3]

Mr Kenyon has sent me a poem entitled "Rhymes on Tolerance". The proper title would be "Intolerant (I will not say intolerable) Rhymes on Tolerance". Ought not a man, who writes a book expressly to inculcate tolerance, learn to treat with respect or at least with indulgence articles of faith which tens of thousands ten times told of his fellow subjects or fellow creatures believe with all their souls, and upon the truth of which they rest their tranquillity in this world and their hopes of salvation in the next—those articles being at least maintainable against his arguments, and most certainly innocent in themselves?—Is it fitting to run Jesus Christ in a silly parallel with Socrates?—the being whom thousand millions of intellectual creatures—of whom I am one humbler unit, take to be their Redeemer with an Athenian philosopher, of whom we should know nothing except through his glorification in Plato and Xenophon? And then to hitch Latimer and Servetus together! To be sure there was a stake and a fire in either case, but where the rest of the resemblance is, I cannot see. What ground is there for throwing the odium of Servetus' death upon Calvin alone? Why, the mild Melancthon wrote to Calvin in the name of all the Reformed churches in Germany to thank him for the act—Zwingli did the same in the name of the Swiss churches, and the Archbishop of Canterbury did the like in the name of the Church of England. Before a man deals out the popular slang of the day about the great leaders of the Reformation, he should learn to throw himself back to the age of the Reformation—when the two great parties in the Church were eagerly on the watch to charge heresy on the other. Besides if ever a poor fanatic thrust himself into the fire—it was Servetus. He was a rabid enthusiast, and did every thing he could in the way of insult and ribaldry to provoke the feelings of the Christian Church.

At the same time he still finds disturbing the absence of a community with which he can identify himself.[4]

Am I or is the non-existence of a Christian Community, in fault— — God knows how much I feel the want of Church Fellowship! But where can I find it? Among the <u>Methodists</u>? <u>Vide</u> the Cuts & Frontispieces to the Methodist, Arminian, Evangelical &c Magazines. The <u>Quakers</u>?— I want the heart of Oak—& here is <u>the Rind</u> & Bark in wondrous pre-servation, counterfeiting a <u>tree</u> to the very life/—. <u>The C. of Eng</u>?—The Churches, and Chapels? O yes, I can go to a Church, & so I can to a Theatre—& go out again—& know as much as [for "of"?] my fellow-goers in the one as in the other— —The Moravians?—If any where, among them. YET—but I will talk to Dr Oakley. But I fear, that every fancy is tolerated among them but the fancy of free enquiry and the free use of the Understanding on subjects that belong to the Understanding— I fear, a wilful Stupor with the sacrifice of Reason under the name of Faith, instead of a Faith higher than Reason because it includes it as one of it's Co-partners—I fear the Tyranny of <u>Dogmas</u>.

As he moves back towards orthodoxy he considers the extent to which Methodism relies on firm adhesion on the part of its members rather than a true spirit of enquiry.[5]

Sunday Evening, June 17—1810—Read thro' Nightingale's portraiture of Methodism. Think it a fair & comparatively impartial Account, & see no reason in the Book, the super-sufficient cause in the Methodist Preachers, for their abuse of it—I am sure, that it left in my mind a far more favorable view both of the Tenets & Preachers of the Society than I had gathered from the publications of zealous Methodists—The now anti-methodistic tenets of the Author himself ought to be deemed a favorable circumstance by an enlightened Methodist, as increasing the credibility of the account with the public in general—and if there be any learned & thinking men among their Leaders, they should surely be occasioned by this Work to reflect, how many hundreds, nay, thousands of their Preachers, & what myriads of their People must be in the same state as Nightingale with regard to any intellectual perception of the Truth of their Doctrines, & only kept to them by the mighty but unreliable force of positive feelings—faith of adhesion/Limpets on the Rock of Salvation!—In the present day, no man is properly accomplished as a Teacher, who has not made himself acquainted with the arguments & expositions of the Unitarians, whether Arian or Socinian, even as in the days of the Reformers & thence to the Revolution no man could be deemed armed for the watch-tower of Protestant Faith, to whom any of the common arguments of the Romanists would appear new. Indeed, even at the present Day, a learned Minister ought to be thorough Master both of the Catholic and of the Socinian Divinity—in order that he may more readily foresee the tendency of any doctrine to this or to that extreme. I observe, that there is one grievous Deficiency in Nightingale's Portraiture/he has given us no notion of the numbers or comparative weight & activity of the Calvinist Methodists—without which we can have but an imperfect view of Wesleyanism, as to its probable stability &c—Item, his calculation of the number of Methodists is wild indeed! he adds his 100,000's with as little care as if Methodists were grains of Sand, no matter how many in a handfull.

He also locates his antipathy to the sect in its constant emphasis on the personal individual.[6]

Two facts press, in my mind, with insupportable weight on the belief in the perfection, or even peneperfection of the Methodists as well as of the Christians of the second Century/the first, their eager belief of all the impossible abominations attributed to the Heretics—Vide S[t] Epiphanius's account of the Gnostics, of which I dare aver that the belief and the naked narration imply as utter a vileness of the Being in toto, as the perpetration would do, could the things be conceived perpetrable—nay, greater, for this latter would be received as proofs positive of Madness in any court of Chancery in the World—. The second fact is, the change in the physiognomy produced in all countries & all ages by Pietism, whether Moravianism, Quakerism, or Methodism/Now we know by a sort of intuition of our own noble being when we see a highly idealized Countenance, the Magdalenes & Saints of Rafael or Dominicini—or the Apollos & Jupiters of the Ancients—& a denaturalized countenance/—all perfection must be Harmony of the whole animal triplex, Body, Soul, and Spirit—but contemplate the phiz of a Puritan! How indeed can it be otherwise, when the whole phisiognomy is formed by notions & feelings concerning the Supreme Being, & the hopes & fears connected with these notions—& these notions all represent God as glorified in proportion to our baseness—Not the sublime sentiment of Plato, in the Supreme ουκ εστι φθονος [he is not jealous]—to feel ourselves glorious in his Glory, & to to love & honor our nature because it capable of adoring & imitating his perfections—but to represent him as a Jealous Being whose Glories can never be duly honored except by exclusion & the utter vileness of all other Beings—The very foundation of Methodism is a death-blow to General Christianity—Faith (says Wesley in a hundred places) is not merely that God was in Christ, reconciling the World to himself, but that C. died for *my* Sins, that he loved *me*, gave himself for *me*!—"that he had taken away *my* sins, even *mine*, and saved *me* from sin & death"—

Conversation between Wesley & the Bishop of Bristol—

"B.—Sir, what do you mean by Faith?

W.—My Lord, by justifying Faith, I mean, a conviction wrought in a man by the Holy Ghost, that Christ hath loved *him*, and given himself for *him*, and that thro' Christ *his* sins are forgiven."

Compare with this St Paul's constant use of *us*, or *mankind*—and state the psychologic difference between/*for all men*—and therefore *for me* as included & felt in the Enthymemes, rather than *made out* & dissevered.

Trace the progress from the democratic system in the infancy of the Church, when the Churches were few, & distant from each other, & represented the Grecian Republics—to the Aristocracy of *representation*, as they became very numerous, & the intercourse more frequent, & rapid—and hence to absolute monarchy—apply this to Methodism originally, & *now*—shew too, that the present Evils in the *government* of Methodism result from their equivocal state, as Dissenters & pretended non-Dissenters—were they avowedly the former, they ought to have *Presbyters*—Presbyter the best possible form of a religion, the Churches of which are very numerous, and yet not connected with, and under the immediate inspection & ordonnance of the State/while in the Church of England by Law Established the King & his Ministers & the Legislature are *the Presbyters*—This remark appears just & not unimportant to me; and is, I believe, new.

Dissenters who, unlike their predecessors, press for a separation between church and state excite his amazement.[7]

The regular generation of the modern, worldly Dissenter was thus: Presbyterian, Arian, Socinian, Unitarian.

Is it not extraordinary to see these Dissenters calling themselves the descendants of the old Dissenters and yet clamoring for a divorce of Church and State? Why, Baxter, Bates and all the rest of them would have thought a man an atheist, who had proposed such a thing. They were rather for merging the state in the church. But these our modern gentlemen, who are blinded by political passions, give the kiss of alliance to the harlot of Rome and walk arm in arm with those who deny the God who redeemed them, if so they may wreak their insane antipathies on the Church. Well! I suppose they have counted the cost, and know what they would have.

Their hatred of the Anglican Church marks an abdication from true catholicity of religion.[8]

I have known and know many Dissenters who profess to have a zeal for Christianity—and I dare say they have: but I have known very few indeed who did not hate the Church of England a thousand times more than ever they loved Christianity. There never was an age since the Apostles, in which the catholic spirit of Religion was so dead, and put aside for love of sects and parties.

He finds himself drawn to the Quaker spirit in certain respects.[9]

I should never be very forward in offering to pour spiritual consolation into any one in distress or disease; I believe, to be of any service, such resources must be self-evolved in the first instance. I am something of the Quaker's mind in this, and am inclined to *wait* for the Spirit.

In spite of this natural inclination, he cannot find it in himself to approve of modern Quakerism.[10]

The Quakers educate upon a principle of suppressing all appearance of passion, where the exhibition of it can be injurious to their worldly interests; but they neither teach nor practise any inward subduing of the appetites; and accordingly they are the most sensual of any race of men I ever knew, within the sanction of certain public ordinances. A Quaker is made up of Ice and Flame—he has no composition, no kindly mean temperature, no Christian gentleness and cheerful charity. Hence he is never interested about any public measure, but he becomes a downright fanatic, and oversteps in his furious irrespective zeal every decency and every right opposed to his course. Of course there are some exceptions, especially amongst the women, but I believe what I say is true of Quakers in general—and I have seen a good deal of them.

Their affecting not to pay tithes is actual dishonesty; they buy for a price calculated on its payment. *Their* duty is to pay their own debts: they have nothing to do with the dedication of the money, the tenth part, which is not theirs, nor formed any part of their purchase. In truth the Quakers, who, though they pretend to be persecuted, are and have been the most petted of the Protestant sects, cultivate with intense correctness a little worldliness of their own: and I once ventured to tell a party of them that I thought they were like a string of double hunched camels trying to get through a needle's eye.

I have never known a trader in philanthropy, who was not wrong somewhere or other: individuals so distinguished are usually unhappy in their family relations—men *not* benevolent to individuals, but almost hostile to them, yet lavishing money and labour and time on the race, the abstract notion.

In contrast to the sacraments of Baptism and the Eucharist which he now believes to be intimately identified with Christianity, modern Quakerism seems to have lost touch entirely with its historical roots.[11]

My doubt is whether Baptism and the Eucharist are properly any *parts* of Christianity, or not rather Christianity itself;—the one the initial conversion or Light, the other the sustaining and invigorating Life—both together the φῶς καὶ ζωὴ [light and life] which are Christianity. A line can only *begin* once; hence there can be no repetition of Baptism; but a line may be endlessly prolonged by fresh additions; hence the sacrament of love and life lasts for ever. But there is no knowing what the modern Quakers are or believe, excepting this, that they are altogether degenerated from their ancestors of the seventeenth century. I should call modern Quakerism a Socinian Calvinism. Penn was a Sabellian, and seems to have disbelieved even the historic fact of the life and death of Jesus—most certainly Jesus of Nazareth was not Penn's Christ, if he had any. It is amusing to see the modern Quakers appealing now to history for a confirmation of their tenets and discipline—by so doing in effect abandoning the strong hold of their founders. As an imperium in imperio [a dominion within a dominion] I think Quakerism a conception of Lycurgus. Modern Quakerism is like one of those gigantic trees which are seen in the forests of North America—apparently flourishing and preserving all its greatest stretch and spread of branches; but when you have cut through an enormously thick and gnarled bark, you find the whole inside hollow and rotten. Quakerism, like such a tree, stands by its inveterate bark alone. *Bark* a Quaker, and he is a poor creature.

At the other extreme he cannot bring himself to believe that Roman Catholics are the only true catholics.[12]

Answer to Papists.—Before we can return a rational answer to the question—What is the Catholic Church—we must first ask, What is a Church?—Ans. A number of persons who are accustomed to meet together for the purpose of openly confessing, of preserving, and of improving, their faith in Christ, as their Saviour and Redeemer. Redemption from Sin and its consequences thro' Jesus Christ is the common Hope & the specific Faith of all Christians.—

What is the *visible* Catholic Church?—The aggregate of all Christian Churches throughout the World—Why do we attribute unity to it? First and chiefly, because they all are members of one Head, Jesus Christ—and secondly, because they are all united in the bond of brotherly Love, by the command of their Head & King.—What is the invisible Church? The aggregate of the actually Redeemed by Faith in Christ, whether men or departed Spirits.—What then is a Heretic? *What* a Heretic is is not difficult to say, generally, tho' there may be difficulty in defining, whether this or that be Heresy, and this or that class of persons Heretics.—Heresy signifies a wilful choice of some doctrine incompatible with or highly injurious to, the Faith in Redemption thro' Jesus Christ—N.B. Every Error is not an Heresy.—

Does an heretical church cease to be a part of the Catholic Church?—
This depends on the definition of Heresy—If the Heresy consist in the
denial of Christ as our Saviour, doubtless. For this is not Christianity,
ergo, &c—If it mean only doctrines more or less erroneous,—no! For
Christ has no where promised Freedom from Error to the Church/
It must be left as the Tares with the Corn till the last Harvest, and like
the distinction between the visible & invisible Church, cannot be
certainly *known*, tho' in many instances it may be conjectured, except
by the Judge of all./Where was the C. of England before Luther? It was
a just & witty answer of Sir H. Wotton/Here where the C. of Rome is
not—in the Gospel & N. T.—but the fair answer is—*in England*; only
with a great deal of Filth & Folly floating on it, which defecated itself in
the Time of Luther.—Does a Stream cease to be a stream, because in
a particular part of its Channel it suddenly purifies itself, and deposits
a vast sediment? With better reason may I ask where the Church of
Rome was—supposing that the C. of E. & of R. flowed together in one
stream/& disparting at an Islet one part retained, the other part dropped
its filth/but this is nonsense/The Church of England was always the C.
of England—& the name of *Roman Catholic* is downright Contradiction
in terms.

The point is refined a little after a few years.[13]

The present adherents of the Romish Church were not Catholics; we are
the Catholics. We can prove that we hold the doctrines of the primitive
Church for the first 300 years. The council of Trent made the Papists
what they are. A foreign Romish Bishop had declared that the Protestants were more like the Catholics before the Council of Trent, than
their present descendants. The course of Christianity and the Christian
Church may be likened to a great river which covered a large channel
and bore along with its waters mud and gravel and weeds, till it met a
great rock in the middle of the stream; by some means or other the
water flows purely and separated from the filth in a deeper and
narrower course on one side of the rock, and the refuse of the dirt and
troubled waters went off on the other, and then cries out, "We are the
River!" A person said, "But you will call them civilly Catholics?" "No, I
will not! I will not tell a lie upon so solemn an occasion! They are not
Catholics! If they were, then we are heretics, and *Roman* Catholics makes
no difference. Catholicism is not capable of degrees. Properly speaking
there can only be one body of Catholics ex vi termini [from the meaning

of the term]; if Roman Catholics be allowed, then there may be English, Irish &c; which with respect to a difference in religious tenets is absurd."

He produces his own definition, for the benefit of Protestants.[14]

Groundwork

of

the Defensio Fidei

of an orthodox Protestant.

1. I believe whatever the Catholic Church believes as Catholic.

2. The Church does not cease to be Catholic because a number or even (as in the time of Athanasius) a majority of those who name themselves Christians, dissent or differ from the sum of her doctrines.

3. Those Doctrines are not Catholic, (i.e. imperative on the faith of every Christian) the unbelief or disbelief of which being deemed heretical would convict the first three Centuries of the Church of Heresy.—

Scholium. This is not precisely the same as, and it is far safer than, the position: I hold the belief of the first 3 Centuries of the Church. For tho' their ignorance or disbelief of a doctrine proves such doctrine not to be Catholic, it does not necessarily follow that the contrary, i.e. the un- or dis-belief of every point of their belief is heretical. For there is a third case possible—it may have been, or it may have become, indifferent. Ex. gr. the administration of the Eucharistic Elements to infants. The Post-nicene Church is as much a negative corrective of the ante-nicene as the Ante of the Post.—/

After the passing of Roman Catholic Emancipation in 1829 and the promulgation of his own view of Church and State Coleridge's conviction of Rome's errors becomes more pronounced, as several comments in his 1833 Table Talk demonstrate.[15]

In my judgment Protestants lose a great deal of time in a false attack when they labor to convict the Roman Catholics of false doctrines. Destroy the *Papacy* and help the Priests to wives, and I am much mistaken if the doctrinal errors—such as there really are—would not very soon pass away. They might remain in terminis [in terminology], but they would lose their sting and body, and lapse back into figures of rhetoric and warm devotion from which they most of them—such as Transubstantiation and Prayer for the Dead and to Saints—originally sprang. But so long as the Bishop of Rome remains Pope, and he has an army of Mamelukes all over the world—we can do little by fulminating against doctrinal tenets. In the Milanese and elsewhere in the north of Italy I am told there is a powerful feeling abroad against the Papacy; they seem to be something in the state of England in Henry VIII's reign. How deep a wound to morals and social purity has that accursed article of the celibacy of the Clergy been! Even the best men in Roman Catholic countries attach a notion of impurity to the marriage of a Clergyman—and can such a feeling be altogether without its effect on the estimation of the wedded life in general? Impossible, and the morals of both sexes in Spain, Italy and France prove it abundantly.

The Papal Church has been anti-Cæsarean, extra-national, and anti-Christian.

The beneficial influence of the Papacy has been much overrated by some writers; and certainly no country in Europe received less benefit and more harm from it than England. In fact the lawful Kings and Parliaments of England were always essentially Protestant in feeling for a National Church, though Catholic in their Doctrine, and it was only the Usurpers, John, Henry IV, &c. that went against this policy. All the great English Schoolmen—J. Scotus—and Ramus—those morning stars of the Reformation, were heart and soul opposed to Rome, and maintained the Papacy to be Antichrist. The Popes always persecuted with rancorous hatred the national clerisies—the married clergy—and disliked the Universities which grew out of the old monasteries. The Papacy was, and is, essentially extra national and was always so considered in this country, although not believed to be anti-Christian.

The Romans had no national clerisy; their priesthood was entirely a matter of State, and as far back as we can trace it, an evident strong hold of the Patricians against the increasing powers of the Plebeians.

He traces one fault of Dissent in the devotion, however limited, to ceremonies—a devotion given fullest rein in the Roman Catholic Church. In this respect the Quakers are freest from criticism.[16]

One cause of the continuance of two of the Sacraments even in the purest & most doctrinal Protestant Churches—and which I have observed even in the society of "the *Disbelievers only so far, at present*" (Arian and Unitarian Meeting-houses) the Pride, the venial Self-consequence which is naturally felt in the performance of a *Ceremony*/ at other times he is *talking*/in these he is *doing* something, ~~and~~ something that must be done, and which he alone can do. Hence Rome, the undoubted Anti-christ, if there be any sense in the Word (i.e. if Christ mean the uncon-ditional Obedience of the Free Will to the Law of pure Reason, and Anti-christ a systematic actually-existing and most powerful Conspiracy to subvert the *Law*, to introduce in its stead all and every *Tampering* of our sensuous *Nature*, *feelings*/pride, swellings up of Heart, melting fancies, (as Sᵗ Teresa) worldly Importance, Terror, in all their minutiæ) Hence, I say, Rome has almost made up her Church-discipline of *Ceremonies*, and hence too the only Body of Christians who have wholly given up are the Quak-ers who—and because they—gave up the sacerdotal Order. 6 Sept: 1805.

The Comparison between the aims and operation of the Mosaic and Romish Ceremonies would make an interesting, & I believe, new Theol. Tract.—To examine, in the early Fathers, what share of the *Feeling* of Baptism belonged to the essence of *initiation* into Christianity, indeed, most awful & *sacramental*; and how much to the actual mode, the ceremony per se: & how far this latter was or was not confounded with the former, as being the most general *mode* of religious Proselytism. Give your repenting Enemy your right-hand & press *his* in return. Make a Bow to your lawful Superiors.—

Might not a moral "Völkslehrer" ["teacher of the masses"] talk of these as absolutely necessary to Salvation, &c, they having been in his mind Incarnations of the Truths involved?—all expressions belong to the world of Sense—to phænomena/all are contingent, local, here this, there another/but when ennobled into symbols of Noumena, it is a common & venial error to forget the vileness in the worth, to confound not to analyse—the contingent symbol with the divine Necessity = Νουμενον [the Noumenon].

Luther's religion provides a better way. His assertion concerning the inefficacy of free will is approved, but with a significant reservation.[17]

It is of vital importance for a theological Student to understand clearly the utter diversity of the Lutheran, which is likewise the Calvinistic denial of *Free* will in the Unregenerate and the doctrine of the modern Necessitarians and (proh pudor! [for shame!]) of the later Calvinists, which denies the proper existence of Will altogether. The former is sound, scriptural, compatible with the divine justice, a new, yea, a *mighty* motive to Morality, & finally, the dictate of common Sense grounded on common Experience. The former the very contrary of all these.

Luther's further avowal that in times of maximum temptation and assaults of conscience it is best to ignore all considerations except those of grace and deliverance through Christ is enthusiastically endorsed.[18]

Yea, verily, Amen and Amen! For this short heroic Paragraph contains the sum and substance, the heighth and the depth of all true Philosophy—. Most assuredly, right difficult it is for us, while we are yet in the narrow chamber of Death with our faces to the dusky ⟨falsifying⟩ *Looking-glass* that covers the scant end-side of the blind Passage from floor to ceiling, right difficult for us so wedged between its walls that we cannot turn round nor have other escape possible but by walking backward, to understand that all we behold or have any memory of having ever beheld, yea, our very selves as seen by us, are but *shadows*—and when the forms, that we [? lived/loved], vanish, impossible not to feel as if real.

At the same time Luther is also defended against charges of other-worldliness.[19]

Was it only of the world *to come*, that Luther and his Compeers preached? Turn to Luther's Table-talk: and see if the larger part be not of that other world which now *is*, and without the Being and the working of which the world *to come* would be either as unintelligible as Abracadabra, or a mere refraction & elongation of the world of Sense—Jack Robinson between two Looking glasses, with a series of Jack Robinsons in secula seculorum.

As to Judaism, Coleridge argues that the best tenets of its religion have been maintained and further fulfilled only by what he regards as the superior truth of Christianity.[20]

Hyman Hurwitz said he owned he did not expect a Messiah; but he thought it might possibly be God's will and meaning that the Jews should remain a quiet light among the nations for the purpose of pointing at the doctrine of the Unity of God.

But this truth of the essential Unity of God has been preserved and gloriously preached by Christianity alone. The Romans never shut up their temples, nor ceased to worship a hundred Gods at the bidding of Jews; the Persians, the Hindus and Chinese learned nothing from the

Jews of this great Truth. From the Christians they did learn it in various degrees—and are still learning it. Indeed the light of the Jews is as the light of a glowworm, which gives no heat and illumines nothing but itself.

The very survival of Judaism, in his view, has been due to the learning of Christian thinkers.[21]

What a blessing Christianity has been to the Jews themselves! Suppose their dispersion to exist when none of the Nations, among whom they were domiciliated & whose several Languages have become their native Mother Tongue, had recognized the divine origin and authority of the Old Testament? What reason is there for supposing that in each Language the comparative Handful of unsettled and wandering Jews would or could have made a Translation? Without the aid of Learning how long ago would the Rabbinical Writers & the Syro-Chaldean Version & Paraphrase have become as much a sealed Book as the original? If even now, the Bible has been almost overwhelmed by Talmudical Rubbish & the Tradition of Man, what would it have been, when no confirmation were given, no ancestral pride awakened, by the equal Faith & Veneration of this same Scripture avowed weekly, daily, proclaimed by the whole *cultivated* World? It is scarcely too much to say, the state of the Jewish Scriptures in the generation before Ezra almost warrants us to infer, that Judaism itself owes its Continuance to Christianity! If then the blessed Redeemer hath extended such Blessings to his Brethren according to the Flesh, even while they reject and solemnly curse him, what may we not hope for them in the day of their Reconcilement? Vide St Paul. . Romans.—

The relationship between the religions of Greece and Egypt, and Time as conceived in the Mosaic writings.[22]

On Time as connected with the Religions of the East, especially the Egyptian, & the post-homeric Greek as its derivative, & the connection between the former and the Mosaic institutions.

The French Savants who went to Egypt in the train of Napoleon (Denon, Fourrier, and Dupuis), have, it is said, triumphantly vindicated the Chronology of Herodotus from documents that cannot lie— namely, the inscriptions & sculptures of those enormous Masses of

Architecture, the gigantic Tomb-stones of the elder World—. It is decided (say they) that the present division of the Zodiac had been arranged by the Egyptians already 15000 years before the Christian Æra—. While according to an Inscription the Temple of Esne is of 8000 years' standing.—Now, first, I do not see the impossibility of an Inscription lying—or the improbability of an Interpreter—misunderstanding it; or the credibility of an Infidel French Savant being free from either—The Inscriptions &c may be & in some instances very likely are, of later date, the Offspring of Vanity & priestly Rivalry—2. The relation of Moses, conveying, in perfect accordance with all we know of analogous facts, the vast progress in civilization & splendor from Abraham & Ahimelech to Joseph & Pharaoh, is worth a cartload of such inferences/—. It is almost universal to speak of the gross Idolatry of Egypt & an argument has been grounded on this assumption in favor of the immediate divine origin of the Mosaic Monotheistic Theocracy. But of this idolatry I find no decisive proof in Moses's own writings—& regard the absence of any such as collate with the passages in the Prophets as an argument of incomparably greater value in support of the Age & authenticity of the Pentateuch—at least, of the documents from which it was formed.

There are three passages that appear to me of highest moment in the enucleation of this problem—one from Herodotus, asserting the identity of the Gods of Greece with those of Egypt—& implying the chronologic or calendar Nature of the latter; & two from Homer—that of the Sacred Sheep & Goats in Trinacria; & that of the Journey of Jupiter with all the Gods to Oceanus & the Ethiopians.—The most convenient order of the discussion will be—1. What is the Homeric Oceanus?—2. What the Sheep & Goats symbolized?—If both 1 and 2 should prove to be measures of *Time*, civil or natural, then it would follow by strongest presumption at least, that the Gods with Jove at their head represented the Divine Power manifested in *"Time & Times & half a Time"*—& this Presumption or Inference would be converted almost to certainty by the passage from Herodotus.—Suppose the above satisfactorily established, the next question would be—Was the scheme originally polytheistic? If so, did the Polytheism itself originate in a Pantheism (i.e. God = World + W = G.)—Or lastly & the opinion to which my own belief inclines, did it begin in Monotheism (World – God = 0. God – World = God + World) but soon degenerated into Pantheism, & thence by means of the ἱρα γραμματα [temple inscriptions] into Polytheism?

—Was it not the subordination of *moral* grounds to Physiology, & the *magical* study of Nature joined with astronomical & meteorological

Observations as the grounds of Prediction, the cause & occasion of this degeneracy into Pantheism?

Writing to Morgan in February 1812 Coleridge records a conversation with a businessman on the difficulty of relating Hinduism to Christianity.[23]

He had the common opinions of the East-India Company's Servants, & the same strength of prejudice against the Missionaries, & the practicability and even the utility of christianizing the natives. None, he affirmed, but the lowest Class with those who from crimes had lost their Cast, would be *christened*: & even these would never be christianized. He admitted Dr Claudius Buchanan to be a man of talents, but seemed to suspect that he had looked on the subject thro' colored, magnifying, & multiplying Glasses—with great Enthusiasm & some Ambition. Any man *wishing* to believe *any* thing might find plenty of seeming facts to confirm him among the Hindoos, from their system of flattery & assentation, & their habitual disregard of Truth. Veracity is a virtue, of which the *best* of them have no idea—they all regard the Tongue as an instrument given to the Weaker for the purpose of escaping from and over-reaching the Stronger; but especially with regard to Europeans, they regard Falsehood as a duty of Politeness, a part of the respect due to their Superiors. That all the most essential Doctrines of Christian Faith exist, and (as the natives at least believe & as it is impossible to disprove) pre-existed in the Hindoo Religion, such as the Trinity, the Incarnation of the second Person in the Trinity, the necessity of Baptism, the article of original Sin & of redemption & regeneration—this agreement instead of facilitating, he thought, must present an almost insurmountable Obstacle to their Conversion—& the Solifidianism of Christianity, i.e. the dogma of exclusive Salvation by Christ, appeared to them at once unphilosophical, inhuman, & derogatory of the divine attributes of the common father of Mankind.—I could not but assent to his opinion, as far as the ordinary notion of Christianity and the ordinary modes of preaching it extended—but I was desirous to believe, that some progress might be made if in Hindostan it were taught as having the same relation to Brahmanism, as Protestantism has to Popery—namely, as a reformation of their Religion, as the same scummed and drawn off from the Dregs.—And surely, the Hindoos are an acute race: and it requires little or no *reasoning*, (that is, links or chain of arguments) but merely common sense, in order to be made to perceive the extreme grossness & cruelty of their present ceremonial rites and sacrifices, not to mention the glaring incongruity of them with their humane & inoffensive character.—O Sir! replied Mr Wilson—common sense they have, & inoffensive & *negatively* humane, they are; but the great & desperate Obstacle is their utter, radical, and constitutional Insensibility. They will not injure a *worm*, but they will let a Cow, their sacred animal, & one from whom they have derived half their nourishment, pine away for hunger without a pang: they will not destroy the deadliest Serpent or Scorpion, but they will stand by and look at a woman or child tortured to death without a single Emotion.—Here ended our friendly dis[course—] all his remarks were sensible; but this latter most excellent—for sensibility, and self-introition, which is impossible without great sensibility, is the conditio sine quâ non of conversion to Christianity, at least, to aught but the name.—

The enigmas of Persian and Indian philosophy in relation to theism and pantheism.[24]

In Sir W. Jones's VIth Diss., that on the Persian's (Vol. I. p. 203 of Dissertation &c relating to the Arts, and Literature of Asia) we have the most pleasing account of the Pantheistic Scheme of Theomonism of the Persian and Indian Philosophers. But here, as in Europe, the System is either the same as religious Idealism, = the Berkleian Scheme: or subject to all the odious consequences of Spinosism, such as the indistinction of good and evil, of moral and physical, of God and blind Fate—and after all, leaving the main problem unsolved & unsolvible, viz. the ground of the existence of Multeity, or the passage from the Infinite to the Finite. The re-union of the Soul after Death with God is a mere Bubble of words and contradictions in a Scheme which makes God all, and all God. If the Body be God, how it can it disjoin from God? If the Body be Maia, i.e. a subjective Illusion, a mad perception or cycle of Imaginations without any correlatives in Being—whence came they? from Finiteness?—But whence came that?—From moral evil? But that supposes a *will*, and that a finite *will*, & this again supposes a plurality of wills, as the bounds, each of other/—for a boundary *from* nothing is as absurd as a boundary *of* Nothing.—

Twenty years before he thought of exploring such enigmas by constructing a dialogue between the relative protagonists.[25]

Had I proceeded in concert with R. Southey with "The Flight and Return of Mohammed" I had intended a Disputation between Mahomet, as the Representative of Unipersonal Theism with the Judaico-Christian Machinery of Angels, Genii, and Prophets; an Idolater with his Gods, Heroes & Spirits of the Departed Mighty; and a Fetisch-Worshipper, who adored the Sensible only, & held no Religion common to all Men or to any Number of men other than as they chanced at the same moment to be acted-on by the same Influence,—as when a hundred Ant-hills are in motion under the same Burst of Sun-shine. And still, chiefly, for the sake of the last Scheme, I should like to do something of this Kind. My enlightened Fetisch-Divine would have been an Okenist + Zoo.-magn[etist] with the Night-side of Nature.

Writing in his 'Opus Maximum' manuscript Coleridge recalls his early intro-duction to Indian philosophy through his reading of the linguists Sir William Jones and Sir Charles Wilkins, and his initial attraction.[26]

...I have myself paid the debt of homage on my first presentation to these foreign potentates by aid of the great linguists above mentioned. But having so done, I sought to purge the sight with the euphrasy of common sense, and took a second and more leisurely view before I put the question to myself, "And what then have I seen?"

> "What are
> These Potentates of inmost Ind?"

He tries to trace the existence of Fancy and Imagination among such early mythologies.[27]

I would fain satisfy myself whether aught of properly <u>imaginative</u> Super-stition is to be found among the ancients—& whether, if such there be, it will not be found connected with the Pelasgic as opposed to the Egyp-tian or State Religion—& grounded on a confused tradition of an Evil Principle—There are terrific circumstances attached by Theocritus to Hecatè—but while Hecatè was a <u>Goddess</u>, the same with Diana, Phoebe, Luna—while Pan was the <u>God</u> of the Woods, and ομοφυλος [of the same stock]. with Jove, Bacchus, Apollo—I find *fancy*, but no ground of imagination/Imagination seems to me to belong to Christianity, or to that patriarchal anticipation of it, implied in the faith in the God-Man, the Desire of Nations—.

In Brahmanism & Buddaism I find grotesque fancy, gigantic little-nesses but no imagination/while in the Arabian Tales & Poems it exists, because Mahomet had adopted the tradition of the Rebellion of Spirits and the Seduction of Man.

A casual glance at the Life of St Teresa proves enlightening on the psychology of the Will.[28]

I must not be too indolent to transcribe the note, I have written, on the final blank leaf of the Life of St Teresa/on opening the second volume casually I met with a curious advice to her friend, Lorenzo, always to keep Holy Water by him, to sprinkle about when he felt any inward confusion, sudden aridity, or under whispers of Temptation, all prob-ably proceeding from the presence of some evil spirit felt by the Soul, tho' not evidenced by the senses—/This led me to reflect on the import-ance of any *act* in restoring the mind from its wanderings, the servitude of mere association, by strengthing & re-enlivening the *Will*—& likewise the indifference of the things, to which a religious power is attached— an Æolian Harp was moaning in my window—what if this had been an appointed part of religious furniture, like the crucifix—and a means, to which a promise of grace had been affixed—in a mind like Teresa's or Mad. Guyon's!— What endless religious applications & accomodations!—

A longer consideration invokes the whole question of the mystics and the validity of their experience, even when received in the course of what he believes to be a mistaken version of Christianity.[29]

Monday, June 25th, 1810—Keswick—Began to read the deeply interest-ing Life & Works of Sta Teresa. She was indeed framed by nature & favored by a very hot-bed in a hot-house of Circumstances, to become a mystic Saint of the first magnitude, a mighty Mother of spiritual Transports, the materia prestabilita of divine Fusions, Infusions, and Confusions.—1. She was a *Woman*—2. a Lady, tenderly & affectionately reared—no toil, no sobering or deadning reality of physical privation or pain, to draw off her self-consciousness from the inward goings on of her Thoughts and Sensations. 3. under a very fond father and Mother, both of them strictly pious, and the mother romantic to boot. 4. She had early sympathy from her Brothers & Sister—& a perfect Convert at 8 years old in her favorite Brother. 5. She was a *Spanish* Woman, a *Spanish* Lady. Reflect on the full import of that word, the Religion, the Government, the Manners, the Climate, the Constitution, the Books implied in it. 6. Accustomed in early Childhood to read the Lives of Saints & of Martyrs—of Spanish Saints & Martyrs who had fought against and suffered under the *Moors*. At about 8 years old She & her Brother were engaged to run away & go to Africa in order to obtain the crown of Martyrdom/She regarded the Martyrs with more Envy than Admiration/they were so very lucky in getting an eternal Heaven at so easy a price. 7. In the habit (and that too without the will or knowlege of the superstitious Father) of reading Volumes of Romance & Chivalry to her Mother/Spanish Romance & Chivalry, before Don Quixote's appearance!—and that by herself all night long. 8. At 14 & 15 by the corruption of a light-minded but favorite Cousin, & her female servants, she opened her fearful heart to Spanish Sweet-heartry, doubtless in the true Oroondates Style—and the giving audience to some dying swain thro' the barred Windows, or having received a Lover's Messages of Flames & flaming Conceits, & Anguish, and Despair—these seem to have been the *mortal* Sins of which she bitterly accuses herself— together with perhaps, a few warm fancies of earthy Love with her aver- sion (at 15 years old) to shut herself up for ever in a Nunnery, to which her Father likewise was obstinately averse. He had doubtless sense enough, with all his superstition, to perceive how utterly unfit such a Nursery of inward Fancies & outward Privations were to a Brain, Heart, & bodily Constitution, like those of innocent, loving, & high- empassioned Theresa. What would come of it but a despairing anguish- stricken Sinner, or a mad Saint? This frame of such exquisite sensibility by nature & by education shaken & ruined by the violence done to her nature by her obstinate resolve to become a nun against her own *Wishes* and against her Father's Will—out of a resolve of Duty/finishing in a burning fever, which ended in Madness for many months or a state very like it—& which left her Brain unsettled, as is evident from the frequent fainting fits, to which she was ever after subject—Previously to this step she had been reading to her over-religious Uncle books of Death, Hell, & Judgment—which made a fearful impression on her tender mind, because out of her exceeding desire to give pleasure she had *affected* to take a delight in reading them to Him, tho' the very contrary was the real case. She at length resolved on nunhood, she says, because she thought it could not be *worse* than the Pains of Purgatory & not so long—& that a Purgatory for this Life was a cheap expiation in exchange for Hell for ever!!—10. Combine these causes only—& as yet I have stated & have read the contents of only eleven pages—& you will see, how almost impossible it was, that a young Spanish Maiden so innocent, & so susceptible, of an imagination so lively by nature & so fever-kindled by disease & its occasions, & thus so well furnished with the requisite images & preconceptions, should not mistake, & often, the less painful and in such a frame the sometimes pleasurable approaches to bodily Deliquium, and her imperfect Fainting-fits for divine Transports, & momentary Union with God—especially if with a thoughtful yet pure psychology you join the force of suppressed Instincts stirring in the heart & bodily frame, of a mind unconscious of their nature/and these in the keenly-sensitive body, in the innocent and loving Soul of a Teresa, with "all her Thirsts, and Lives, and Deaths of Love"—and what remains unsolved, for which the credulity of the Many and the Knavery of a Few will not furnish ample explanation.

11. One other source it is almost criminal to have forgotten—Page the 12th of her Life has brought it back to my recollection—those Effects I mean so supersensual that they might even with wise men venially pass for supernatural, and so glorious for human nature that tho' they be in truth our *Humanity* itself in its contra-distinction from animal nature, it is yet no wonder if conscious of the sad & humiliating Weaknesses blended into one person with this noble Instinct, the Soul attributes* them to Divinity acting on us & from without.

The need to distinguish the valuable insights of such mystics from the errors and delusions incident on their particular religious allegiance.[30]

It were greatly to be wished, for the sake of tender & pious Protestants, that some one of steady Judgment yet affectionately devout & who delights in quiet meditation, should make an extract from the writings of Teresa, Madame Guyon, Franc. De Sales—& even perhaps the best parts of Bœhmen & his Followers—which would perhaps win its way with the Public still more, if to each *Extract* the Life were given to the

---

* (a mistake this of the sensuous imagination relatively to Place and to Space, rather than a misnomer of the thing itself, which is verily & in fact the το Θειον εφ' ημιν, Θεος οικειος [the God upon us, the domestic God]!) the Effects, I say, of the *moral* Being after difficult Conquest, the total State of the Spirit after the victorious Struggle, in which and by which *the* WILL has preserved its perfect Freedom by a deep and vehement Energy of perfect Obedience to the pure, practical Reason, or Conscience! Thence flows in upon and fills the Soul that Peace,

Author or Authoress—exposing the delusions & the after impostures & interpolations—For Teresa's Life & Works were not written under the eye of a watchful Dominican, but afterwards 12 years in the Inquisition—& that there are various *Interpolations*, there can be no doubt.

In Chapter XI. Vol. I. prettily comparing the business of Prayer to that of watering a Garden for the Lord, she elucidates the four states of Prayer—1. by the drawing up water from a well with the bucket by mere force of the arm—2. by *the wheel* & pully—3. by the drawing off streamlets from a River & great Fountain—4ᵗʰ—by copious rains from Heaven/ —the first the seemingly unassisted poor laboring Will—the last, the will swallowed up in the full descent of Grace on the soul—She adds judiciously, p. 68. The true Love of God doth not consist in having Tears, or Tenderness, or Spiritual Gusts; but to serve him with uprightness, Fortitude of mind, and Humility. Not that we are to reject or undervalue those aidances & refreshments when given/under the notion that they are of the nature of sensuality—For we are Body & Soul as well as Soul & Body—but still we must remain Lords of ourselves, when they are withheld, & reflect, that *the will* may wax and strengthen under the greatest dryness of our sensitive nature, nay, far more under frequent & grievous Dyspathy & Reluctions of the Body, than it *could do* amid its perpetual Sympathy.—Of Kant's two divisions of *Religious Sects* as distinguished from ecclesiastical, I prefer the latter on many

---

which passeth Understanding! that State which would be affronted and calumniated by the name of Pleasure, which is degraded & misrepresented even by that of Happiness—the corner stone, say rather, the living Fountain of that Religion & that Morality, which cannot even in thought be distinguished the one from the other; and which secures Religion to Man, as long as anywhere in the partakers of human Nature there remains that instinctive craving, dim & blind tho' it may be, of the moral being after this unknown Bliss, or Blessedness—known only & anticipated by the Hollowness where it is. (The Plant in its dark Chamber turns & twists its stem & grows toward the Light-Cranny, the sensation of the want supplying the sense of the Object wanted!) Under all forms of Religion, positive or the growth of philosophic Meditation, this divine *Humanity* has developed itself, has had its Epiphanies & Incarnations, too glorious an attribute of man, too specifically the Image of his unwithholding Father & Creator, to be confined to any name or race, but which it is but Truth & Fact of History to declare, is more especially fostered & favored by Christianity. Its frequent "manifestations in the flesh" even under the most selfish & unchristian of its Forms (the Roman Catholic) carries to my Understanding as well as Heart a more forcible Argument for its Divinity, than all the miracles of Veeshnoo would afford tho' each miracle had tenfold the support of outward Testimony that has hitherto been adduced by the Writers on the miraculous facts of the Gospel, from Grotius to Paley.

accounts; yet dare not say, that there are not persons to whom the former (the heart-crash of Remorse) may not be more appropriate. Prisons have been opened by earthquakes—and the first view which the Soul has of her Destiny & her present unfitness for it may be from a flash of Lightning in a storm/tho' more frequently, I trust, from the sweet & silent Dawn.

Yet in the end, whatever their brand of faith, and however prone to delusion, it is difficult not to believe that such mystics are sharing a common experience.[31]

St Teresa saith (Life, Relation 4. p. 301) "That if any of her Visions, Revelations, or Speeches had incited her to a thing that had been contrary to any point of the CATHOLIC FAITH or God's Law, she should not have been necessitated to seek out persons to have resolved her: for hence she should soon have perceived it to be the Devil."—a fair example of my former remark on the assumption that miraculum esse, et a Deo vocem afferre [to be a miracle, and to report a voice from God], is one & the same thing—&c. What? if God had worked a Miracle to convince St Teresa of the falsehood of the Roman Superstitions & Abuses—would she not, like the Jews, have made it a test of her Love & Obedience to God that she had attributed it without hesitation to the Devil?

Charity. What man of penetration can read the works of Teresa, Whitfield, and Wesley or Flechier, whom I mention as familiar names and representatives of the doctrines of the pious Catholics, the pious Calvinists, and the pious Arminians, the last holding a power in the will to accept & co-operate with the Grace of God, yet not presuming any other merit than the mere diminution of demerit—the second abhorring the very name both of Merit & Free Will and the third holding both & naming both with open mouth & Joyousness—yet who, I say, can read these authors, & not perceive that they all felt the same feelings, and *meant* the very same things!—N.B. To dwell with especial force, and that re-iterated on every fit occasion, on the possible, nay, probable difference between a Unitarian, and Unitarianism, between a Papist and Popery—to prove with a pen of fire the fusion of Love, and Piety, melting down and blending into transient harmony the most intractable and discordant materials/Read Sta Teresa's Life & Tracts, Francesco de Sales, &c &c for the latter/and describe the former from the recollection of Mrs Danvers—the life of Firmin—the spirit breathed thro' the writings of Lardner—& a still more forcible illustration, the life & second Vol. of Hartley compared with the inevitable consequences (in logic) of his first

Vol.—Not what may be drawn, but what is—determines on the character of the Individual—not what has been drawn in particular instances
and under antidote & over-balances particular, but what naturally
would follow, considering the thing per se or Lord of the Ascendant,
must determine on the character of a doctrine—Have adder[s] ceased to
be poisonous, because Paul took them up uninjured? Even whole classes
of Beings are something armed as with inborn antidote—Thus Women
in general with regard to enthusiastic notions in piety—and breathe
sweet music thro' a Hemlock Pipe.

*The psychological critique which underlies many of his statements concerning
the egotistical tendency of exclusive religious beliefs is set forth boldly at one
point in* Aids to Reflection.[32]

He, who begins by loving Christianity more than Truth, will proceed by
loving his own Sect or Church better than Christianity, and end by loving himself better than all.

Conclusions

At intervals in his life Coleridge would try to sum up what it was that he hoped he was achieving. In previous sections it has been argued that in his early career he had high hopes of bringing about a revolution in psychological thinking by demonstrating the working of a level in the subconscious that was in direct communication with the divine, but over the years this conviction was modified. At its highest, as already mentioned above, it amounted to an alignment of the creative principle in the artist with the creative power of God himself: an aspiration which seems to haunt a poem such as 'Kubla Khan', but which was modified in time to refer rather to the primary imagination, and the assertion in *Biographia Literaria* that it was 'a repetition in the finite mind of the eternal act of creation in the infinite I AM'.[1] Even this reduced form, however, was stroked out by him in one copy, according to his daughter[2]—presumably as over-presumptuous. Ideas of the kind proved nevertheless to be insuppressible in his work, however swiftly they might be checked by a self-deprecating humility.

From time to time Coleridge would take the simple course of trying to justify his aims in a single formulation, as in some notebook entries. In the same way, attempts at finality could be shot through with shadows of uncertainty. From time to time he inserted entries in his notebooks reminding future readers of the provisional quality of all the thinking in these 'fly-catchers'—as he sometimes called them. This was a bold acknowledgement of the continuing need for more adequate formulation of his beliefs; yet he could also, paradoxically, make statements about the overriding adequacy of his 'system' with a finality that seemed to belie the heuristic quality he elsewhere claimed for them.

In conclusions provided for two of his works, again, he tried in different ways to sum up what he had been saying in longer terms, providing a religious setting in each case. At the end of *Biographia Literaria* he maintained that his object in recounting the vicissitudes of his life had been to rescue the young from the permanent habits of contempt into which they were in danger of falling and to demonstrate the reasonableness of the teachings of the Church. What was there indicated in brief and broad terms was then set out in much more detailed argument at the end of *Aids to Reflection*, with a long discussion of the short-comings inherent in recent science. Both conclusions alike involved self-defence against charges of mysticism, coupled with an attempt to distinguish the false and true versions of mystical experience.

These two major statements concerning his aims were accompanied by various shorter statements and assertions which attested the complexity of his views. The letter quoted above in which he saw the progression in one's career from youth to age as marked by a long losing battle between the youthful imagination and the nature it tried to subdue was a vivid instance of his steadily increasing disillusionment concerning the possibilities of moral progress. Yet in one respect at least nature had left her mark. The years of his contact with the Wordsworths had left him with a permanent sense of the necessary distinction between the mechanical view of the mind which he felt to have characterized eighteenth-century philosophy and a sense of the mind as living organism which he believed to be the true one.

The ramifications of this insight gave Coleridge an unusual power in identifying the deficiencies of what was at present offered to his contemporaries. The period during which he explored the possibility of devising a religion of life had made him unusually sensitive to the difference between the linguistic instruments appropriate to the discussion of vital processes and those that were adequate to mechanical operations—which in turn had made him an unusually sensitive and intelligent literary critic. He believed an equivalent recognition to lie at the root of all genuine Christianity. Accordingly, he was always impatient with religious doctrines that seemed to address human beings as if they were themselves mechanical in their faculties rather than endowed with the processes of life. Such treatment amounted to a deficient regard for what should be alive in its recipients.

His desire that the living philosophy he valued should also result in an equally living communication between human beings he found exemplified in the writings of St Paul. While he continued to regard the early chapters of the gospel of St John as providing the most important and succinct version of the doctrines he regarded as central ('In Him was life, and the life was the light of men') he found the qualities of the

Pauline writings to be also of great value, displaying an ability to communicate with human frailty that was appealing. This grace, which he characterized as 'gentlemanliness', he recommended to members of his family as a model for their own human conduct.

In other aspects of his religious thinking he was more bound by the presuppositions of his contemporary culture. While he was always delighted by the processes of development, and indeed of living evolution, he could not accept the idea that human beings were themselves the product of an evolution through time and no more. However much he may have been delighted by the idea of the 'living filament' that worked through the whole animal creation in the thinking of Erasmus Darwin[3] he could not for a moment accept the further step that would enable Darwin's grandson to propose a cognate model including human beings. He remained convinced of the existence of an impassable gulf between the illuminated Reason of human beings that was capable of responding to divine moral imperatives and the ingenious, problem-solving understanding they possessed in common with the rest of the animate creation.

He wrote little on the question of immortality—mainly, perhaps, because he never really questioned its validity. 'All intense passions,' he wrote in 1811, 'have faith in their own eternity, & thence in the eternity of their objects'[4] and what he believed to be true of the passions was even more true of the sense of Being that underlay all such emotions. The point, made directly in a late note on immortality, remained a crucial element in his philosophy to the end. His last message ('he articulated with difficulty, but his mind was clear and powerful') was given to J. H. Green the night before his death and reaffirmed for the last time his belief in the absolute quality of the 'I am', both as a divine and human statement, as well as the equivalently vital need for communication of all such Beings with each other—and with the Divine.

Set in that form, the nature of the third person of the Trinity was still undetermined; it was the relationship between the Creative Father and the generated son that remained his most important concern and subject of affirmation. He had no difficulty, in other words, in affirming a Divine Binity—the supreme Being and the generated Word—but he could achieve a Trinity only by way of an oblique further move, as when he tried to identify the third person with the Spirit of Love. Yet in terms of his lasting quest this was peculiarly appropriate. As often in his writings, whether in poetry or prose, love proved once again to be for him the ultimate and necessary key to human existence.

In 1803 he turns aside from discussion of evil to assert the virtue and positiveness of his own endeavours.[1]

What is it, that I employ my Metaphysics on? To perplex our clearest notions, & living moral Instincts? To extinguish the Light of Love & of Conscience, to put out the Life of Arbitrement—to make myself & others *Worthless, Soul*-less *God*less?—No! To expose the Folly & the Legerdemain of those who have thus abused the blessed Organ of Language, to support all old & venerable Truths, to support, to kindle, to project, to make the Reason spread Light over our Feelings, to make our Feelings diffuse vital Warmth thro' our Reason—these are my Objects—& these my Subjects. Is this the metaphysics that bad Spirits in Hell delight in?

Above all he argues for the ability of true love to establish itself as a universal feeling, affecting the quality of human ideas, and approached only in its effects by the not dissimilar potency of fear in certain circumstances.[2]

On Friday Night, 8th Feb/1805, my feeling, in sleep, of exceeding great Love for my Infant/seen by me in the Dream/yet so as that it might be Sara, Derwent or Berkley/and still *it was an individual Babe and mine.*
Of Love in Sleep, the seldomness of the Feeling, scarcely ever in short absences, or except after very long Absence/a certain indistinctness, a sort of *universal-in-particularness* of Form, seems necessary—vide the note preceding, and my Lines. "All Look or Likeness caught from Earth, All accident of Kin or Birth, Had pass'd Away: there seem'd no Trace of Aught upon her brighten'd Face Uprais'd beneath the rifted Stone, Save of one Spirit, all her own/She, she herself, and only she Shone in her body visibly." This abstract Self is indeed in its nature a Universal personified—as Life, Soul, Spirit, &c. Will not this prove it to be a *deeper* Feeling, & of such intimate affinity with ideas, so to modify them & become one with them, whereas the appetites and the feelings of Revenge and Anger co-exist with the Ideas, ~~in~~ not combine with them; and alter the apparent effect of the Forms not the Forms themselves./Certain modifications of Fear seem to approach nearest to this Love-sense, in its manner of acting.—

At the end of his Biographia Literaria *Coleridge attempts an adequate conclusion to everything he has been saying, ending in a prose poem of adoration to the Deity.*[3]

CONCLUSION

IT sometimes happens that we are punished for our faults by incidents, in the causation of which these faults had no share: and this I have always felt the severest punishment. The wound indeed is of the same dimensions; but the edges are jagged, and there is a dull underpain that survives the smart which it had aggravated. For there is always a consolatory feeling that accompanies the sense of a proportion between antecedents and consequents. The sense of Before and After becomes both intelligible and intellectual when, and *only* when, we contemplate the succession in the relations of Cause and Effect, which like the two poles of the magnet manifest the being and unity of the one power by relative opposites, and give, as it were, a substratum of permanence, of identity, and therefore of reality, to the shadowy flux of Time. It is Eternity revealing itself in the phænomena of Time: and the perception and acknowledgement of the proportionality and appropriateness of the Present to the Past, prove to the afflicted Soul, that it has not yet been deprived of the sight of God, that it can still recognize the effective presence of a Father, though through a darkened glass and a turbid atmosphere, though of a Father that is chastising it. And for this cause, doubtless, are we so framed in mind, and even so organized in brain and nerve, that all confusion is painful.—It is within the experience of many medical practitioners, that a patient, with strange and unusual symptoms of disease, has been more distressed in mind, more wretched, from the fact of being unintelligible to himself and others, than from the pain or danger of the disease: nay, that the patient has received the most solid comfort, and resumed a genial and enduring chearfulness, from some new symptom or product, that had at once determined the name and nature of his complaint, and rendered it an intelligible effect of an intelligible cause: even though the discovery did at the same moment preclude all hope of restoration. Hence the mystic theologians, whose delusions we may more confidently hope to separate from their actual intuitions, when we condescend to read their works without the presumption that whatever our fancy (always the ape, and too often the adulterator and counterfeit of our memory) has not made or cannot make a picture of, must be nonsense,—hence, I say, the Mystics have joined in representing the state of the reprobate spirits as a dreadful dream in which there is no sense of reality, not even of the pangs they are enduring—an eternity without time, and as it were below it—God present without manifestation of his presence. But these are depths, which we dare not linger over. Let us turn to an instance more on a level with the ordinary sympathies of mankind. Here then, and in this same healing influence of *Light* and distinct Beholding, we may detect the final cause of that instinct which in the great majority of instances leads and almost compels the Afflicted to communicate their sorrows. Hence too flows the alleviation that results from "*opening out* our griefs:" which are thus presented in distinguishable forms instead of the mist, through which whatever is shapeless becomes magnified and (literally) *enormous*.

This has been my Object, and this alone can be my Defence—and O! that with this my personal as well as my LITERARY LIFE might conclude! the unquenched desire I mean, not without the consciousness of having earnestly endeavoured to kindle young minds, and to guard them against the temptations of Scorners, by shewing that the Scheme of Christianity, as taught in the Liturgy and Homilies of our Church, though not discoverable by human Reason, is yet in accordance with it; that link follows link by necessary consequence; that Religion passes out of the ken of Reason only where the eye of Reason has reached its own Horizon; and that Faith is then but its continuation: even as the Day softens away into the sweet Twilight, and Twilight, hushed and breathless, steals into the Darkness. It is Night, sacred Night! the upraised Eye views only the starry Heaven which manifests itself alone: and the outward Beholding is fixed on the sparks twinkling in the aweful depth, though Suns of other Worlds, only to preserve the Soul steady and collected in its pure *Act* of inward Adoration to the great I AM, and to the filial WORD that re-affirmeth it from Eternity to Eternity, whose choral Echo is the Universe.

ΘΕΩι ΜΟΝΩι ΔΟΞΑ. [to God alone be the glory]

In a fragment of the subsequent period he surveys the loss of his early optimism concerning the necessary progress of a moral ascent, yet refuses to abandon his belief in an ascent of humanity, as a whole.[4]

... tho' I have out lived the Optimism of my Youth and early Manhood, when my fancy and my ingenuity were strained to find good in every thing, and I strove to think even

> Guilt and Anguish and the wormy Grave
> Shapes of a Dream—

I still retain, I dare not forego, the faith in a continued tho' spiral Ascent of Humanity. How indeed in the absence of this faith could we without mockery prefer the prayer—Thy Kingdom come! Thy Will be done on Earth as it is in Heaven! Evil is not eternal. It *began*, and not from God. Therefore it must end and by God.—

This one might infer from reason. And by the same Light we recognizes, tho' by it we could never have discovered, the further truth, that God, "the Word that was in the beginning, in whom is Life and that Life the Light of Man", i.e. the ground of that Reason which constitutes our proper Humanity, must take up our human Nature into himself in order to act as a renewing principle of moral Life on the fallen humanity in us. For "since by Man came Death, by Man must come the Resurrection".

As far, therefore, as a firm faith in a redemptive process, never suspended, tho' not always apparent, may be called Optimism, so far I still remain an Optimist. But that the process consists in a moral and intellectual progression of the Mass of Mankind, or of a whole People or Nation—this no longer appears to me so clear a point as it did during that period of Life when the Head took the Heart for its Chief Counsellor, and when whatever of Good was stirring within me I supposed myself to have in common with all men. But I have since then been made to reflect . . .

To set forth the evil of the time, when we know of no adequate yet practicable remedy, is at all times a *thankless* office. But that it is in *all* cases an idle one, or that the Physician is worthy of no thanks, who determines the true name and nature of the Malady and refers it to its right seat and source, even tho' he should confess himself unable to prescribe for it—of this I am not so clearly convinced—If he draws off those, who have been losing themselves on a wrong scent, if he guard the Patient against unprincipled Empirics and Remedies worse than the Disease, I do not see why those, who in all other things so highly extol the division of Labor, can consistently deny him the credit of having *paid in* to the Public his contingent of utility. But be this as it may! It is but an individual Concern, and this too respecting the most shadowy of Boons, contemporary reputation. As such, I feel that it is below the deep interest of the present Question.—Not to mention, that it takes for granted the existence of an evil, characteristic of the times, that requires its appropriate Remedy.

Some years later he attempts a fuller and more adequate defence of his position in a concluding section for his Aids to Reflection *where he again tries to outline a proper view of the mystical tradition.*[5]

I AM not so ignorant of the temper and tendency of the age in which I live, as either to be unprepared for the *sort* of remarks which the literal interpretation of the Evangelist will call forth, or to attempt an answer to them. Visionary Ravings, Obsolete Whimsies, Transcendental Trash, &c. &c., I leave to pass at the price current among those who are willing to receive abusive phrases as substitutes for argument. Should any Suborner of anonymous Criticism have engaged some literary Bravo or Buffoon beforehand, to vilify this work, as in former instances, I would give a friendly hint to the operative Critic that he may compile an excellent article for the occasion, and with very little trouble, out of Warburton's Tract on Grace and the Spirit, and the Preface to the same.—There is, however, one—objection, shall I say? or accusation? which will so often be heard from men, whose talents and reputed moderation must give a weight to their words, that I owe it both to my own character and to the interests of my readers, not to leave it unnoticed. The charge will probably be worded in this way:—There is nothing new in all this! (*as if novelty were any merit in questions of Revealed Religion!*) It is *Mysticism*, all taken out of WILLIAM LAW, after he had lost his senses, poor Man! in brooding over the Visions of a delirious German Cobbler, Jacob Behmen.

Of poor Jacob Behmen I have delivered my sentiments at large in another work. Those who have condescended to look into his writings must know, that his characteristic errors are; first, the mistaking the accidents and peculiarities of his own over-wrought mind for realities and modes of thinking common to all minds: and secondly, the confusion of Nature, *i.e.* the active powers communicated to matter, with God, the Creator. And if the same persons have done more than merely looked into the present volume, they must have seen, that to eradicate, and, if possible, to preclude both the one and the other stands prominent among its avowed objects.

Of William Law's Works I am acquainted with the SERIOUS CALL; and besides this I remember to have read a small tract, on Prayer, if I mistake not, as I easily may, it being at least six-and-twenty years since I saw it. He may in this or in other tracts have quoted the same passages from the fourth Gospel as I have done. But surely this affords no presumption that my conclusions are the same with his; still less, that they are drawn from the same premises; and least of all, that they were adopted from his writings. Whether Law has used the phrase, assimilation by faith, I know not; but I know that I should expose myself to a just charge of an idle parade of my Reading, if I recapitulated the tenth part of the Authors, Ancient and Modern, Romish and Reformed, from Law to Clemens Alexandrinus and Irenaeus, in whose works the same phrase occurs in the same sense. And after all, on such a subject how worse than childish is the whole dispute!

Is the fourth Gospel authentic? And is the interpretation, I have given, true or false? These are the only questions which a wise man would put, or a Christian be anxious to answer. I not only believe it to be the true sense of the texts; but I assert that it is the only true, rational, and even *tolerable* sense. And this position alone I conceive myself interested in defending. I have studied with an open and fearless spirit the attempts of sundry learned Critics of the Continent, to invalidate the authenticity of this Gospel, before and since Eichhorn's Vindication. The result has been a clearer assurance, and (as far as this was possible) a yet deeper conviction of the genuineness of *all* the writings, which the Church has attributed to this Apostle. That those, who have formed an opposite conclusion, should object to the use of expressions which they had ranked among the most obvious marks of spuriousness, follows as a matter of course. But that men, who with a clear and cloudless assent receive the sixth chapter of this Gospel as a faithful, nay, *inspired* Record of an actual discourse, should take offence at the repetition of words which the Redeemer himself, in the perfect foreknowledge that they would confirm the disbelieving, alienate the unsteadfast, and transcend the present capacity even of his own Elect, had chosen as the *most* appropriate; and which, after the most decisive proofs, that they *were* misinterpreted by the greater number of his Hearers, and not understood by any, he nevertheless repeated with stronger emphasis and *without comment*, as the *only* appropriate symbols of the great truth he was declaring, and to realize which ἐγένετο σάρξ [he became flesh]*— that in their own discourses these men should hang back from all express reference to these words, as if they were afraid or ashamed of them, though the earliest recorded ceremonies and liturgical forms of the primitive Church are absolutely inexplicable, except in connexion

---

*Of which our *he was made flesh*, is perhaps the best that our language admits, but is still an inadequate translation. The Church of England in this as in other doctrinal points, has preserved the golden mean between the superstitious reverence of the Romanists, and the avowed contempt of the Sectarians, for the Writings of the Fathers, and the authority and unimpeached traditions of the Church during the first three or four Centuries. And how, consistently with this honorable characteristic of our Church, a minister of the same could, on the sacramentary scheme now in fashion, return even a plausible answer to Arnauld's great Work on Transubstantiation, (not without reason the Boast of Catholicism,) exceeds my powers of conjecture.

with this discourse, and with the *mysterious* and *spiritual*, not allegorical and merely ethical, import of the same; and though this import is solemnly and in the most unequivocal terms asserted and taught by their own Church, even in her Catechism, or compendium of doctrines necessary for all her Members; *this* I may, perhaps, *understand*; but *this* I am not able to vindicate or excuse!

There is, however, one opprobrious phrase which it may be profitable for my younger Readers that I should explain, viz. Mysticism. And for this purpose I will quote a sentence or two from a Dialogue . . .

MYSTICS AND MYSTICISM

"*Antinöus*.—What do you call Mysticism? And do you use the word in a good or in a bad sense?"

"*Nöus*.—In the latter only: as far, at least, as we are now concerned with it. When a Man refers to *inward feelings* and *experiences*, of which Mankind at large are not conscious, as evidences of the truth of any opinion—such a Man I call a A MYSTIC: and the grounding of any theory or belief on accidents and anomalies of individual sensations or fancies, and the use of peculiar terms invented or perverted from their ordinary significations, for the purpose of expressing these *idiosyncracies*, and pretended facts of interior consciousness, I name MYSTICISM. Where the error consists simply in the Mystic's attaching to these anomalies of his individual temperament the character of *Reality*, and in receiving them as Permanent Truths, having a subsistence in the Divine Mind, though revealed to himself alone; but entertains this persuasion without demanding or expecting the same faith in his neighbours—I should regard it as a species of ENTHUSIASM, always indeed to be deprecated, but yet capable of co-existing with many excellent qualities both of Head and Heart. But when the Mystic by ambition or still meaner passions, or (as sometimes is the case) by an uneasy and self-doubting state of mind that seeks confirmation in outward sympathy, is led to impose his faith, as a duty, on mankind generally: and when with such views he asserts, that the same experiences would be vouchsafed, the same truths revealed, to *every man* but for his secret wickedness and unholy will—such a Mystic is a FANATIC, and in certain states of the public mind a dangerous Member of Society. And most so in those ages and countries in which Fanatics of elder standing are allowed to persecute the fresh competitor. For under these predicaments, Mysticism, though originating in the singularities of an individual Nature, and therefore essentially anomalous, is nevertheless highly *contagious*. It is apt to collect a swarm and cluster *circum fana*, around the new *Fane*: and therefore merits the name of FANATICISM, or as the Germans say, Schwärmerey, i.e. *Swarm-making."*

We will return to the harmless species—the enthusiastic Mystics: a species that may again be subdivided into two ranks. And it will not be other than germane to the subject, if I endeavour to describe them in a sort of allegory, or parable. Let us imagine a poor pilgrim benighted in a wilderness or desart, and pursuing his way in the starless dark with a lantern in his hand. Chance or his happy genius leads him to an Oasis or natural Garden, such as in the creations of my youthful fancy I supposed Enos* the Child of Cain to have found. And here, hungry and thirsty, the way-wearied Man rests at a fountain; and the Taper of his Lantern throws its Light on an over-shadowing Tree, a Boss of snow-white Blossoms, through which the green and growing Fruits peeped, and the ripe golden Fruitage glowed. Deep, vivid, and faithful are the impressions, which the lovely Imagery comprised within the scanty Circle of Light, makes and leaves on his Memory! But scarcely has he eaten of the fruits and drunk of the fountain, ere scared by the roar and howl from the desart he hurries forward: and as he passes with hasty steps through grove and glade, shadows and imperfect beholdings and vivid fragments of things distinctly seen

---

*Will the Reader forgive me if I attempt at once to illustrate and relieve the subject by annexing the first stanza of the Poem composed in the same year in which I wrote the Ancient Mariner and the first book of Christabel?

> "Encinctur'd with a twine of Leaves,
> That leafy twine his only Dress!
> A lovely Boy was plucking fruits
> In a moonlight wilderness.
> The Moon was bright, the air was free,
> And Fruits and Flowers together grew
> On many a Shrub and many a Tree:
> And all put on a gentle hue,
> Hanging in the shadowy air
> Like a Picture rich and rare.
> It was a Climate where, they say,
> The Night is more belov'd than Day.
> But who that beauteous Boy beguil'd,
> That beauteous Boy! to linger here?
> Alone, by night, a little child,
> In place so silent and so wild—
> Has he no friend, no loving mother near?"
> WANDERINGS OF CAIN

blend with the past and present shapings of his Brain. Fancy modifies Sight. His Dreams transfer their forms to real Objects; and these lend a substance and an *outness* to his Dreams. Apparitions greet him; and when at a distance from this enchanted land, and on a different track, the Dawn of Day discloses to him a Caravan, a troop of his fellow-men, his memory, which is itself half fancy, is interpolated afresh by every attempt to recall, connect, and *piece out* his recollections. His narration is received as a Madman's Tale. He shrinks from the rude Laugh and contemptuous Sneer, and retires into himself. Yet the craving for Sympathy, strong in proportion to the intensity of his Convictions, impels him to unbosom himself to abstract Auditors; and the poor Quietist becomes a Penman, and, all too poorly stocked for the Writer's trade, he borrows his phrases and figures from the only Writings to which he has had access, the sacred Books of his Religion. And thus I shadow out the enthusiast Mystic of the first sort; at the head of which stands the illuminated Teutonic Theosopher and Shoemaker, honest JACOB BEHMEN, born near Gorlitz, in Upper Lusatia, in the 17th of our Elizabeth's Reign, and who died in the 22nd of her Successor's.

To delineate a Mystic of the second and higher order, we need only endow our Pilgrim with equal gifts of Nature, but these developed and displayed by all the aids and arts of Education and favorable Fortune. *He* is on his way to the Mecca of his ancestral and national Faith, with a well-guarded and numerous Procession of Merchants and Fellow-pilgrims, on the established Track. At the close of Day the Caravan has halted: the full moon rises on the Desert: and he strays forth alone, out of sight, but to no unsafe distance; and Chance leads *him* too, to the same Oasis or Islet of Verdure on the Sea of Sand. He wanders at leisure in its maze of Beauty and Sweetness, and thrids his way through the odorous and flowering Thickets into open "Spots of Greenery," and discovers statues and memorial characters, grottos, and refreshing Caves. But the Moonshine, the imaginative Poesy of Nature, spreads its soft shadowy charm over all, conceals distances, and magnifies heights, and modifies relations; and fills up vacuities with its own whiteness, counterfeiting substance; and where the dense shadows lie, makes solidity imitate Hollowness; and gives to all objects a tender visionary hue and softening. Interpret the Moonlight and the Shadows as the peculiar genius and sensibility of the Individual's own Spirit: and here you have the other sort: a Mystic, an Enthusiast of a nobler Breed—a FENELON. But the residentiary, or the frequent visitor of the favored spot, who has scanned its beauties by steady Day-light, and mastered its true proportions and lineaments, he will discover that both Pilgrims have indeed been there! *He* will know, that the delightful Dream, which the latter tells, is a Dream of Truth; and that even in the bewildered Tale of the former there is Truth mingled with the Dream.

But the source, the Spring-head, of the Charges which I anticipate, lies deep. Materialism, conscious and avowed Materialism, is in ill repute: and a confessed Materialist therefore a rare character. But if the faith be ascertained by the fruits: if the predominant, though most often unsuspected, persuasion is to be learnt from the influences, under which the thoughts and affections of the Man move and take their direction; I must reverse the position. ONLY NOT ALL ARE MATERIALISTS. Except a few individuals, and those for the most part of a single Sect: every one, who calls himself a Christian, holds himself to have a Soul as well as a Body. He distinguishes Mind from Matter, the *Subject* of his consciousness from the *Objects* of the same. The former is his MIND: and he says, it is immaterial. But though *Subject* and *Substance* are words of kindred roots, nay, little less than equivalent terms, yet nevertheless it is exclusively to sensible OBJECTS, to Bodies, to modifications of Matter, that he habitually attaches the attributes of reality, of substance. Real and Tangible, Substantial and Material, are Synonymes for him. He never indeed asks himself, what he means by MIND? But if he did, and tasked himself to return an honest answer—as to what, at least, he had hitherto meant by it—he would find, that he had described it by negatives, as the opposite of Bodies, *ex. gr.* as a somewhat opposed to solidity, to visibility &c. as if you could abstract the capacity of a vessel, and conceive of it as a somewhat by itself, and then give to the emptiness the properties of containing, holding, being entered, and so forth. In short, though the proposition would perhaps be angrily denied in words, yet *in fact* he thinks of his *Mind*, as a *property*, or *accident* of a something else, that he calls a *Soul* or *Spirit*: though the very same difficulties must recur, the moment he should attempt to establish the difference. For either this Soul or Spirit is nothing but a thinner Body, a finer Mass of Matter: or the attribute of Self-subsistency vanishes from the Soul on the same grounds, on which it is refused to the Mind.

I am persuaded, however, that the dogmatism of the Corpuscular School, though it still exerts an influence on men's notions and phrases, has received a mortal blow from the increasingly *dynamic* spirit of the physical Sciences now highest in public estimation. And it may safely be predicted, that the results will extend beyond the intention of those, who are gradually effecting this revolution. It is not Chemistry alone that will be indebted to the Genius of Davy, Oersted, and their compeers: and not as the Founder of Physiology and philosophic Anatomy alone, will Mankind love and revere the name of John Hunter. These men have not only *taught*, they have compelled us to admit, that the immediate objects of our *senses*, or rather the grounds of the visibility and tangibility of all Objects of Sense, bear the same *relation* and similar proportion to the *intelligible* object—i.e. to the Object, which we actually *mean* when we say, "*It is such or such a thing*," or "*I have seen this or that*,"—as the paper, ink, and differently combined straight and curved lines of an Edition of Homer bear to what we understand by the words, Iliad and Odyssey. Nay, nothing would be more easy than so to construct the paper, ink, painted Capitals, &c. of a printed disquisition on the Eye, or the Muscles and Cellular Texture (*i.e.* the Flesh) of the human Body, as to bring together every one of the sensible and ponderable *Stuffs* or Elements, that are *sensuously* perceived in the Eye itself, or in the Flesh itself. Carbon and Nitrogen, Oxygen and Hydrogen, Sulphur, Phosphorus, and one or two Metals and Metallic Bases, constitute the whole. It cannot be these, therefore, that we mean by an *Eye*, by our *Body*. But perhaps it may be a particular *Combination* of these? But here comes a question: In this term do you or do you not include the *Principle*, the *Operating Cause*, of the Combination? If *not*, then detach this Eye from the Body! Look steadily at it—as it might lie on the Marble Slab of a dissecting Room. Say it were the Eye of a Murderer, a Bellingham: or the Eye of a murdered Patriot, a Sidney!—Behold it, handle it, with its various accompaniments or constituent parts, of Tendon, Ligament, Membrane, Blood-vessel, Gland, Humors; its Nerves of Sense, of Sensation, and of Motion. Alas! all these names, like that of the Organ itself, are so many Anachronisms, figures of Speech, to express that which has been: as when the Guide points with his finger to a heap of Stones, and tells the Traveller, "That is Babylon, or Persepolis."—Is this cold Jelly "the Light of the Body?" Is this the Micranthropos in the marvellous Microcosm? Is this what you *mean* when you well define the Eye as the Telescope and the Mirror of the Soul, the Seat and Agent of an almost magical power?

Pursue the same inquisition with every other part of the Body, whether integral or simply ingredient; and let a *Berzelius* or a *Hatchett* be your interpreter, and demonstrate to you what it is that in each actually meets your Senses. And when you have heard the scanty catalogue, ask yourself if *these* are indeed the living *Flesh*, the *Blood* of Life? Or not far rather—I speak of what, as a Man of Common Sense, you really *do*, not what, as a philosopher, you *ought* to believe—is it not, I say, far rather the distinct and individualized Agency that by the given combinations utters and bespeaks its Presence? Justly and with strictest propriety of language may I say, *Speaks*. It is to the coarseness of our Senses, or rather to the defect and limitation of our percipient faculty, that the *visible* Object appears the same even for a moment. The characters, which I am now shaping on this paper, abide. Not only the forms remain the same, but the particles of the coloring stuff are fixed, and, for an indefinite period at least, remain the same. But the particles that constitute the *size*, the visibility of an organic structure are in perpetual flux. They are to the combining and constitutive Power as the pulses of air to the Voice of a Discourser; or of one who sings a roundelay. The same words may be repeated; but in each second of time the articulated air hath passed away, and each act of articulation appropriates and gives momentary form to a new and other portion. As the column of blue smoke from a cottage chimney in the breathless Summer Noon, or the stedfast-seeming Cloud on the edge-point of a Hill in the driving air-current, which momently condensed and recomposed is the common phantom of a thousand successors;—such is the flesh, which our *bodily* eyes transmit to us; which our *Palates* taste; which our Hands touch.

But perhaps the material particles possess this combining power by inherent reciprocal attractions, repulsions, and elective affinities; and are themselves the joint Artists of their own combinations? I will not reply, though well I might, that this would be to solve one problem by another, and merely to shift the mystery. It will be sufficient to remind the thoughtful Querist, that even herein consists the essential difference, the contra-distinction, of an Organ from a Machine; that not only the characteristic Shape is evolved from the invisible central power, but the material Mass itself is acquired by assimilation. The germinal power of the Plant transmutes the fixed air and the elementary Base of Water into Grass or Leaves; and on these the Organific Principle in the Ox or the Elephant exercises an Alchemy still more stupendous. As the unseen Agency weaves its magic eddies, the foliage becomes indifferently the Bone and its Marrow, the pulpy Brain, or the solid Ivory. That what you see *is* blood, *is* flesh, is itself the work, or shall I say, the translucence, of the invisible Energy, which soon surrenders or abandons them to inferior Powers, (for there is no pause nor chasm in the activities of Nature) which repeat a similar metamorphosis according to *their* kind;—These are not fancies, conjectures, or even hypotheses, but *facts*; to deny which is impossible, not to reflect on which is ignominious. And we need only reflect on them with a calm and silent spirit to learn the utter emptiness and unmeaningness of the vaunted Mechanico-corpuscular Philosophy, with both its twins, Materialism on the one hand, and Idealism, rightlier named *Subjective Idolism* on the other: the one obtruding on us a World of Spectres and Apparitions; the other a mazy Dream!

Let the Mechanic or corpuscular Scheme, which in its absoluteness and strict consistency was first introduced by DES CARTES, be judged by the results. *By its fruits shall it be known.*

In order to submit the various phenomena of moving bodies to geometrical construction, we are under the necessity of abstracting from corporeal substance all its *positive* properties, and obliged to consider Bodies as differing from equal portions of Space* only by figure and mobility. And as a *Fiction of Science*, it would be difficult to overvalue this invention. It possesses the same merits in relation to Geometry that the atomic theory has in relation to Algebraic Calculus. But in contempt of Common Sense, and in direct opposition to the express declarations of the inspired Historian (Genesis I.), and to the tone and spirit of the

---

*Such is the conception of Body in Des Cartes' own system. *Body* is every where confounded with *Matter*, and might in the Cartesian sense be defined, Space or Extension with the attribute of Visibility. As Des Cartes at the same time zealously asserted the existence of intelligential Beings, the reality and independent Self-subsistence of the Soul, Berkleianism or Spinosism was the immediate and necessary Consequence. Assume a *plurality* of self-subsisting Souls, and we have Berkleianism; assume one only, (unam et unicam Substantiam), and you have Spinosism, *i.e.* the Assertion of one infinite Self-subsistent, with the two Attributes of Thinking and Appearing. "Cogitatio infinita sine centro, et omniformis Apparitio." [Infinite cogitation without a centre and omniform apparition] How far the Newtonian Vis inertiae [the power of inertia] (interpreted any otherwise than as an arbitrary term = x y z, to represent the unknown but necessary supplement or integration of the Cartesian Notion of Body) has patched up the Flaw, I leave for more competent Judges to decide. But should any one of my Readers feel an interest in the speculative principles of Natural Philosophy, and should be master of the German Language, I warmly recommend for his perusal the earliest known publication of the Great Founder of the Critical Philosophy, (written in the twenty-second Year of his Age!) on the then eager controversy between the Leibnitzian and the French and English Mathematicians, respecting the Living Forces—"Gedanken von der wahren Schätzung der lebendigen Kräfte: 1747"—in which Kant demonstrates the *right reasoning* to be with the latter; but the Truth of *Fact*, the evidence of *Experience*, with the former; and gives the explanation, namely: Body, or Corporeal Nature, is something else and more than geometrical extension, even with the addition of a Vis inertiae. And Leibnitz, with the Bernouillis, erred in the attempt to demonstrate geometrically a problem not susceptible of geometrical construction.—This Tract, with the succeeding Himmels-system, may with propriety be placed, after the Principia of Newton, among the striking instances of early Genius; and as the first product of the Dynamic Philosophy in the Physical Sciences, from the time, at least, of Giordano Bruno, whom the Idolaters burnt for an Atheist, at Rome, in the year 1600.

Scriptures throughout, Des Cartes propounded it as *truth of fact*, and instead of a World *created* and filled with productive forces by the Almighty Fiat, left a lifeless Machine whirled about by the dust of its own Grinding: as if Death could come from the living Fountain of Life; Nothingness and Phantom from the Plenitude of Reality! the Absoluteness of Creative Will!

Holy! Holy! Holy! let me be deemed mad by all men, if such be thy ordinance: but, O! from *such* Madness save and preserve me, my God!

When, however, after a short interval, the Genius of Kepler, expanded and organized in the soul of Newton, and there (if I may hazard so bold an expression) refining itself into an almost celestial Clearness, had expelled the Cartesian Vortices; then the necessity of an active power, of positive forces present in the Material Universe, forced itself on the conviction. For as a Law without a Lawgiver is a mere abstraction; so a *Law* without an Agent to realize it, a *Constitution* without an abiding Executive, is, in fact, not a Law but *an Idea*! In the profound Emblem of the Great Tragic Poet, it is the powerless Prometheus fixed on a barren Rock. And what was the result? How was this necessity provided for? God himself—my hand trembles as I write! Rather, then, let me employ the word, which the religious Feeling, in its perplexity, suggested as the substitute—the *Deity itself* was declared to be the real Agent, the actual Gravitating Power! The Law and the Law-giver were identified. God (says Dr. Priestley) not only does, but *is* everything. Jupiter est quodcunque vides. And thus a system, which commenced by excluding all life and immanent activity from the visible Universe and evacuating the natural World of all Nature, ended by substituting the Deity, and reducing the Creator to a mere Anima Mundi: a scheme that has no advantage over Spinosism but its inconsistency, which does indeed make it suit a certain Order of Intellects, who, like the Pleuronectae (or Flat Fish) in Ichthyology that have both eyes on the same side, never see but half of a subject at one time, and forgetting the one before they get to the other are sure not to detect any inconsistency between them.

And what has been the consequence? An increasing unwillingness to contemplate the Supreme Being in his *personal* Attributes: and thence a Distaste to all the peculiar Doctrines of the Christian Faith, the Trinity, the Incarnation of the Son of God, and Redemption. The young and ardent, ever too apt to mistake the inward triumph in the detection of error for a positive love of truth, are among the first and most frequent victims to this epidemic *fastidium* [loathing]. Alas! even the sincerest seekers after light are not safe from the contagion. Some have I known, constitutionally religious—I speak feelingly; for I speak of that which for a brief period was my own state—who under this unhealthful influence have been so estranged from the heavenly *Father*, the *Living* God, as even to shrink from the personal pronouns as applied to the Deity. But many do I know, and yearly meet with, in whom a false and sickly *Taste* co-operates with the prevailing fashion: many, who find the God of Abraham, Isaac, and Jacob, far too *real*, too substantial; who feel it more in harmony with their indefinite sensations

> "To worship NATURE in the hill and valley,
> Not knowing what they love:—"

and (to use the language, but not the sense or purpose of the great Poet of our Age) would fain substitute for the Jehovah of their Bible

> "A sense sublime
> Of something far more deeply interfused,
> Whose dwelling is the Light of setting suns,
> And the round Ocean and the living Air;
> A Motion and a Spirit, that impels
> All thinking things, all objects of all thought,
> And rolls through all things!"
>
> WORDSWORTH

And this from having been educated to understand the Divine Omnipresence in any sense rather than the alone safe and legitimate one, the presence of all things to God!

Be it, however, that the number of such men is *comparatively* small! And be it (as in fact it often *is*) but a brief stage, a transitional state, in the process of intellectual Growth! Yet among a numerous and increasing class of the higher and middle Ranks, there is an inward withdrawing from the Life and Personal Being of God, a turning of the Thoughts exclusively to the so called physical Attributes, to the Omnipresence in the counterfeit form of Ubiquity, to the Immensity, the Infinity, the Immutability!—the attributes of space with a notion of Power as their Substratum!—A FATE, in short, not a Moral Creator and Governor! Let intelligence be imagined, and wherein does the conception of God differ essentially from that of Gravitation (conceived as the Cause of Gravity) in the understanding of those, who represent the Deity not only as a necessary but as a *necessitated* Being! those, for whom Justice is but a scheme of General Laws; and Holiness, and the divine Hatred of Sin, yea and Sin itself, are words without meaning or accommodations to a rude and barbarous race! Hence, I more than fear, the prevailing taste for Books of Natural Theology, Physico-theology, Demonstrations of God from Nature, Evidences of Christianity, &c. &c. *Evidences* of Christianity! I am weary of the Word. Make a man feel the *want* of it; rouse him, if you can, to the self-knowledge of his *need* of it; and you may safely trust it to its own Evidence—remembering only the express declaration of Christ himself: No man cometh to me, unless the Father leadeth him! Whatever more is desirable—I speak now with reference to Christians generally, and not to professed Students of Theology—may, in my judgment, be far more safely and profitably taught, without controversy or the supposition of infidel antagonists, in the form of Ecclesiastical History.

The last fruit of the Mechanico-corpuscular Philosophy, say rather of the mode and direction of feeling and thinking produced by it on the educated class of society; or that result, which as more immediately connected with my present theme I have reserved for the last—is the habit of attaching all our conceptions and feelings, and of applying all the words and phrases expressing reality, to the objects of the Senses: more accurately speaking, to the images and sensations by which their presence is made known to us. Now I do not hesitate to assert, that it was one of the great purposes of Christianity, and included in the process of our Redemption, to rouse and emancipate the Soul from this debasing Slavery to the outward Senses, to awaken the mind to the true Criteria of Reality, viz. Permanence, Power, Will manifested in Act, and Truth operating as Life. "My words," said Christ, "are Spirit: and they (*i.e.* the spiritual powers expressed by them) are Truth;"—*i.e. very* Being. For this end our Lord, who came from Heaven to "take Captivity captive," chose the words and names, that designate the familiar yet most important Objects of Sense, the nearest and most concerning Things and Incidents of corporeal nature:—Water, Flesh, Blood, Birth, Bread! But he used them in Senses, that could not without absurdity be supposed to respect the mere *phaenomena*, Water, Flesh, &c., in senses that by no possibility could apply to the colour, figure, specific mode of Touch or Taste produced on ourselves, and by which we are made aware of the presence of the Things, and *understand* them—Res, quae *sub* apparitionibus istis *statuenda* sunt [the things which are under apparitions are to be erected]. And this awful Recalling of the drowsed soul from the dreams and phantom world of sensuality to *actual* Reality,— how has it been evaded! These words, that were Spirit! these Mysteries, which even the Apostles must wait for the Paraclete, (*i.e.* the Helper, the Strengthener) in order to comprehend! these spiritual things which can only be *spiritually* discerned,—were mere Metaphors, Figures of Speech, Oriental Hyperboles! "All this means *only* MORALITY!" Ah! how far nearer to the truth would these men have been, had they said that Morality means all this!

In the course of such self-defences he affirms that the words preserved in his notebooks must be regarded not as final statements on his part but simply as provisional stages in his gropings toward the Truth.[6]

If I should die without having destroyed this & my other Memorandum Books, I trust, that these Hints & first Thoughts, often too cogitabilia [thinkable] rather than actual cogitata a *me* [thought by me], may not be understood as my fixed opinions—but merely as the suggestions of the disquisition; & acts of obedience to the apostolic command of Try all things: hold fast that which is good.

This is reiterated several years later.[7]

If any Stranger should light on this or the preceding Numbers of the "Flycatcher," let him read them not as asserted truths but as processes of a mind working toward truth—& construe the occasional <u>positiveness</u> of the language as expressing only the conviction of the moment, which however lively is yet quite compatible with an unfeigned, yea, at the very moment co-present, sense of the probability of my being in error, or at least of half-truth. And in fact he will find often a later Number, now correcting, now overthrowing the expressed convictions of a former—not I trust without due thankfulness to God for the increase of Light.

In spite of this, he also argues in his last years that in his best writings he is master of a great system, superior to all others.[8]

My system is the only attempt that I know of ever made to reduce all knowledges into harmony; it opposes no other system, but shows what was true in each, and how that which was true in the particular in each of them became error because it was only half the truth. I have endeavored to unite the insulated fragments of truth and frame a perfect mirror. I show to each system that I fully understand and rightfully appreciate what that system means; but then I lift up that system to a higher point of view, from which I enable it to see its former position where it was indeed, but under another light and with different relations; so that the fragment of truth is not only acknowledged, but explained. So the old astronomers discovered and maintained much that was true, but because they were placed on a false ground, and looked from the wrong point of view, they never did—they never could—discover *the* truth—that is the whole truth. As soon as they left the earth—their false centre—and took their stand in the Sun—immediately they saw the whole system in the true light—and their former station remaining— but remaining a part of the prospect. I wish in short, to connect by a moral copula Natural History with Political History—or in other words, to make History scientific, and Science historical—to take from History its accidentality—and from Science its fatalism.

As might be inferred from the shape of that affirmation, he has never lost faith in the existence of an Ascent through Creation.[9]

In the several Classes and orders that mark the scale of Organic Nature from the Plant to the highest order of Animals each higher implies a lower in order to it's actual *existence*—and the same position holds good equally of the vital and organic Powers. Thus: without the 1st Power, that of growth, or what Bichat & others name the Vegetive Life, or Productivity, the 2nd. power, that of total and loco-Motion (commonly but most infelicitously called, Irritability) could not exist— i.e. *manifest* it's being. Productivity is the necessary Antecedent of Irritability: and in like manner, Irritability of Sensibility. But it is no less true, that in the *idea* of each power, the lower derives it's *intelligibility* from the higher: and the highest must be presumed to inhere latently or potentially in the lowest, or this latter will be wholly unintelligible, inconceivable. You can have no *conception* of it. Thus in Sensibility we see a power that in every instant *goes out* of itself & in the same instant retracts and falls back on itself: which the great Fountains of pure Mathesis, the Pythagorean and Platonic Geometricians illustrated in the production or self-evolution of the Point into the Circle. Imagine the going-forth and the retraction as two successive Acts, the Result would be an infinity of angles, a growth in zig-zag; in order to the imaginabil- ity of a circular line the extroitive and the retroitive must co-exist in one and the same act and moment, the curve line being the Product. Now what is *ideally* true in the generations or productive Acts of the intuitive Faculty (τῆς Αἰσθήσεως καθαρᾶς, or *pure* Sense) must be assumed as truth of fact in all living growth: or wherein would the Sport of a Plant differ from a chrystal? The latter is formed wholly by apposition ab extra: in the former the movement ab extra is consequent on (i.e. in order of thought) and yet coinstan[tan]eous with the movement ab intra.—Thus, the specific Character of Sensibility, the highest of the three powers, is found to be the general Character of Life; and supplies the only way of *conceiving*, supplies the only insight into the *possibility* of, the first and lowest power.

Lastly (that I may complete the ascent of Powers for my own satisfaction and not as expecting or in the present habit of your thoughts even *wishing* you to follow me to a Height, dizzy for the strongest spirit, it being the apex of all human, perhaps of angelic knowlege to know, that *it must be*: since all absolute Ultimates can only be seen by a Light thrown backward from the Penultimate—John's Gosp. I. 18)—Lastly, I say, the Self-*containing* Power supposes a self-*causing* Power. *Causa sui*, αἰτία ἡ ὑπερούσιος. Here alone we find a Problem which in it's very statement contains it's own solution—the one self-solving Power, beyond which no question is *possible*. Yet short of this we dare not rest: for even the ὁ ὤυ [being], the supreme Reality, if it were contemplated abstractly from the Absolute Will, whose essence it is to be causative of all *Reality*, would sink into a Spinozistic Deity. That this is not evident to us arises from the false notion of Reason (ὁ Λόγος [the Word]) as a quality, property, or faculty of the Real, whereas Reason *is* the supreme Reality, the only true *Being* in all things visible and invisible! the Pleroma, in whom alone God loveth the World! Even in Man *Will* is deeper than *Mind*: for mind does not cease to be *mind*, by having an antecedent; but Will is either the First (τὸ ἀεὶ πρόπρωτον, τό nunquam *positum*, semper *sup*ponendum [the ever initial first, the never posited, always *sup*posed]) or it is *not* Will at all.—

His sense of the 'Idea' and of Ascent is elaborated in a letter to Edward Coleridge, where he compares the spiritual sense of Human Beings with the room left for their future evolution in organisms such as insects.[10]

... that an other World is inshrined in the *Microcosm*, I not only believe but at certain depths of my Being, during the solemner Sabbaths of the Spirit, I have held commune therewith, in the power of that Faith which is 'the substance of the things hoped for', the living Stem that will itself expand into the flower, which it now foreshews. How should it not be so, even on grounds of natural Reason and the Analogy of inferior Life? Is not Nature prophetic up the whole vast Pyramid of organic Being? And in which of her numberless predictions has Nature been convicted of a Lie? Is not every Organ announced by a previous instinct or act? The Larva of the Stag-beetle lies in it's Chrysalis like an infant in the Coffin of an Adult, having left an empty space half the length, it occupies—and this space is the exact length of the Horn that distinguishes the perfect animal, but which, when it constructed it's temporary Sarcophagus, was not yet in existence. Do not the Eyes, Ears, Lungs of the unborn Babe give notice and furnish proof of a transuterine, visible, audible, atmospheric world?—We have eyes, ears, touch, taste, smell. And have we not an answerable World of Shapes, Colors, Sounds, and sapid and odorous bodies? But likewise—alas for the Man, for whom the one has not the same evidence of Fact as the other!—the Creator has given us spiritual Senses and Sense-organs—Ideas I mean! the Idea of the Good, the Idea of the Beautiful, Ideas of Eternity, Immortality, Freedom, and of that which contemplated relatively to WILL is Holiness, in relation to LIFE is Bliss: and must not these too infer the existence of a World correspondent to them? There is a Light, saith the Hebrew Sage, compared with which the glory of the Sun is but a cloudy Veil: and is it an ignis fatuus given to mock us and lead astray? And from a yet higher authority we know that it is a Light that lighteth every man that cometh into the world: and are there no Objects to reflect it? Or must we seek it's analogon in the Light of the Glow-worm, that simply serves to distinguish one reptile from all the rest, and lighting inch by inch it's mazy path through weeds and grass, leaves all else before, behind, and around it in darkness? No! Another and answerable World there is: and if any man discern it not, let him not, whether sincerely or in contemptuous irony, pretend a defect of faculty as the cause. The Sense, the Light, and the conformed Objects are all there, and for all men, and the difference between man and man in relation thereto results from no difference in their several gifts & powers of *intellect*, but in the WILL. As certainly as the Individual is a Man, so certainly should this other world be present to him: yea, it is his proper Home. But he is an absentee, & *chooses* to live abroad.

At the level of social intercourse, he increasingly stresses the virtues of the gentlemanly.[11]

Religion is the most gentlemanly thing in the world.

On this score, his great exemplar is St. Paul.[12]

I have been very much interested in the account of Bishop Sandford …He seems to have been a thorough gentleman upon the model of Sᵗ Paul, whose manners were the finest of any man upon record.

Meanwhile, he has explained to James Gillman's son how the idea of the gentlemanly is fulfilled in Christianity.[13]

Believe me, that He who takes his footing on the notion of the *Gentlemanlike*, will hardly attain, much less realize, the *idea* of a Gentleman: while the Christian—supposing the same social *Manège*, the same advantages of outward training—the Christian, respectful or forbearing to other men thro' the consciousness of his own actual defects and deficiencies, yet standing in awe of Himself from the knowlege of what he is *called* to be, is capable of becoming and aspires to become, who not overlooking the hues and qualities that difference man from man still looks thro' them; and in every exercise of prayer is compelled to lose them in the contemplation of the Reason, one and the same in all men, and the responsible Will and mysterious permanent Identity common to all men, and constituting while they contra-distinguish our Humanity— the Christian, for whom in this very habit of feeling respect for every man, even because he is a Man, there arises that *manner* of shewing respect to others which implies & with the ease and unconsciousness of all *continual* feelings claims & anticipates respect for himself—the Christian *comprehends, includes* the Gentleman. Or shall I not rather say, he is the *Apotheosis* of a Gentleman?

As death approaches he writes to Miss Lawrence, finding it more urgent to affirm his belief in orthodox Christianity and the necessity of the Redeemer, as opposed to the Unitarian beliefs he once held.[14]

I have for more than 18 months been on the brink of the grave, under sufferings which have rendered the Grave an object of my wishes, & only not of my prayers, because I commit myself, poor dark Creature, to an omniscient & all-merciful, in whom are the issues of Life and Death—content, yea, most thankful if only his Grace will preserve within me the blessed faith, that He *is*, and is a God, that heareth prayer, abundant in forgiveness, & THEREFORE to be feared—no *fate*, no

God, as imagined by the Unitarians; a sort of I know not what *law-giving Law* of Gravitation, to whom Prayer would be as idle as to the Law of Gravity if an undermined Wall were falling upon me; but a God, that made the Eye, & therefore shall *he* not see? who made the Ear, and shall he not hear? who made the heart of man to love him, and shall he not love that creature, whose ultimate end is to love him?—A God, who *seeketh* that which was lost, who calleth back that which had gone astray—who calleth thro' his own Name, Word, Son, from everlasting the *Way*, and the TRUTH, and who became Man that for poor fallen Mankind he might *be* (not merely announce, but *be*) the RESURRECTION and THE LIFE—Come unto *me*, all ye that are weary and heavy-laden, and *I* will give you rest!—O my dear Miss Lawrence! prize above all earthly blessings the faith—I trust, that no Sophistry of shallow Infra-socinians has quenched it within you—that God is a God that heareth Prayer.—If varied Learning, if the assiduous cultivation of the reasoning Powers, if an accurate & minute acquaintance with all the arguments of controversial writers; if an intimacy with the doctrines of the Unitarians which can only be obtained by one who for a year or two in his early life had been a convert to them, yea, a zealous, and by themselves deemed powerful, Supporter of their opinions;—lastly, if the utter absence of any imaginable wordly interest that could sway or warp the mind and affections;—if all these combined can give any weight or authority to the opinion of a fellow-creature, they will give weight to my adjuration, sent from my sick-bed to you, in kind love—O trust, o trust, in your *Redeemer!* In the Co-eternal *Word*, the only-begotten, the living NAME of the Eternal I AM, Jehovah, Jesus!—

Disappointed by her reply he nevertheless modifies his condemnation of Unitarianism.[15]

I was affected, not surprised, not disappointed, by her answer, but yet through great affection could not wholly suppress the feeling of regret to find her and her family still on that noiseless sand-shoal and wrecking shallow of Infra-Socinianism, yclept most calumniously and insolently, Unitarianism: as if a Tri-unitarian were not as necessarily Unitarian as an apple-pie must be a pie. But you have done me the honour of looking through my *Aids to Reflection*; and you will therefore, perhaps, be aware that though I deem Unitarian*ism* the very *Nadir* of Christianity, and far, very far worse in relation either to the *Affections*, the *Imagination*, the Reason, the Conscience, nay even to the UNDERSTANDING, than several of the forms of *Atheism*—*ex. gr.* than the Atheism of Spinoza—whose pure spirit may it be my lot to meet, with St. John and St. Paul smiling on him and loving him—yet I make an impassable chasm between *an* and *ism*, and while I almost yield to the temptation of despising Priestleyianism as the only *sect* that feels and expresses contempt or slander of all that differ from them; the poison of hemlock for the old theological whiskey and its pugnacious effects; yet I am persuaded that *the Word* works *in* thousands, to whose ears the *words* never reached, and remained in the portal at the unopened door.

Meanwhile, he argues with Green about what he thinks to be a 'change of Pole' on his part, insisting on the necessity of reconciling Reason with Revelation.[16]

My principle has ever been, that Reason is *subjective* Revelation, Revelation *objective* Reason—and that *our* business is not to *derive* Authority from the *mythoi* of the Jews & the first Jew-Christians (i.e. the O. and N. Testament) but to *give* it to them—never to assume their stories as facts, any more than you would Quack Doctors' affidavits on oath before the Lord Mayor—and verily in point of old Bailey Evidence this is a flattering representation of the Paleyian Evidence—but by *science* to confirm the *Facit*, kindly afforded to beginners in Arithmetic. If I lose my faith in *Reason*, as the perpetual revelation, I lose my faith altogether. I must deduce the objective from the subjective Revelation, or it is no longer a revelation for me, but a beastly fear, and superstition.

In increasing weakness, he restates once again his central religious belief and stresses the need for a regeneration of natural philosophy in an awakened science.[17]

God's will be done! He knows that my first prayer is not to fall from Him, and the faith that He is God, the I AM, the God that heareth prayer—the Finite in the form of the Infinite = the Absolute Will, the Good; the Self-affirmant, the Father, the I AM, the Personeity;—the Supreme Mind, Reason, Being, the *Pleroma*, the Infinite in the form of the Finite, the Unity in the form of the Distinctity; or lastly, in the synthesis of these, in the *Life*, the *Love*, the Community, the Perichoresis, or Intercirculation—and that there is *one* only God! And I believe in an apostasis, absolutely necessary, as a *possible* event, from the absolute perfection of Love and Goodness, and because WILL is the only ground and antecedent of all Being. And I believe in the descension and con-descension of the Divine Spirit, Word, Father, and Incomprehensible Ground of all—and that he is a God who *seeketh* that which was lost, and that the whole world of Phaenomena is a revelation of the Redemptive Process, of the Deus *Patiens*, or Deitas *Objectiva* beginning in the separation of Life from Hades, which under the control of the Law = Logos = Unity—becomes *Nature*, i.e., that which never *is* but *natura* est, is to be, from the brute Multeity, and Indistinction, and is to end with the union with God in the Pleroma. I dare not hope ever to see you again in the flesh—scarcely expect to survive to the hearing of you. But be assured I have been comforted by the fact you have given me, that there are men of profound science who yet feel that *Science*, even in its most flourishing state, needs a *Baptism*, a Regeneration in Philosophy—

To a protagonist of slave emancipation he contends that the alienation of such human beings is to be explained by another belief of which he is assured, that of a Fall requiring an awakening of their moral nature leading to discovery of the source of true freedom.[18]

Now next to the knowlege—for in this case Faith *is* Knowlege—of an Almighty God, the Father of Spirits, and best conveyed—for even to little children it is adequately conveyed—as a Father and Universal Governor, the most momentous truth is the Fact of a FALL, and that all the miseries of the World are the consequences of this Fall—and thence to deduce the true notion of human Freedom—viz. that Control from with-out must ever be *inversely* as the Self-government or Control from within, unless men are to fall abroad into the state of wild beasts, or more truly of wild Fiends. Now as in the very lowest state a man cannot be forced into action by mere physical force, like the parts of a machine, but must act by the determinating of his Will, the moral forces nearest to physical must be substituted—bodily pain, and Fear from the experience & anti-cipation of Pain. Man is made a Beast—& alas! by Man in defiance of and most impious contradiction to the common Creator's Fiat. But this is not all that this great truth involves. It can be to awake in the mind of the *Slave* by human Law, that even in Slavery he may be free with a freedom, compared with which his oppressor is a pitiable Slave—

The awakened self, by contrast, is capable of making the statement 'I am', which brings with it the assurance of its own immortality.[19]

The faith in Immortality!/ What is but the impossibility of believing the contrary? The inevitable Rebound of the I am—itself the fearful Rebound of Life. The moment that the Soul affirms, I am, it asserts, I cannot cease to be—For the I am owns no antecedent, it is an act of absolute Spontanëity & of absolute necessity. No cause existing why it is, no cause can be imagined why it should cease to be. It is an impossible Thought as long as the I am is affirmed—By one means only can the fearful burthen of the Future I be removed, by an act of freedom equally transcendent denying the I am—and by seeking it elsewhere. And this is the Birth in his Spirit to the Word.—Fearful—what finite & fallen Creature that thinks, reflects, can find the clinging thought of imperishable Self-being other than most fearful?—I was born a healthy infant—yet what have I become—? Who shall deliver me from the Body of this Death—and what tho' I should not recollect the sufferings & circumstances of the past!—I can find no comfort in this thought. It will be still the I that suffers, but none know that a few years hence I shall have the tortures of the Stone—but that the pain will be such that I shall have no memory of my present Being—will that console me?—

Speaking with difficulty to J.H. Green on the evening before his death, and shortly before falling into his final coma, he urges him, in any posthumous writing, to keep a firm hold of what he believes to be his central beliefs.[20]

And be thou sure in whatever may be published of my posthumous works to remember that, first of all is the Absolute Good whose self-affirmation is the 'I am,' as the eternal reality in itself, and the ground and source of all other reality.

And next, that in this idea nevertheless a distinctivity is to be carefully preserved, as manifested in the person of the Logos by whom that reality is communicated to all other beings.

Notes

1 The Early Intellectual Quest

1 *CL* I 347–8.
2 Letter to Mrs Evans, 22 February 1792, *CL* I 33.
3 Reported by Lawrence Hanson, *Life of S.T. Coleridge* (1938) p. 510.
4 *CL* I 279–85.
5 Essay 'My First Acquaintance with Poets' in *The Spirit of the Age*. *HW* XVII, 108.
6 For good accounts, see H.W. Piper, *The Active Universe* (1962) and Ian Wylie, *Young Coleridge and the Philosophers of Nature* (1989).

Textnotes

1 Lines 1–24: *Poems* (Beer) 88–9.
2 Lines 13–49: ibid., 126–7.
3 *Lects* (1795) 89–93.
4 Ibid., 93–116.
5 Ibid., 141.
6 Ibid., 145.
7 Ibid., 150.
8 Ibid., 152.
9 Ibid., 161–2.
10 Ibid., 175–7.
11 Ibid., 195.
12 Ibid., 206–8.
13 Ibid., 208–9.
14 Ibid., 228–9.
15 *CL* I 279–85. The passages in square brackets were inked out in the manuscript.
16 *BL* I 200.

2 A Religion of Life?

1 *Poems* (Beer) 72–3.
2 Letter of January 1796 to Wade: *CL* I 177.
3 Letter of May 1798 to J.P. Estlin: ibid., 410.
4 *Henry Crabb Robinson on Book and their Writers*, ed. E.J. Morley (3 vols 1938) I 112.
5 See his letter of 10 March 1815: *CL* IV 548 and note.

Textnotes

1 *CL* I 145–6.
2 *Poems* (Beer) 73.

3 Letter to George Coleridge, 10 March 1798: *CL* I 397–8.
4 *CN* I 258.
5 Ibid., 553; *SWF* I 110.
6 *CL* II 948–9.
7 Ibid., 949; 960; 961.
8 Ibid., 1008 (October 1803).
9 *CN* I 1616.
10 *CL* II 1034.
11 Ibid., II 1037.
12 Ibid., II 1039.
13 Ibid., II 1022–3.
14 *CN* I 1379.
15 Ibid., I 556.
16 Ibid., III 3869.
17 *TT* I 265.
18 *Poems* (Beer) 210.
19 *CN* II 2540.
20 Ibid., II 2546.
21 Ibid., III 4040.
22 Ibid., III 4088.
23 Ibid., III 4153.
24 Ibid., II 3156.
25 Ibid., II 3159.
26 Ibid., II 2444.

3 Self-Examinings

1 *Poems* (Beer) 73–4.
2 *Life of John Sterling* (1851) chapter viii.

Textnotes

1 Letter to George Coleridge, 8 February 1794: *CL* I 63.
2 To the same, 11 February 1794: ibid., I 65.
3 To the same, 30 March 1794: ibid., I 78.
4 *CN* II 2091.
5 Ibid., II 2453.
6 To George Coleridge, April 1807: *CL* III 6.
7 *CN* II 3353.
8 To Thomas Roberts, December 1813: *CL* III 463.
9 To Joseph Cottle, April 1814: ibid., 478.
10 *CM* III 512.
11 Ibid.
12 *CN* IV 5000.
13 Ibid., V 5001.
14 Ibid., V 5275.
15 Ibid., V 6675.
16 Ibid., V 6784.
17 Ibid., V 5704.

4 Psychological Speculations

1 There, where it was still more influential, the fashion was associated with the ferment that surrounded the revolutionary events. See Robert Darnton, *Mesmerism and the End of the Enlightenment in France* (Cambridge, Mass., 1968).

2 *CL* I 192–3.

3 See my *Coleridge the Visionary* (1959), chapter 2, and *Coleridge's Poetic Intelligence* (1977) p. 73. As mentioned in the first, the contemporary relevance of 'that, which comes out of thine eye' (addressed to the Mariner) in the first version was first noticed long ago, notably in Lane Cooper's 1901 article 'The Power of the Eye in Coleridge' (in *Studies Presented to J.M. Hart* (N.Y.), pp. 78–121; reptd in his *Late Harvest* (Ithaca, N.Y., 1952)). Rather surprisingly, however, Cooper did not perceive any further significance in Coleridge's use of the phenomenon, concluding, 'It is disappointing to find his "poet's eye" so continually "fixed" by so trivial a "fact of mind". (1952 edn, 95)

4 Letter to Thelwall, 19 November 1796: *CL* I 260.

5 *Friend* I 146.

6 Lines 121 6: *Poems* (Beer) 128–9.

Textnotes

1 *CN* I 186.

2 Ibid., I 212.

3 Ibid., I 918.

4 Ibid., I 923.

5 Ibid., I 920.

6 Ibid., I 921.

7 Ibid., I 1412.

8 Ibid., I 1414.

9 Ibid., I 1416.

10 Ibid., I 1417.

11 Ibid., I 1554.

12 Ibid., I 1575; 1597; 1600; 1620.

13 Ibid., I 1710.

14 Ibid., I 1827.

15 Ibid., I 1832–3.

16 Ibid., II 2060.

17 Ibid., II 2061.

18 Ibid., II 2090.

19 Ibid., III 4046.

20 Ibid., III 4396.

21 Ibid., III 4409.

22 Ibid., V 5999.

23 Ibid., V 6257.

24 *TT* I 107–8.

25 *CL* V 97–9.

26 Ibid., V 5671.

27 Ibid., V 6291.

28 Ibid., V 6523.

29 *CL* V 19.
30 *CN* II 2112.
31 Ibid., III 3295.

5 The Existence and Nature of God

1 *CL* I 20.
2 Ibid., I 153.
3 Ibid., I 366.
4 *CN* I 922.
5 Ibid., II 2448, below, pp. 86–7.
6 *CL* II 1189.
7 *Paradise Lost* IV 520.
8 Letter of 25 July 1800, *CL* I 612.
9 Quoted, J.R. Barth, *Coleridge and Christian Doctrine* (Cambridge, Mass., 1969) p. 94.
10 Marginal comment on p. 389 of Daniel Waterland's *Importance of the Doctrine of the Holy Trinity* (2nd edn., 1734): *Notes on English Divines* (1853) p. 210, to be re-edited in *CM* VI.
11 Further discussion may be found in chapter 4, 'The One and Triune God', of Barth's book.

Textnotes

1 *BL* I 179–80.
2 *TT* I 488–9.
3 *CN* III 3743.
4 Ibid., II 2448.
5 Ibid., II 1188–90.
6 Ibid., II 1192.
7 *CL* II 1193–9.
8 *SWF* I 259–60.
9 *CL* III 480–6.
10 Ibid., IV 545.
11 Ibid., IV 849–51.
12 Ibid., V 86–7.
13 *CN.*, III 3813.
14 Ibid., III 3820.
15 *SWF* I 415–16.
16 *CN* II 2445.
17 *TT* I 278–9.
18 *SWF* II 1510–12.
19 *CN* III 4087.
20 *SWF* I 411.
21 *CN* IV 4816.
22 *TT* 22 February 1834: I 462–3.

6   Questions of Evil and the Will

1   See e.g. his letters to Southey, 11 December 1794 (*CL* I 139) and to Thelwall in May 1796 (ibid., I 213).
2   Ibid., II 706.
3   Ibid., I 238.
4   See, e.g. *Paradise Lost* II 555–61; V 519–43.

Textnotes

1   'The Destiny of Nations', lines 60–3; 80–91.
2   *CN* IV 4283.
3   *CL* I 114–15.
4   Ibid., I 192–3.
5   Ibid., I 396.
6   Ibid., II 1032.
7   *CN* I 1619.
8   Ibid., I 1622.
9   Ibid., I 1640–1.
10   Ibid., I 1770.
11   Ibid., II 2537.
12   *CL* III 466.
13   Ibid., III 467.
14   *TT* I 106–7.
15   *AR* 139–41.
16   *CN* IV 5271.
17   Ibid., III 3675.
18   Ibid., III 3701.
19   *SWF* I 256–9.
20   *CN* II 2208.
21   Ibid., IV 5195.
22   Ibid., IV 5243.

7   'Science, Freedom and the Truth ... '

1   For an account of Coleridge's interest in *Naturphilosophie*, including its relation to his Trinitarianism, see Raimonda Modiano, *Coleridge and the Concept of Nature* (1985) pp. 138–206.

Textnotes

1   *CL* I 320–1.
2   Ibid., I 244–5.
3   Ibid., II 727.
4   *CN* II 2330.
5   To Dorothy Wordsworth, November 1807: *CL* III 38.
6   Ibid., III 128–9.
7   Ibid., III 146.
8   Ibid., III 171–2.
9   *Friend*, I 470.

10   *CN* II 2640.
11   To Mary Cruikshank, 1807: *CL* III 32.
12   *CN* III 3885 (cf. 3892; 3893; 3896; 3897).
13   *SWF* I 807.
14   Ibid., I 589–94; *CN* IV 4512.
15   Ibid., V 5930.
16   Marginal annotation on Southey's *Life of Wesley*: *CM* V 141–2.
17   *CL* IV 760–1.
18   *CL* IV 574–5.
19   *Lects* (1818–19) I 316–17.
20   *SWF* II 894–8.
21   *CN* III 4377.
22   Ibid., III 4378.
23   Ibid., III 3593.
24   Ibid., III 3619.
25   *CL* IV 767–9.
26   Ibid., IV 770.
27   Ibid., IV 775.

8   Original Sin and the True Reason

1   MS Letter of 13 April 1814 in Perkins Library, Duke University. I am grateful to Heather Jackson for having drawn my attention to this; see also her head-note at *CM* III 507.
2   *CM* III 507–13.

Textnotes

1   *AR* 250–7.
2   Ibid., 265–85 (quoting from Jeremy Taylor).
3   Ibid., 288.
4   Ibid., 291–2.
5   Ibid., 216–25; 236.
6   Ibid., 236–8.
7   Ibid., 351–4.
8   Ibid., 357–9.

9   Doctrines and Illuminations

1   *Table Talk*, 25–6 August 1827: *TT* I 87. A previous record for 8 July conveys a more reasoned critique: 'first persecuting, then tautological, and lastly heretical. Author unknown'. Ibid., 78.
2   Ibid., II 433.
3   Apart from the examples quoted below, examples of such confessions can be found in *CN* III 3581, 4005, 4340; *CL* IV 631 (cf. 686) and *AR* 197–8.
4   See below, pp. 190–1.
5   *Christian Observer* XLIV (1845) 262. A long and valuable footnote to *TT* I 152–3 contains this quotation along with many further references.

Textnotes

1 *CN* III 3964.
2 *SWF* I 570–1.
3 Ibid., II 1484–6.
4 *CN* III 3857.
5 *TT* I 313.
6 *CL* IV 81–2; *CN* IV 4750 (cf. *AR* 361–7).
7 *CL* V 444–5.
8 *SWF* II 9012.
9 *TT* I 134–6.
10 *Poems* (Beer) 61n.
11 *CN* I 257.
12 *Poems* (Beer) 424.
13 Ibid., 442.
14 *CL* III 478–9.
15 *TT* I 152–3.
16 Ibid., I 138.
17 *CL* VI 684–5.
18 Ibid., V 496–7.
19 *Poems* (Beer) 472–4.
20 *CN* II 2440, 2469.
21 Ibid., V 5492.
22 *SWF* I 156.
23 *Poems* (Beer) 486.
24 *CN* II 2921.

10 Other Faiths

1 See *CL* IV 751, Gillman, *Life of Coleridge* (1838) 21–2, and his table talk of 21 July 1832 and 21 April 1811: *TT* I 310 and 12.
2 See ibid., I 415–16, 457–9.
3 Ibid., I 417.
4 *Anima Poetae*, ed. E.H. Coleridge (1895), p. 159.
5 NB 17.78v: *Anima Poetae*, p. 143.
6 *CN* I 864.
7 *C & S* 56.
8 See my *Coleridge's Poetic Intelligence* (1977) pp. 109–11, 227–8, 268.
9 *CN* I 204; see also his own temptation to 'adopt the Brahman creed': *CL* I 350.
10 See my *Coleridge the Visionary* (1959) pp. 96, 102, 113, 247.

Textnotes

1 *SWF* I 454–5.
2 Ibid., I 322–4.
3 *TT* I 454–5.
4 *CN* V 5637.
5 Ibid., III 3900, discussing Joseph Nightingale's *Portraiture of Methodism*.
6 Ibid., III 3901.

7 *TT* I 492–3.
8 Ibid., I 236–40.
9 Ibid., I 430.
10 Ibid., I 415–16.
11 Ibid., I 458–9.
12 *CN* III 3872.
13 *TT* I 49–50.
14 *CN* IV 4338.
15 *TT* I 368–71.
16 *CN* II 2664.
17 *CM* III 737.
18 Ibid., III 740.
19 To Edward Coleridge, *CL* VI 596.
20 *TT* I 100.
21 *CN* IV 4769.
22 Ibid., IV 4794.
23 *CL* III 373–4.
24 *CN* IV 4737.
25 Ibid., IV 4973.
26 Ms 'On the Divine Ideas', quoted in John Muirhead's *Coleridge as Philosopher* (1930) p. 284. The source of the quotation is untraced.
27 *CN* V 6615.
28 Ibid., III 3909.
29 Ibid., III 3911.
30 Ibid., III 3925.
31 Ibid., III 3907.
32 *CAR* 107.

Conclusions

1 *BL* chapter 13, I 304.
2 Ibid., 304n.
3 See Erasmus Darwin's *Zoonomia* (1794–6) II 240.
4 *CN* III 4056.

Textnotes

1 *CN* I 1623.
2 Ibid., I 2441.
3 *BL* II 234–5; 247–8.
4 *SWF* I 419–21.
5 *AR* 383–407.
6 *CN* III 3881.
7 *CN* V 6450.
8 *TT* I 248–9.
9 *CL* VI 597–8; 600.
10 Ibid., VI 595–6.
11 *TT* I 116.
12 *TT* I 496–7 (cf. 389 and n.).

13   *CL* VI 928.
14   Ibid., VI 890–1.
15   Ibid., VI 893.
16   Ibid., VI 895.
17   Ibid., VI 897.
18   To Thomas Pringle, ibid., VI 940–1.
19   *CN* V 5995.
20   From J.A. Heraud's posthumous oration, quoted by Lucy E. Watson, *Coleridge at Highgate* (1925) p. 158.

Index

Abraham, 220
Adam, 111, 159, 164, 170
aether, 60, 145
Africa, 199
Ahimelech, 220
Aids to Reflection, 2, 111, 179, 187, 190, 196, 204, 231, 254
Aleph, 76
Alexandrinus, Clemens, 238
'All look or likeness', 233
alogi, 157
Alps, 42
Anabaptists, 187, 207
anatomy, 243
'Ancient Mariner', 61, 193, 196, 240n
angels, 201
Anglican Church, 1, 194, 205; *see also* Church of England
Anima Mundi, 246
animal magnetism, 60, 137
Anthropomorphites, 83
Anti-christ, 217
Antioch, 181
ants, 171
Apocrypha, 185
Apollo, 61, 210, 223
Apostles' Creed, 181, 182
apparitions, 62, 72, 131, 240
Arabian Nights' Entertainments, 196
Arabian Tales, 224
Arians, 181, 209, 211
Aristotle, 65, 156n
Arminian, 186, 190, 228
Arnauld, A., 192, 238n
art, 156n
'Assertion of Religion', 155
association, 16, 118
astronomer, 18
Athanasian creed, 179
Athanasius, 179, 215
atheism, 12, 168, 255
atheist, 11, 245n
atonement, 125, 186

Augustine, 190
Autenrieth, J.H.F., 73

Babylon, 243
Bacon, Francis, 65, 96, 149
Baptism, 187, 192, 212, 221
Barabbas, 138
Barrow, Isaac, 177
Barth, J.R., 261
Bates, 211
Baxter, Richard, 211
Beddoes, Dr, 131
bees, 138, 171
Beethoven, 196
Behmen, Jacob, 153, 237, 240
Being, 107, 150, 151, 157n, 201, 232, 248
Bellarmino, R.F.R., 206
Bellingham, J., 243
benevolence, 11, 14, 15
Berkeley, George, Berkleian, 114, 222, 245n
Bernouilli, J., 245n
Berzelius, J.J. von, 140, 243
Bethlehem, 7
Beverly, R., 132
Bible, 94, 185, 195
Bichat, M.X.-V., 73, 250
Biographia Literaria, 5, 47, 83, 231, 233
Blanchard's Medical Dictionary, 56
blasphemy, 10
Blumenbach, J.F., 61, 130
Boehme, Jacob, 2, 203
Botany Bay, 5, 25
Bowyer, J., 55
Boyle, R., 121, 132
Brahmin, Brahmanism, 167, 168, 205, 221, 224, 264
Brande, W.T., 140
Bristol, 4, 128, 154
Bristol, Bishop of, 210
Browne, Sir Thomas, 137
Bruno, Giordano, 153, 245n